AI and the Future

How AI is reshaping industries, the
skills required for the workforce of tomorrow.

Disclaimer

The information provided in this book, "AI and the Future of Work," is intended for general informational purposes only. While we have made every effort to ensure the accuracy and reliability of the content, the field of Artificial Intelligence (AI) and technology is continually evolving. Therefore, we cannot guarantee that the information presented here is free from errors or omissions or that it is up-to-date with the latest developments in the field.

The content in this book should not be considered as professional, legal, financial, or technical advice. Readers are encouraged to seek advice and guidance from qualified professionals and experts in their respective fields for specific and individualized concerns.

Furthermore, the views and opinions expressed within this book are those of the authors and contributors and do not necessarily reflect the views of the publisher or any affiliated organizations. The authors and publisher disclaim any liability for any loss, damage, or injury caused by the information presented in this book or its application.

Readers are advised to conduct their own research and due diligence when making decisions or taking actions related to the topics discussed in this book. Any reliance on the information provided herein is done at the reader's own risk.

Lastly, this book may contain references or links to external websites, resources, or third-party content. These references are provided for convenience and informational purposes. The authors and publisher do not endorse or control the content of these external sources and are not responsible for their accuracy or reliability.

By reading and using the information in this book, you acknowledge and accept these disclaimers and understand that you are solely responsible for any actions or decisions you make based on the content presented herein.

Contents

Introduction: "AI and the Future of Work" 4

Chapter 1: The Dawn of a New Era 5

    1.1. The Transformative Power of AI 6

    1.2. Historical Context: A Continuum of Innovation 14

    1.3. An Exploration Ahead: Impact on Industries, Jobs, and Skills 17

Chapter 2: Exploring the World of Artificial Intelligence 26

    2.1. A Primer on AI Technologies 26

    2.2. Narrow AI and General AI: Unveiling the Distinction 33

    2.3. Real-World Applications of AI Across Industries 39

Chapter 3: AI's Disruption across Industries 48

    3.1. Healthcare: Diagnostics, Personalized Medicine, and Telehealth 48

    3.2. Manufacturing: Automation, Predictive Maintenance, and Supply Chain Optimization 55

    3.3. Finance: Algorithmic Trading, Fraud Detection, and Customer Service 93

    3.4. Retail: E-commerce, Recommendation Systems, and Inventory Management 115

    3.6. Education: Personalized Learning, Virtual Classrooms, and Educational AI Tools 133

Chapter 4: Shifting Job Landscapes 140

    4.1. AI's Impact on Jobs: A Complex Interplay of Displacement, Augmentation, and Creation 140

    4.2. Job Categories Vulnerable to Transformation: Routine Tasks, Manual Labor, Data Entry 142

4.3. Job Categories on the Cusp of Expansion: AI Programming, Data Analysis, Ethical Oversight 144

4.4. Unveiling Industry Case Studies Exhibiting Profound Job Transformations 146

4.5. Confronting Workforce Challenges and Embracing Opportunities 148

Chapter 5: Skills for the AI Era: Navigating the Evolving Landscape 149

5.1. The Interplay of Soft and Technical Skills: A New Hierarchy 150

5.2. Reskilling and Upskilling: Lifelong Learning Redefined . 152

Chapter 6: The Human-AI Collaboration 162

6.2. Examples of Successful Human-AI Collaboration in Various Fields 165

6.3. Ethical Considerations: Bias, Privacy, and Responsible AI Development 167

Chapter 7: Navigating Ethical and Societal Challenges 170

7.1. Upholding Ethical AI: Fairness, Transparency, and Accountability 171

7.2. Mitigating Job Displacement: Universal Basic Income, Reskilling, and Social Safety Nets 172

Chapter 8: Preparing for the AI-Driven Future 223

8.2. Government Policies: Balancing Innovation, Regulation, and Collaboration 234

8.3. Individual Actions: The Transformative Role of Lifelong Learning and Adaptability 289

8.4. A Tapestry of Preparedness: Weaving Together Businesses, Government, and Individuals 306

8.5. A Dynamic Future Unveiled: Navigating the Uncharted with Unity..309

Chapter 9: Case Studies of AI Implementation........................312

Chapter 10: Envisioning Tomorrow's Workforce......................324

10.1. Remote Work and Augmented Reality Offices: Bridging Distances..325

10.2. The Evolving Nature of Leadership: Adaptive and Empathetic...328

10.3. Collaboration and Team Dynamics: Beyond Boundaries331

10.4. The Interplay of AI, Creativity, and Human Ingenuity.334

Conclusion: Embracing the AI-Enhanced Future......................338

Introduction: "AI and the Future of Work"

In the not-so-distant past, the idea of machines that could think, learn, and make decisions like humans belonged to the realm of science fiction. Today, it's a reality—a reality that is transforming industries, reshaping job markets, and revolutionizing the very nature of work. Welcome to "AI and the Future of Work," a journey into the heart of this technological revolution.

As we stand on the precipice of an AI-driven future, it's crucial to understand the profound changes underway. Artificial Intelligence (AI) is more than a buzzword; it's a powerful force reshaping our world. It's in the algorithms that recommend what you should watch next on Netflix, the chatbots that provide instant customer support, the autonomous vehicles that navigate our streets, and the machines that diagnose diseases faster and more accurately than human doctors.

This book is your guide to understanding AI's transformative power, its historical context, and its impact on industries, jobs, and the skills required in tomorrow's workforce. It delves into the intricacies of AI technologies, from machine learning to natural language processing, and explores real-world applications across sectors like healthcare, finance, agriculture, and education.

But this journey doesn't stop at the technical aspects. We delve into the human dimension, exploring how AI is shifting job landscapes. Some roles may be displaced, while new ones emerge, requiring a blend of technical skills and soft skills like creativity and critical thinking. We navigate the ethical and societal challenges, from bias in AI algorithms to the implications of job displacement and explore solutions like Universal Basic Income and lifelong learning.

As we venture deeper, we discover the collaborative potential of AI. It's not about machines replacing humans; it's about AI enhancing human capabilities. We explore how AI can be a creative partner, how it's revolutionizing leadership and team dynamics, and how it's blurring the lines between physical and virtual workspaces.

This book isn't just about AI; it's about envisioning a future where humans and technology collaborate to build a better world. It's about preparing for the AI-driven era with adaptability and continuous learning. It's about embracing change and viewing AI as a catalyst for positive change.

So, embark on this journey with an open mind and a curious spirit. The future is here, and it's exciting. "AI and the Future of Work" is your roadmap to navigate this transformative landscape, uncover its opportunities, and shape a future where human potential and AI capabilities amplify one another.

Chapter 1: The Dawn of a New Era

1.1. The Transformative Power of AI

In the expansive realm of technological progress, there exist a select few innovations that have managed to capture the collective imagination and present a profound potential for reshaping society as we know it. Among these, none stands out quite as prominently as Artificial Intelligence (AI). Its ascent has heralded a fresh chapter in our history, characterized by unprecedented capabilities, prospects, and trials. This section embarks on an exploration of the remarkably transformative influence that AI wields, not only within the confines of workplaces but also in broader domains, casting light on its profound ramifications across industries, economies, and even the very essence of labor itself.

1.1.1. AI: A Catalyst for Change

Artificial Intelligence (AI) stands as a powerful catalyst, sparking transformation across various aspects of our lives. It is not merely a collection of advanced algorithms; rather, it represents a seismic shift in how we approach problems, make decisions, and innovate. At its core, AI mirrors human cognitive functions such as learning, reasoning, and problem-solving, bestowing machines with the ability to process massive volumes of data and derive meaningful insights. This capacity to analyze data swiftly and accurately positions AI as a game-changer across diverse sectors.

The workplace is undergoing a revolution, guided by the transformative potential of AI. Automation, once confined to monotonous and routine tasks, now encompasses intricate activities previously reserved for human experts. AI-powered algorithms can discern complex patterns within data, predict future trends, and even generate imaginative solutions. This metamorphosis is evident in AI's growing presence across industries spanning healthcare, finance, manufacturing, and entertainment.

AI's impact extends beyond mere efficiency; it's a harbinger of innovation. With the power to sift through vast datasets and unearth intricate correlations, AI opens new pathways for discovery and invention. Drug discovery accelerates through AI-enabled simulations, while scientific research gains momentum from machine learning algorithms parsing complex data sets.

Even in creative fields, AI-generated art challenges conventional notions of human creativity. Collaborative robots (cobots) collaborate alongside human artists and designers, offering fresh perspectives and approaches. This interplay between human ingenuity and AI's analytical prowess stimulates innovation in domains that were once deemed solely within the purview of human expertise.

Amidst AI's transformative prowess, the human element remains indispensable. AI can automate tasks and processes, but it cannot replicate the depth of human emotions, context, and creativity. This realization ushers in a paradigm shift in how we perceive work. Instead of fearing displacement, individuals and organizations are redefining roles, emphasizing human qualities like empathy, intuition, and critical thinking.

In this new era, collaboration between humans and AI takes center stage. AI augments human capabilities, aiding professionals in making informed decisions and concentrating on value-added tasks. It liberates employees from mundane chores, empowering them to engage in higher-order thinking and creativity. The future of work isn't a contest between humans and machines; it's a partnership leveraging the strengths of both.

In conclusion, AI's transformative might reshapes industries, redefines roles, and propels society into uncharted territories. As AI continues to evolve, its impact will permeate economies and societies, warranting thoughtful navigation. Subsequent chapters will delve into the intricate facets of this transformation, from the historical journey to ethical considerations and strategies for embracing a future where AI and human collaboration thrive. The AI era is upon us, rewriting the future of work with every algorithm and innovation.

1.1.2. Reshaping Industries and Processes

The advent of Artificial Intelligence (AI) is instigating a seismic wave of change that is profoundly reshaping industries and revolutionizing the very processes that underpin them. This transformation isn't just a minor shift; it's a profound alteration that is challenging traditional paradigms and ushering in new modes of operation. This section delves into the remarkable impact of AI on various industries and the processes that drive economies forward.

Industries spanning healthcare, finance, manufacturing, and beyond are experiencing a profound metamorphosis thanks to the infusion of AI. In healthcare, AI-driven diagnostic tools are revolutionizing medical care, enhancing accuracy in detecting and diagnosing medical conditions. The financial landscape is also undergoing a shift, as algorithms powered by AI execute intricate investment strategies with unprecedented precision and speed. Manufacturing processes are being streamlined and optimized through AI-driven robotics, boosting efficiency and reducing costs. Even entertainment is not immune to AI's influence, with recommendation systems that personalize user experiences, enhancing engagement.

The ripple effects of AI extend beyond industries to the very processes that drive economies. Supply chains are being meticulously optimized, reducing waste and enhancing efficiency. Customer service experiences are elevated through AI-powered chatbots, providing assistance round the clock. Data-driven insights are shaping marketing strategies, enabling businesses to tailor their offerings to specific customer segments, thereby improving overall business performance and fostering a more customer-centric approach.

However, the impact of AI isn't just confined to increasing efficiency; it's also about igniting innovation. AI's capability to analyze vast datasets and uncover intricate patterns is spurring new avenues for discovery. In fields like drug discovery and scientific research, AI is accelerating progress by simulating experiments and processing complex data. The creative realm is also witnessing AI-generated art that challenges conventional boundaries, while collaborative robots (cobots) are collaborating with human artists, infusing new perspectives into the creative process.

As industries and processes adapt to this new era, it's important to recognize that the human factor remains essential. AI may automate tasks, but it cannot replicate the depth of human emotions, empathy, and creative thinking. This realization is leading to a reevaluation of roles, with a shift towards emphasizing uniquely human qualities that complement AI's analytical prowess.

In this evolving landscape, collaboration between humans and AI emerges as a central theme. AI augments human capabilities, allowing professionals to make more informed decisions and focus on tasks that require human intuition and creativity. It liberates individuals from mundane tasks, freeing them to engage in higher-order thinking. This synergy between humans and AI is not a competition; it's a partnership that capitalizes on the strengths of both entities.

In conclusion, AI's transformative impact is altering industries, reshaping processes, and propelling society into new frontiers. As AI continues its evolution, its effects will reverberate through economies and societies, necessitating thoughtful navigation. Subsequent chapters will delve deeper into the nuances of this transformation, spanning historical evolution, ethical considerations, and strategies for embracing a future where AI and human collaboration thrive. The age of AI is here, rewriting the narrative of work with every algorithm and innovation.

1.1.3. Beyond Efficiency: Pioneering Innovation

The emergence of Artificial Intelligence (AI) isn't merely confined to enhancing efficiency; it's a dynamic force that is driving the vanguard of innovation. AI's impact extends far beyond streamlining existing processes; it's igniting the spark of creativity and opening new avenues for exploration and invention. This section delves into the remarkable ways in which AI is not just optimizing, but pioneering innovation across various domains.

AI's capacity to process vast datasets and unveil intricate correlations is redefining the boundaries of discovery. It's accelerating progress in fields like drug discovery by simulating experiments and analyzing complex data, thereby revolutionizing the pace of scientific breakthroughs. In creative industries, AI-generated art challenges established notions of human creativity, pushing the envelope of artistic expression. Collaborative robots (cobots) are venturing into uncharted territories, working alongside human artists and designers to offer fresh insights and novel approaches.

This interplay between AI's analytical prowess and human ingenuity is breathing new life into domains that were once the sole province of human expertise. Machine learning algorithms, inspired by the architecture of the human brain, are revolutionizing tasks like image recognition and natural language processing. This synergy is not about replacing humans; it's about enhancing human potential by leveraging AI's computational power to unravel complexities that were previously beyond our grasp.

Yet, amid this wave of innovation, the essence of the human touch remains indispensable. AI can process data, but it can't replicate the depth of human emotions, empathy, and creativity. This realization is prompting a reevaluation of roles, with a renewed emphasis on qualities that make us uniquely human, such as intuition, empathy, and critical thinking. Instead of fearing displacement, individuals and organizations are leveraging AI to augment their capabilities and amplify their impact.

In this era of innovation, the partnership between humans and AI emerges as the cornerstone of progress. AI complements human decision-making by providing data-driven insights and automating routine tasks. This liberates individuals to focus on tasks that require emotional intelligence, strategic thinking, and creative problem-solving. The future isn't about humans versus machines; it's about a collaborative coexistence where the strengths of both entities are harnessed for collective advancement.

In conclusion, AI's transformative influence goes beyond efficiency, permeating the realm of innovation and discovery. Its role as a catalyst for creativity is redefining industries, expanding the horizons of research, and reimagining the creative process. As AI continues to evolve, its impact will reshape the trajectory of progress, demanding a thoughtful approach. Subsequent chapters will delve deeper into the intricate dimensions of this transformation, including historical context, ethical considerations, and strategies for embracing a future where AI and human collaboration flourish. The AI era is here, painting a new landscape of work with every algorithm and innovation.

1.1.4. The Human Element: Redefining Roles

Amidst the rise of Artificial Intelligence (AI), the human element stands as an unwavering cornerstone, guiding the transformation of roles and redefining the value that individuals bring to the table. While AI can automate tasks and processes, it falls short in replicating the complexity of human emotions, context, and creativity. This section delves into the profound shift occurring in the world of work as the interplay between humans and AI redefines roles and highlights the distinctive qualities that set us apart.

AI's integration isn't about supplanting humans; rather, it's an opportunity to recalibrate the role that individuals play in the workforce. Automation might handle routine and repetitive tasks, but it's the depth of human empathy, intuition, and critical thinking that shapes the trajectory of innovation and problem-solving. As AI takes over mundane chores, it affords us the chance to channel our energies into tasks that demand human insight, creativity, and nuanced decision-making.

In this era of collaboration, AI serves as a tool to enhance human capabilities, augmenting our expertise and helping us make more informed choices. Professionals are empowered to engage in high-level reasoning and strategic thinking, unburdened from the routine tasks that can be automated. The result is a workforce that is more agile, adaptable, and capable of embracing the complex challenges that define the modern world.

The evolving landscape is leading to a redefinition of traditional roles. Instead of fearing displacement, individuals and organizations are recognizing the potential for AI to free us from the constraints of the mundane, enabling us to engage in tasks that demand the full spectrum of human intelligence. As roles evolve, the emphasis shifts from rote tasks to skills that AI can't replicate, such as emotional intelligence, empathy, creativity, and ethical decision-making.

Furthermore, AI's rapid evolution necessitates a commitment to lifelong learning. As new roles emerge and existing ones evolve, the ability to adapt and upskill becomes essential. This isn't a burden but an opportunity for personal and professional growth, as individuals and organizations embrace a culture of continuous learning to stay ahead in the ever-changing landscape.

In conclusion, the human element remains integral in the age of AI, redefining the roles we play and shaping the value we contribute. AI serves as a powerful ally, amplifying our capabilities and empowering us to focus on tasks that require uniquely human qualities. As we navigate this new era of collaboration, AI and humans are not competing forces; they are partners in progress, building a future where the harmonious integration of our strengths paves the way for unprecedented innovation and advancement.

Conclusion: 1.1. The Transformative Power of AI

The transformative might of AI is orchestrating a profound reshaping of industries, prompting a reevaluation of roles, and propelling society into uncharted domains. As the trajectory of

AI technology continues its trajectory of advancement, the repercussions will reverberate across economies and societies, necessitating deliberate contemplation and meticulous navigation. The subsequent chapters of this literary venture will delve even deeper into the multifaceted aspects of this transformation, charting the historical voyage that has culminated in this juncture, scrutinizing the intricate ethical dilemmas, and proposing strategies for embracing a future characterized by the harmonious coexistence of AI and human ingenuity. We're standing at the threshold of the AI era, and with each algorithm and innovation, the landscape of labor is being rewritten, promising a future that amalgamates human acumen with the prowess of AI.

1.2. Historical Context: A Continuum of Innovation

The trajectory of technological progress resembles a rich tapestry woven with intricate threads of innovation, each contributing to the grand narrative of human advancement. The rise of Artificial Intelligence (AI) as a transformative influence isn't an isolated occurrence but rather a crucial juncture in a continuum of innovation that has spanned across centuries. This section embarks on a journey to trace the historical evolution from early mechanization to the digital age, culminating in the current era defined by AI-driven automation.

1.2.1. Mechanization: The First Steps

The roots of automation were planted during the era of the industrial revolution, a time that marked the advent of mechanization and the inception of modern industry. The introduction of steam-powered machinery and mechanized processes brought about a revolution in manufacturing, significantly enhancing production capabilities and reshaping economies. Tasks that previously demanded manual labor were now undertaken with a precision fueled by mechanical prowess, laying the groundwork for the automation that would eventually emerge.

1.2.2. Digitalization: The Rise of Computers

The mid-20th century witnessed the ascent of computers, ushering in a new phase of data processing and automation. The arrival of digital computers introduced the concept of programmability, enabling humans to provide machines with instructions through coded commands. This era ushered in the automation of intricate calculations, data storage, and retrieval of information, streamlining both administrative and computational operations.

1.2.3. From Algorithms to AI: The Emergence of Artificial Intelligence

The transition from digitalization to AI was marked by a shift from rule-based algorithms to machines imbued with the capacity to learn and reason. The concept of AI emerged in the mid-20th century, championed by trailblazers like Alan Turing and John McCarthy. Early AI systems showcased symbolic reasoning, striving to simulate human thought processes. However, constraints related to computational power and data availability restrained significant advancements.

The late 20th century and early 21st century brought forth noteworthy breakthroughs. The evolution of machine learning algorithms was propelled by the abundance of data and the progression of computational capabilities. Neural networks, inspired by the structural design of the human brain, gained prominence. This period witnessed AI systems excelling in domains such as image recognition and natural language processing, paving the way for the AI-driven automation that characterizes our present age.

1.2.4. AI-Driven Automation: The Present Era

The culmination of this historical progression leads us to the contemporary era marked by AI-driven automation. Narrow AI, distinguished by its expertise in specific domains, has permeated various industries. Equipped with advanced deep learning algorithms and vast datasets, AI systems excel in tasks that were once the exclusive domain of human expertise. This includes tasks as varied as medical condition diagnosis, steering autonomous vehicles, and analyzing intricate financial trends.

The common thread interwoven through this continuum of innovation is the pursuit of efficiency, accuracy, and innovation. Mechanization sought to amplify physical labor, while digitalization aimed to streamline data-related processes. AI represents the zenith of this journey, introducing systems that are not only capable of learning but also of adapting and reasoning. The historical context underscores that AI isn't a sudden departure from the past but rather a natural progression, showcasing humanity's persistent endeavor to harness technology for its advancement.

Conclusion: 1.2. Historical Context: A Continuum of Innovation

Gaining insight into the historical context of AI's rise deepens our understanding of its significance. From the mechanization of tasks during the industrial revolution to the digitalization of processes in the mid-20th century, we now stand at a pivotal juncture in the ongoing story of human innovation. The upcoming chapters of this book venture further into the multifaceted impact of AI on industries, jobs, and skills, providing a comprehensive view of the dynamic landscape shaped by AI. Just as AI builds upon the foundations laid by the past, it beckons us to co-create a future where the potential of humanity converges harmoniously with the potential of technology in unprecedented ways.

1.3. An Exploration Ahead: Impact on Industries, Jobs, and Skills

The emergence of Artificial Intelligence (AI) ushers in a fresh era of transformation, creating ripples that touch every facet of our lives. As AI technologies continue their rapid advancement, it becomes essential to closely examine how they influence industries, jobs, and the skills that the evolving landscape demands. This section lays the groundwork for comprehending the extensive implications of AI, shedding light on how it is reshaping the very fabric of our economic and social systems.

1.3.1. The Canvas of Industries: AI's Disruptive Strokes

The domains of industries are undergoing a profound transformation due to the disruptive influence of Artificial Intelligence (AI). This technological force is leaving its mark across various sectors, reshaping the way business is conducted and revolutionizing traditional models. This section delves into the far-reaching consequences of AI's integration, showcasing its capacity to redefine industries and open up new avenues of progress.

Industries that once adhered to established norms and methods are now experiencing a metamorphosis fueled by AI's innovative capabilities. The healthcare sector, for instance, is witnessing a revolution as AI-driven diagnostic tools offer unmatched accuracy in detecting diseases. Manufacturing is embracing change through the infusion of AI-powered robotics and automation, optimizing production processes for efficiency and precision. Similarly, the financial sector is not immune to this transformative wave, with algorithms executing intricate trading strategies and portfolio management with exceptional speed and accuracy.

In this evolving landscape, AI's impact extends far beyond these examples. Sectors such as agriculture, transportation, energy, and entertainment are all being touched by AI's disruptive strokes. The canvas of industries is being reimagined, with AI as the paintbrush that brings innovation and efficiency to the forefront. As AI continues to push boundaries and explore new possibilities, industries are being challenged to adapt, evolve, and harness the potential of this technology to their advantage.

The real-world applications of AI across industries are not only impressive but also indicative of a broader shift toward a technologically advanced future. As we delve deeper into the intricate workings of AI's transformative influence, we uncover a tapestry of change that is altering industries at their core. This section invites readers to contemplate the implications of AI's disruptive strokes on the industries we rely on, setting the stage for a comprehensive understanding of the broader AI revolution.

1.3.2. Job Market Dynamics: Displacement, Augmentation, Creation

The influence of Artificial Intelligence (AI) on the job market is nothing short of transformative, ushering in a complex landscape characterized by displacement, augmentation, and creation. As AI technologies continue to advance, they are reshaping the world of work in multifaceted ways, sparking debates, and prompting both excitement and concerns. In this section, we delve into the intricate dynamics of this evolving job landscape, highlighting the challenges and opportunities it presents.

1.3.2.1. Displacement: The Changing Face of Work

One of the most palpable impacts of AI on the job market is the displacement of certain roles and tasks that were once the exclusive domain of humans. Automation, powered by AI and robotics, has made significant strides in areas that involve routine, repetitive, and rule-based tasks. Manufacturing, data entry, and customer support are just a few examples where machines and algorithms have taken over, raising valid concerns about job displacement.

However, it's essential to recognize that the story of displacement is not one of unmitigated loss. While certain tasks may be automated, the broader impact on employment is more nuanced. Displaced workers often have opportunities to reskill and transition into roles that require uniquely human qualities such as creativity, empathy, critical thinking, and complex problem-solving. The challenge lies in facilitating this transition and providing the necessary support and training.

1.3.2.2. Augmentation: Enhancing Human Capabilities

AI's transformative power extends beyond displacement; it lies in its capacity to augment human capabilities. AI systems excel at processing vast amounts of data, identifying patterns, and providing insights in real time. This augmentation allows professionals across various industries to make more informed decisions, increasing efficiency and productivity.

In healthcare, AI augments the diagnostic abilities of medical professionals by analyzing medical images and patient data with remarkable accuracy. In finance, it enhances the abilities of analysts and traders by processing market data at incredible speeds. In education, it personalizes learning experiences, catering to individual student needs.

The augmentation narrative is one of collaboration between humans and machines, where AI serves as a powerful tool, amplifying human potential. Professionals are liberated from mundane and time-consuming tasks, enabling them to focus on higher-level responsibilities that require creativity, judgment, and empathy.

1.3.2.3. Creation: Forging New Opportunities

Perhaps one of the most exciting dimensions of AI's impact on the job market is the creation of entirely new job categories and industries. As AI technologies continue to evolve, they give rise to a demand for specialized skills and expertise. These new opportunities extend across various domains:

- **AI Programming and Development:** The development and maintenance of AI systems require skilled programmers and engineers proficient in machine learning, neural networks, and natural language processing.
- **Data Analysis and Interpretation:** The exponential growth of data necessitates professionals who can extract meaningful insights, inform decision-making, and ensure data privacy and security.
- **Ethical Oversight:** With AI's increasing influence, there's a growing need for professionals who can ensure responsible and ethical AI development, addressing concerns related to bias, fairness, and transparency.
- **AI-Enhanced Roles:** Existing job roles, from marketing to journalism, are evolving as professionals incorporate AI tools and techniques into their work.

Conclusion: 1.3.2. Job Market Dynamics: Displacement, Augmentation, Creation

The AI-driven transformation of the job market is a multifaceted phenomenon that cannot be reduced to simple narratives of displacement or automation. Instead, it calls for a nuanced understanding of the interplay between displacement, augmentation, and creation. As certain tasks become automated, new opportunities emerge, demanding adaptability, reskilling, and a commitment to lifelong learning from both workers and organizations.

Government policies, education and training programs, and industry initiatives will play pivotal roles in helping society navigate this evolving landscape. Embracing AI as a collaborative partner and harnessing its potential for the betterment of work and society is the key to thriving in the AI-augmented future. The challenges are real, but so are the opportunities for those prepared to embrace them.

1.3.3. Skills for the AI-Driven Ecosystem: Navigating Uncharted Terrain

The advent of an AI-powered future necessitates a fundamental recalibration of the skills individuals require to thrive in the workforce. While technical proficiency remains crucial, the evolving landscape places a premium on a new set of skills – skills that enable individuals to harness the potential of AI as a collaborative partner rather than a replacement. In this section, we explore the critical skills necessary for navigating the AI era, emphasizing the value of both technical and soft skills, and offer insights into strategies for both individuals and organizations to reskill effectively.

1.3.3.1. Technical Proficiency: The Foundation

Technical proficiency, particularly in areas related to AI and data science, forms the foundation of success in the AI-driven ecosystem. This includes:

- **AI Literacy:** A fundamental understanding of AI principles, algorithms, and their applications is essential. Even for non-technical professionals, a basic grasp of how AI functions empowers informed decision-making.
- **Data Literacy:** With data being the lifeblood of AI, the ability to collect, analyze, and interpret data is invaluable. This skill ensures that data is used effectively to drive insights and innovation.
- **Programming and Coding:** Proficiency in programming languages like Python, R, and Java is crucial, especially for AI developers and data scientists.
- **Machine Learning and Deep Learning:** A deeper understanding of machine learning techniques, neural networks, and natural language processing is essential for those working directly with AI systems.
- **Data Privacy and Ethics:** In an era where data privacy and ethical considerations are paramount, individuals must be well-versed in the principles of ethical AI development, responsible data handling, and privacy regulations.

1.3.3.2. Soft Skills: The Human Touch

In the AI era, soft skills take on new significance. These uniquely human qualities are irreplaceable and complement the technical foundation. They include:

- **Creativity:** While AI can optimize processes and generate ideas, true creativity remains a human trait.

Creative thinking drives innovation, problem-solving, and the development of novel solutions.
- **Critical Thinking:** The ability to analyze complex situations, identify patterns, evaluate information, and make informed decisions is invaluable. Critical thinking is the linchpin of effective problem-solving in a data-rich world.
- **Adaptability:** The rapid pace of AI advancements demands adaptability. Individuals who can pivot, learn quickly, and embrace change will thrive in this dynamic environment.
- **Emotional Intelligence:** In roles that involve human interaction, such as healthcare and customer service, emotional intelligence becomes indispensable. Empathy, understanding, and the ability to connect on an emotional level remain uniquely human strengths.
- **Interdisciplinary Collaboration:** AI projects often require multidisciplinary teams. The ability to collaborate effectively with professionals from diverse backgrounds is essential for driving innovation.

1.3.3.3. Lifelong Learning: The Cornerstone of Adaptation

In the AI era, learning doesn't end with formal education; it's a lifelong endeavor. The rapid evolution of technology means that skills become outdated quickly. To stay relevant, individuals must commit to continuous learning and upskilling:

- **Online Courses and Certifications:** A plethora of online courses and certifications, often offered by top universities and institutions, provide opportunities to acquire new skills and stay updated.
- **Professional Development:** Employers can play a pivotal role in supporting their workforce's

development by providing opportunities for ongoing training and skill enhancement.
- **Self-Directed Learning:** Individuals can take the initiative to explore new topics, experiment with AI tools, and engage in self-directed learning to adapt to the changing landscape.
- **AI-Powered Learning:** AI itself can be a tool for learning. Adaptive learning platforms and AI-powered educational resources cater to individual needs and learning styles.

Conclusion: 1.3.3. Skills for the AI-Driven Ecosystem: Navigating Uncharted Terrain

The AI-driven ecosystem presents both challenges and opportunities. While it automates routine tasks, it opens doors to innovation, efficiency, and collaboration. The key to success lies in embracing AI as a partner, not a replacement, and cultivating a skill set that complements AI's capabilities.

As the workforce evolves, organizations must invest in reskilling their employees to equip them with the necessary technical and soft skills. Individuals, on the other hand, must embark on a journey of lifelong learning, adapting to the ever-changing AI landscape. In this transformative era, those who blend technical expertise with uniquely human skills will not only navigate uncharted terrain but also thrive in the AI-driven future.

Conclusion: 1.3. An Exploration Ahead: Impact on Industries, Jobs, and Skills

The exploration ahead entails a journey through the multifaceted impact of AI on industries, jobs, and skills. By dissecting AI's influence on diverse sectors, understanding its repercussions on the job market, and identifying the skills demanded for success, our goal is to provide readers with a comprehensive grasp of the challenges and opportunities intrinsic to this unparalleled technological leap. The ensuing chapters of this book will delve even further into each of these dimensions, unraveling complexities, and offering a roadmap for embracing a future that is enriched by the augmentation of AI. As we embark on this journey of exploration, let us acknowledge that the trajectory of AI's influence is malleable; it is shaped by the collective decisions and actions we take.

Chapter 2: Exploring the World of Artificial Intelligence

2.1. A Primer on AI Technologies

In the landscape of technological innovation, Artificial Intelligence (AI) stands as a pivotal force, bringing to life a range of capabilities that were once the stuff of science fiction. This section serves as a foundational introduction to the core technologies that serve as the bedrock of AI's incredible abilities. By shedding light on concepts like machine learning, neural networks, natural language processing, and more, our aim is to unveil the intricate mechanisms that power AI's transformative impact.

2.1.1. Machine Learning: Revealing the Algorithms of Learning

In the realm of Artificial Intelligence (AI), machine learning stands as a luminous pillar, illuminating the path to advanced capabilities through learning algorithms. This section provides an insightful glimpse into the world of machine learning, where computers acquire knowledge from data and refine their performance over time. By exploring the intricacies of supervised learning, unsupervised learning, and reinforcement learning, we uncover the mechanisms that enable machines to grasp patterns and make informed decisions.

At its essence, machine learning is the art of empowering computers to learn autonomously. In the realm of supervised learning, algorithms are trained with labeled data, enabling them to discern patterns and associations. Once trained, these algorithms can predict outcomes for new, unseen data, such as predicting the weather based on historical weather patterns. Unsupervised learning takes a different route, uncovering hidden patterns within unlabeled data. This approach has applications in diverse fields, from clustering similar customer behaviors for targeted marketing to identifying groupings in astronomical data.

Reinforcement learning adds a dimension of interaction. Inspired by behavioral psychology, this approach involves training algorithms through a system of rewards and penalties. Just as humans learn from consequences, reinforcement learning algorithms refine their strategies based on the outcomes of their actions. This method is particularly potent in training AI agents for tasks like game playing or robotics, where trial and error lead to improved decision-making.

Machine learning's potential applications are astounding. In financial markets, algorithms analyze historical data to forecast stock prices, aiding investors in making informed decisions. In healthcare, they process vast datasets to identify potential drug candidates, revolutionizing the drug discovery process. Image recognition thrives through machine learning, with algorithms learning from massive datasets to distinguish objects, faces, and scenes.

This capacity to learn from data propels AI into realms that were once considered the domain of human expertise. As machines learn and adapt, they enhance their proficiency, making them indispensable partners in decision-making, analysis, and problem-solving. This section serves as a gateway to understanding the fundamental principles behind machine learning, laying the foundation for delving further into AI's impact on industries, job markets, and the skill landscape.

2.1.2. Neural Networks: Mirroring the Complexity of the Human Brain

In the captivating world of Artificial Intelligence (AI), neural networks shine as a remarkable endeavor to emulate the intricate workings of the human brain. This section offers a glimpse into the fascinating realm of neural networks, where layers of artificial neurons collaborate to process information and unravel complex patterns. By understanding the structure and function of neural networks, we uncover the driving force behind AI's capabilities and innovations.

At its core, a neural network is a network of interconnected artificial neurons, inspired by the neurons that compose the human brain. These neurons work in harmony, processing and transmitting information through layers that progressively extract higher-level features from raw data. Deep learning, a subset of neural networks, introduces multiple layers that autonomously learn intricate features and hierarchies, empowering algorithms to excel in tasks that demand perceptual understanding.

The power of neural networks is vividly evident in image recognition. Through exposure to countless images, a neural network learns to distinguish various objects, such as identifying a cat in a photograph. This technology is integral to self-driving cars, enabling them to interpret their surroundings and navigate safely. Similarly, in natural language processing, neural networks decode the complexities of language, facilitating translation, sentiment analysis, and text generation.

The growth of neural networks is fueled by the abundant availability of data and the exponential increase in computing power. This has led to a renaissance in AI, with neural networks at the forefront of breakthroughs in speech recognition, medical diagnoses, and more. As these networks evolve, their capabilities grow, transforming AI from a tool that performs specific tasks to a partner that comprehends and interacts with the world.

Neural networks, in their emulation of the human brain, open doors to innovations that were once the realm of science fiction. This section serves as a portal into the heart of neural networks, providing a foundation to delve deeper into their role in reshaping industries, influencing job markets, and redefining the skills demanded in the modern workforce. As we explore the frontiers of AI, we uncover a new era of collaboration between human intelligence and artificial cognition.

2.1.3. Natural Language Processing: Deciphering Human Communication

In the realm of Artificial Intelligence (AI), Natural Language Processing (NLP) emerges as a key to bridging the gap between human language and machine understanding. This section delves into the intricate world of NLP, where machines decode and generate human language with contextual significance. By unraveling the complexities of NLP, we gain insights into how AI transforms the way we interact with technology and communicate with machines.

NLP equips computers with the ability to comprehend, interpret, and generate human language in a manner that mirrors human communication. From chatbots engaging in lifelike conversations to sentiment analysis gauging public opinion on social media platforms, NLP plays a pivotal role in shaping human-AI interactions. This technology has moved beyond mere text-based communication to encompass speech recognition and language translation, enabling seamless communication across languages and cultures.

The evolution of NLP involves grappling with the nuances of language, such as idioms, context, and even emotional undertones. Sentiment analysis algorithms, for instance, can discern the emotions behind text, gauging whether a statement is positive, negative, or neutral. This has applications in diverse fields, from understanding customer feedback to tracking public sentiment on social and political issues.

Machine translation is another remarkable facet of NLP. By analyzing vast bilingual datasets, algorithms can automatically translate text from one language to another. This technology has revolutionized global communication, enabling people to connect and collaborate across linguistic barriers.

As NLP advances, so does our capacity to communicate with machines in a more natural and intuitive manner. Voice assistants like Siri and Alexa are manifestations of NLP, allowing users to interact with technology through spoken language. This technology isn't just about understanding words; it's about comprehending context, intent, and even humor.

The journey into NLP opens a gateway to understanding how machines grasp the intricacies of human language. This section lays the groundwork for deeper exploration into how NLP reshapes industries, influences the job market, and demands new skills from the workforce. As we navigate the landscape of AI, we uncover a world where machines not only understand what we say but also how we say it.

2.1.4. Computer Vision: AI's Visual Perception

In the expansive realm of Artificial Intelligence (AI), Computer Vision stands as a window through which machines gain the power of visual perception. This section offers an illuminating view into the world of Computer Vision, where AI systems analyze images and videos, mirroring the human sense of sight. By delving into the intricacies of Computer Vision, we uncover how AI processes visual data to navigate and understand the world.

Computer Vision empowers AI to interpret and make sense of visual information from the environment. Just as humans rely on their eyes to perceive the world, AI algorithms process images and videos, identifying objects, patterns, and even emotions. This technology has transcendent applications, from medical imaging that aids in diagnosing diseases to self-driving cars that recognize traffic signs and pedestrians.

At the heart of Computer Vision lies deep learning, a subset of AI that involves neural networks with multiple layers. These networks autonomously learn to recognize features within images, progressively identifying more complex structures. This enables algorithms to identify objects, faces, and even scenes with remarkable accuracy. Image recognition technology not only transforms industries like manufacturing and agriculture but also finds its way into everyday applications, such as facial recognition for unlocking smartphones.

Computer Vision is integral to augmented reality experiences, overlaying digital information onto the physical world. This technology enables users to interact with their surroundings in novel ways, enhancing gaming, education, and even remote assistance scenarios. In the realm of healthcare, Computer Vision assists in surgeries, allowing doctors to visualize internal organs with greater precision.

As the field advances, the applications of Computer Vision continue to expand. Surveillance systems become more intelligent, identifying suspicious activities in crowded places. Robots equipped with Computer Vision navigate complex environments, enabling tasks like warehouse management and precision agriculture. This technology even extends its reach to art conservation, helping experts analyze paintings and artifacts.

This section unveils the potential of Computer Vision, serving as a foundation for deeper exploration into its role in transforming industries, influencing job markets, and shaping the skills demanded by the evolving workforce. As we peer through the lens of AI's visual perception, we embark on a journey that merges the capabilities of technology with the artistry of human sight.

Conclusion: 2.1. A Primer on AI Technologies

This primer serves as a gateway into the realm of AI technologies propelling our world into uncharted territories. The intricacies of machine learning, neural networks, natural language processing, and computer vision collectively lay the groundwork for AI's capabilities. With this knowledge in hand, readers can approach subsequent chapters, delving deeper into how these technologies reshape industries, influence the job market, and redefine the skills essential for the workforce of tomorrow.

2.2. Narrow AI and General AI: Unveiling the Distinction

As we embark on a journey through the realm of Artificial Intelligence (AI), it becomes essential to illuminate the contrast between two pivotal concepts: Narrow AI and General AI. These terms serve as beacons along the AI spectrum, casting light on the diversity of AI capabilities and their far-reaching implications for our technological landscape and society at large.

2.2.1. Narrow AI: Precision in Specialization

In the dynamic realm of Artificial Intelligence (AI), Narrow AI emerges as a beacon of precision within the vast sea of possibilities. This section delves into the concept of Narrow AI, often referred to as Weak AI, where the focus lies on specialized expertise in a specific domain. By uncovering the nuances of Narrow AI, we gain insights into how these specialized AI systems are meticulously crafted to excel in targeted tasks, enhancing efficiency and effectiveness in various applications.

Narrow AI is intentionally designed to master well-defined tasks within a limited context. These AI systems are meticulously trained to accomplish singular tasks or a cluster of closely related activities with remarkable accuracy and efficiency. From the voice-activated personal assistants that engage in seamless conversations with us, such as Siri and Google Assistant, to the algorithms that curate personalized recommendations on our favorite streaming platforms, Narrow AI seamlessly integrates into our daily lives.

It's important to note that Narrow AI operates within its defined boundaries. Its expertise is tailored to a specific task or domain and does not inherently possess the capacity to generalize its skills beyond these parameters. While its performance within its designated realm is remarkable, Narrow AI lacks the comprehensive cognitive capabilities that humans possess. It does not have the capacity for abstract reasoning, contextual understanding, or creative thinking that define human cognition.

However, the significance of Narrow AI lies in its precision. By channeling its capabilities into focused tasks, it achieves levels of accuracy and speed that surpass human capacities. Whether it's analyzing vast datasets for medical diagnoses, optimizing supply chain logistics, or recognizing patterns in financial data, Narrow AI delivers results that are consistent, reliable, and finely tuned.

This section serves as a portal to understanding how Narrow AI operates within its niche, paving the way for deeper exploration into AI's impact on industries, jobs, and skills. As we continue our journey through the landscape of AI, we discover the potential of Narrow AI to elevate efficiency and accuracy while recognizing the boundaries that differentiate it from the realm of human-like cognition.

2.2.2. General AI: The Horizon of Human-Like Intellect

In the vast landscape of Artificial Intelligence (AI), the concept of General AI emerges as a beacon illuminating the quest for machines with human-like cognitive abilities. This section unveils the essence of General AI, often termed Strong AI, where AI systems aspire to emulate the breadth and depth of human intelligence. By delving into General AI, we explore the tantalizing possibility of machines that possess understanding, learning, and reasoning capabilities akin to human beings.

General AI transcends the boundaries of specialized tasks, envisioning AI systems with a scope of cognition that parallels human intellect. Unlike Narrow AI, which excels within confined domains, General AI is designed to understand, learn, and reason across a diverse spectrum of tasks and contexts. This conceptual AI entity possesses a level of consciousness and adaptability that echoes human cognition. It's not bound by rigid limitations; rather, it holds the capacity to transfer knowledge and skills from one field to another, exhibiting profound understanding and creative problem-solving.

In the realm of General AI, machines would not merely execute tasks; they would comprehend the intricacies of situations, grasp the underlying context, and formulate nuanced solutions. This paradigm shift extends beyond automated actions, inviting machines to partake in human-like reasoning and creativity. Imagine AI systems that seamlessly transition from diagnosing medical conditions to composing music, demonstrating a versatility that mirrors human capabilities.

However, the journey to General AI is complex and laden with challenges. Replicating the entirety of human cognitive abilities requires traversing uncharted territories of consciousness, adaptability, and emotional understanding. Ethical considerations, technical hurdles, and questions about accountability converge, underlining the intricate path toward achieving General AI.

As we explore General AI, it's imperative to acknowledge that this horizon is a future aspiration rather than a present reality. While Narrow AI thrives in specialized tasks, General AI remains a pursuit that sparks philosophical debates and necessitates responsible development. As we navigate the terrain of AI's potential, we must tread carefully, guided by ethical principles and conscious decision-making.

This section provides a glimpse into the far-reaching scope of General AI, setting the stage for deeper exploration into its implications for industries, jobs, and skills. As we move forward, we hold both the promise of machines that approach human-like cognition and the profound responsibilities entailed in shaping AI's trajectory for the betterment of society.

2.2.3. Implications and Forging Ahead

The distinction between Narrow AI and General AI carries profound implications that ripple across industries, economies, and the very fabric of society. This section sheds light on the far-reaching consequences of these two distinct forms of AI and outlines the ethical and strategic considerations as we navigate the evolving landscape of artificial intelligence.

Narrow AI, with its specialized expertise, is already shaping industries and revolutionizing processes within confined domains. Its precision and efficiency contribute to enhanced productivity and effectiveness. Industries ranging from healthcare and finance to manufacturing and entertainment are witnessing the transformational impact of Narrow AI. However, its limitations in terms of broader reasoning and understanding underscore the distinction between these AI forms.

On the horizon lies the tantalizing promise of General AI, where machines approach human-like cognition. This potential opens avenues for innovation that span beyond specialized tasks, revolutionizing the nature of work, creativity, and problem-solving. The implications are profound; General AI has the capacity to redefine entire industries, enable novel forms of human-machine collaboration, and unlock solutions to complex challenges that transcend the boundaries of individual domains.

However, the path to General AI is a complex journey. Ethical considerations loom large, encompassing questions about consciousness, accountability, and the potential social impact. The ethical development of AI systems that approach human-like cognition requires navigating uncharted terrain while ensuring transparency, fairness, and respect for human values.

As we forge ahead, responsible AI development becomes paramount. Guided by ethical frameworks, industry collaboration, and the wisdom of experts, we can harness the transformative potential of AI while mitigating risks. Open dialogue about the potential and limitations of General AI fosters a collective understanding that empowers informed decision-making.

This section serves as a touchstone for contemplating the implications of AI's evolution, urging us to navigate the path ahead with foresight and responsibility. The dialogue between Narrow AI and General AI enriches our understanding of AI's current capabilities and beckons us to envision a future where AI augments human capacities while respecting the ethical foundations that underpin our societies.

Conclusion: 2.2. Narrow AI and General AI: Unveiling the Distinction

In the dichotomy between Narrow AI and General AI, we encounter the full spectrum of AI's promise, spanning from specialized expertise to the aspiration of human-like cognition. As we traverse the forthcoming chapters of this book, where we delve into AI's impact on industries, jobs, and skills, let us be mindful of this dual narrative. While Narrow AI elevates our present, General AI tantalizes us with potential futures, grounded in ethical considerations that underscore our collective responsibility in shaping the contours of AI's unfolding narrative.

2.3. Real-World Applications of AI Across Industries

The canvas of Artificial Intelligence (AI) is no longer confined to theoretical musings—it has materialized as a tangible force that is reshaping industries on a global scale. This section delves into the practical applications of AI's transformative prowess across various sectors, illuminating its capacity to optimize processes, elevate decision-making, and redefine conventional practices.

2.3.1. Healthcare: Precision Diagnosis and Enhanced Care

Within the healthcare realm, Artificial Intelligence (AI) emerges as a game-changing force, imbuing precision into diagnoses and elevating patient care to unprecedented heights. This section delves into the applications of AI that are reshaping the medical landscape, showcasing its ability to enhance diagnostic accuracy, streamline treatment processes, and empower healthcare professionals to provide exceptional care.

AI's impact is most pronounced in medical imaging analysis, where algorithms trained on extensive datasets excel in detecting intricate patterns indicative of various conditions. This capability leads to early detection of diseases such as cancer, enabling timely intervention and improving patient outcomes. By scrutinizing medical images with a level of scrutiny that transcends human capacity, AI contributes to the accuracy and speed of diagnoses.

Predictive analytics powered by AI are revolutionizing the way healthcare providers identify potential health risks in patients. These AI models can process a multitude of patient data, from medical history to genetic markers, to predict the likelihood of diseases or complications. Such proactive insights empower medical professionals to devise preventative strategies and interventions, ultimately fostering a culture of proactive healthcare.

Virtual health assistants, equipped with AI-driven natural language processing, usher in a new era of patient engagement and management. These virtual companions interact with patients, providing personalized health information, reminding them of medication schedules, and addressing common inquiries. This personalized touch enhances patient adherence to treatment plans, ultimately contributing to improved outcomes.

Moreover, AI's prowess extends to medical research, where it expedites the analysis of vast datasets, identifies potential drug candidates, and predicts disease outbreaks. AI-driven simulations aid drug discovery by testing compounds' effectiveness and toxicity in silico, accelerating the drug development process.

In conclusion, the fusion of AI and healthcare has ushered in an era of precision diagnosis and elevated care. From early disease detection through advanced imaging analysis to predictive insights that shape preventative interventions, AI's contributions resonate across the entire healthcare spectrum. By amplifying healthcare professionals' capabilities and streamlining processes, AI is transforming patient outcomes and the way we perceive medical care.

2.3.2. Finance: The Data-Driven Financial Frontier

In the financial landscape, Artificial Intelligence (AI) emerges as a transformative force, propelling the domain into an era defined by data-driven decision-making and unparalleled efficiency. This section delves into the applications of AI in the realm of finance, illuminating its role in optimizing trading strategies, revolutionizing customer interactions, and safeguarding the integrity of financial operations.

AI's impact is palpable in algorithmic trading, where machine learning models analyze massive datasets to identify market trends and execute trades with unrivaled speed and precision. These algorithms, guided by AI, adapt to market fluctuations in real time, making strategic decisions that maximize returns. The infusion of AI in trading reshapes traditional investment strategies, harnessing the power of predictive analytics and pattern recognition.

Customer interactions within the financial sector are redefined through AI-powered chatbots. These virtual assistants engage customers in real-time conversations, addressing queries, providing assistance, and facilitating transactions. By offloading routine inquiries from human agents, these AI-driven chatbots enhance the efficiency of customer service operations while maintaining a high level of responsiveness.

AI is a key player in the realm of fraud detection, where its analytical capabilities excel in identifying unusual patterns and anomalies in transactions. These AI-driven systems monitor transactions in real time, flagging potentially fraudulent activities and safeguarding financial integrity. The precision of AI in spotting irregularities reduces false positives and enhances the accuracy of fraud identification.

Additionally, AI's applications extend to risk assessment and portfolio management. AI models analyze vast datasets to evaluate risk profiles, enabling financial institutions to make informed decisions about lending and investment. This data-driven approach enhances the accuracy of risk assessments and contributes to sound financial strategies.

In conclusion, the integration of AI in finance heralds a new era of data-powered decision-making and operational excellence. From revolutionizing trading strategies to enhancing customer interactions and fortifying security measures, AI's presence in the financial landscape is transformative. As the financial sector embraces AI-driven insights, it ushers in a future where accuracy, efficiency, and innovation are the hallmarks of financial operations.

2.3.3. Manufacturing: Redefining Automation and Efficiency

The manufacturing sector is undergoing a profound transformation with the infusion of Artificial Intelligence (AI), redefining automation and elevating operational efficiency to unprecedented levels. This section delves into the realm of manufacturing, unveiling the ways in which AI is reshaping production processes, predicting maintenance needs, and optimizing supply chain management.

AI's impact is most pronounced in the realm of automation. Robotic arms imbued with AI algorithms are revolutionizing production lines by executing intricate tasks with unparalleled precision. These AI-powered robots enhance operational efficiency by minimizing errors and accelerating production cycles. Their adaptability and ability to learn from real-time data ensure that manufacturing processes remain agile and responsive.

Predictive maintenance, empowered by AI, is redefining equipment upkeep. By analyzing real-time machine data, AI models can predict when machinery is likely to experience breakdowns or require maintenance. This proactive approach minimizes downtime, reduces operational disruptions, and extends the lifespan of equipment. The integration of AI in maintenance practices shifts the manufacturing landscape from reactive to preventative strategies.

Supply chain optimization represents another domain where AI's impact is transformative. AI-driven algorithms analyze vast datasets to forecast demand, optimize inventory levels, and dynamically adjust distribution strategies. This data-powered approach ensures that supply chains remain agile and responsive to market fluctuations, reducing waste and enhancing cost-effectiveness.

Furthermore, AI augments quality control processes. Machine learning models scrutinize product data to detect defects and irregularities, ensuring that only products of the highest quality reach consumers. This level of precision enhances customer satisfaction and reduces recalls, bolstering brand reputation.

In conclusion, the synergy of AI and manufacturing is ushering in an era of redefined automation and heightened operational efficiency. From precision-driven automation to predictive maintenance and supply chain optimization, AI's contributions resonate across the entire manufacturing spectrum. By elevating production capabilities and streamlining processes, AI is not just transforming how products are made—it's shaping the future of manufacturing itself.

2.3.4. Retail: Tailored Customer Experiences

In the dynamic world of retail, Artificial Intelligence (AI) emerges as a transformative force that is reshaping the landscape by offering personalized customer experiences tailored to individual preferences. This section delves into the applications of AI within the retail sector, highlighting its role in revolutionizing customer engagement, enhancing sales strategies, and optimizing inventory management.

One of the most striking applications of AI in retail is personalized recommendation systems. AI-powered algorithms analyze customer behaviors, preferences, and purchase history to offer product suggestions that align with individual tastes. These recommendations enhance the shopping experience, fostering a sense of personalization that encourages customer engagement and boosts sales.

Virtual shopping assistants, equipped with AI capabilities, elevate the level of customer service. These assistants engage shoppers in real-time conversations, addressing inquiries, providing product information, and guiding purchasing decisions. By offering immediate assistance and enhancing the shopping journey, these AI-driven virtual assistants contribute to improved customer satisfaction.

AI's role extends to inventory management, a critical facet of the retail industry. AI algorithms analyze historical sales data, market trends, and external factors to optimize inventory levels. This ensures that retailers maintain the right amount of stock, mitigating the risks of overstocking or understocking. The result is an efficient supply chain that adapts dynamically to demand fluctuations.

Additionally, AI-powered visual recognition technology enhances the in-store experience. Smart mirrors equipped with AI analyze customer outfits, suggesting complementary products and driving cross-selling opportunities. This interactive engagement offers a blend of convenience and personalization that resonates with modern shoppers.

In conclusion, AI's presence in retail is a game-changer, shaping customer experiences through personalization, efficiency, and interactive engagement. From tailored product recommendations to virtual shopping assistants and data-driven inventory management, AI's impact is palpable across the entire retail journey. By combining innovation and personalization, AI is revolutionizing how retailers connect with their customers, ensuring that every shopping encounter is a unique and satisfying experience.

2.3.5. Education: Learning Evolution and Beyond

Within the realm of education, Artificial Intelligence (AI) emerges as a transformative agent that is reshaping the way students learn, teachers instruct, and educational institutions operate. This section delves into the applications of AI within the educational sector, highlighting its role in adaptive learning, language acquisition, and creating interactive learning environments.

One of the most remarkable applications of AI in education is adaptive learning. AI-powered platforms analyze individual student performance and preferences, tailoring educational content to suit each learner's pace and learning style. This personalized approach optimizes learning outcomes by ensuring that students engage with material that matches their level of comprehension and challenges them appropriately.

Language acquisition is significantly enhanced through AI-driven Natural Language Processing (NLP) technologies. AI tutors equipped with NLP capabilities assist students in language learning, helping them develop reading, writing, and speaking skills. These AI-driven tutors offer immediate feedback, enabling students to refine their language abilities and gain confidence in their communication skills.

AI is also instrumental in creating interactive and engaging learning experiences. Educational tools powered by AI incorporate gamification, simulations, and multimedia to captivate students' attention and facilitate conceptual understanding. By merging technology and education, AI-driven tools encourage active participation and foster a deeper connection with the learning material.

Additionally, AI contributes to administrative efficiency within educational institutions. Chatbots powered by AI handle routine inquiries from students and parents, allowing administrative staff to focus on more complex tasks. AI-driven data analysis informs institutional decision-making by identifying trends in student performance and satisfaction.

In conclusion, AI's influence in education extends beyond the classroom, shaping learning experiences and administrative operations alike. From adaptive learning that tailors education to individual needs to language acquisition assistance and interactive tools that engage students, AI's impact is profound. As education evolves to meet the needs of modern learners, AI emerges as a pivotal force, redefining how knowledge is imparted and absorbed in the 21st century.

Conclusion: 2.3. Real-World Applications of AI Across Industries

These real-world instances resonate as concrete demonstrations of AI's transformative prowess spanning across sectors. As we venture into subsequent chapters, exploring AI's influence on industries, jobs, and skills, remember these tangible manifestations of AI's potential. The future of AI is not a distant abstract—it's an ongoing revolution that molds how we engage with our work, existence, and interaction with the dynamic world that envelops us.

Chapter 3: AI's Disruption across Industries

3.1. Healthcare: Diagnostics, Personalized Medicine, and Telehealth

The healthcare sector, a cornerstone of human well-being, finds itself at the cusp of a remarkable transformation propelled by the capabilities of Artificial Intelligence (AI). This section takes a comprehensive dive into the multifaceted applications of AI in healthcare, encompassing diagnostics, personalized medicine, and the evolution of telehealth. By delving into these areas, we uncover how AI is reshaping medical practices, enhancing accuracy, accessibility, and overall patient outcomes.

3.1.1. Diagnostics: Elevating Accuracy and Efficiency

In the realm of healthcare, Artificial Intelligence (AI) is taking diagnostics to unprecedented heights by revolutionizing accuracy and efficiency. This section sheds light on the profound impact of AI on medical diagnostics, unveiling how AI-driven technologies are enhancing the interpretation of medical images, detecting subtle anomalies, and ultimately improving patient outcomes.

AI's prowess in image analysis has ushered in a new era of diagnostic precision. Radiology departments harness AI algorithms to meticulously scrutinize intricate medical images like X-rays, MRIs, and CT scans. These algorithms possess an extraordinary ability to identify even the most subtle abnormalities, leading to the early detection of diseases such as cancer. By swiftly flagging potential issues, AI not only expedites diagnoses but also facilitates timely interventions that can significantly influence treatment success.

Moreover, AI acts as a collaborative partner for medical professionals, augmenting their expertise and offering second opinions. This symbiotic relationship between AI and human experts cultivates a synergy that enhances the overall diagnostic process. The fusion of human clinical knowledge with AI's analytical prowess creates a comprehensive diagnostic approach that yields more accurate results.

The efficiency gains from AI-powered diagnostics are equally noteworthy. Traditionally, medical image interpretation could be a time-consuming endeavor. AI's rapid processing capabilities expedite this process, allowing healthcare practitioners to focus more on patient care and treatment planning. By eliminating manual labor-intensive tasks, AI liberates medical professionals to allocate their time and expertise where it matters most.

In conclusion, AI's impact on diagnostics transcends conventional limits, offering a paradigm shift in accuracy and efficiency. From its role in early disease detection to its collaborative partnership with medical professionals, AI is redefining the landscape of medical diagnostics. By leveraging AI's capabilities, healthcare practitioners are equipped with tools that not only enhance their diagnostic accuracy but also optimize their workflow, ultimately translating into improved patient care and outcomes.

3.1.2. Personalized Medicine: A Revolution in Treatment

The landscape of healthcare is undergoing a seismic transformation, thanks to the revolutionary impact of Artificial

Intelligence (AI) on personalized medicine. This section unravels the profound implications of AI in the realm of personalized medicine, showcasing how AI's analytical prowess is revolutionizing treatment approaches by tailoring interventions to individual genetic profiles, medical histories, and lifestyles.

At the heart of personalized medicine lies AI's ability to decipher complex genetic data and medical information. AI algorithms meticulously analyze extensive datasets, unveiling genetic markers that influence disease susceptibility, drug response, and overall health. This intimate understanding of an individual's genetic makeup empowers healthcare providers to craft treatment plans that are uniquely suited to each patient.

The shift from a one-size-fits-all approach to targeted interventions is a hallmark of personalized medicine. By leveraging AI-driven insights, healthcare practitioners can prescribe treatments that maximize efficacy while minimizing adverse effects. This transformation has far-reaching implications for patient outcomes, particularly in areas such as cancer treatment, where therapies can be tailored to the genetic characteristics of the tumor.

Moreover, AI's role in personalized medicine extends beyond treatment to prevention. Predictive analytics, powered by AI, forecast an individual's predisposition to certain diseases based on genetic markers and lifestyle factors. This enables proactive measures, such as lifestyle modifications and early screenings, that can preemptively address potential health risks.

The fusion of AI and personalized medicine doesn't just impact individual patients—it also contributes to the advancement of medical research. By aggregating and analyzing vast datasets, AI-driven studies can identify novel genetic associations, refine treatment protocols, and facilitate drug discovery processes.

In conclusion, personalized medicine's revolution is intricately intertwined with AI's analytical capabilities. By tailoring treatments to individual genetic profiles and medical histories, AI empowers healthcare to transcend the boundaries of traditional medicine. As AI continues to refine its understanding of genetics and medical data, personalized medicine emerges as a cornerstone of healthcare, offering targeted interventions that are not only effective but also promise a new era of patient-centered care.

3.1.3. Telehealth: Bridging Gaps in Access

The evolution of healthcare is marked by the transformative influence of Artificial Intelligence (AI) in the realm of telehealth. This section delves into the profound impact of AI on telehealth, showcasing how it acts as a bridge, closing geographical and accessibility gaps in healthcare delivery while redefining patient-provider interactions.

Telehealth, empowered by AI, presents a paradigm shift in how healthcare is accessed and delivered. Through AI-powered telehealth platforms, patients can connect with healthcare professionals remotely, transcending physical barriers. Video calls, messages, and remote monitoring devices become conduits for consultations and diagnostics, fostering a sense of immediacy and convenience.

AI's role in telehealth begins with preliminary symptom assessments. Chatbots and virtual health assistants equipped with AI algorithms interact with patients, gathering information about symptoms and medical history. This preliminary triage streamlines the healthcare process, ensuring that patients receive appropriate care promptly. Moreover, AI augments healthcare professionals' capabilities by presenting them with synthesized patient information, enabling more informed decisions during consultations.

For regions with limited medical infrastructure, AI-powered telehealth emerges as a lifeline. Geographical distances and resource constraints no longer serve as barriers to quality healthcare. AI-driven platforms connect patients with specialists, allowing them to receive expert opinions and diagnoses without the need to travel.

In addition to diagnostics, AI contributes to remote monitoring. Wearable devices and sensors collect patient data, which is then analyzed by AI algorithms. Any deviations from normal health parameters trigger alerts, prompting healthcare providers to intervene as needed. This proactive approach enhances patient care and fosters early intervention.

However, as telehealth flourishes, ethical and regulatory considerations come to the forefront. Data privacy, security, and the ability to maintain patient-provider relationships in a virtual environment are challenges that require careful navigation.

In conclusion, AI's integration with telehealth is a transformative force, offering a democratization of healthcare access and enhancing patient-provider interactions. By erasing geographical disparities and fostering proactive care, AI-powered telehealth exemplifies the potential of technology to revolutionize healthcare delivery, ensuring that quality medical care is accessible to all, regardless of location.

3.1.4. Challenges and Opportunities on the Horizon

The integration of Artificial Intelligence (AI) into healthcare, while promising remarkable advancements, also presents a spectrum of challenges and opportunities that lie on the horizon. This section delves into these intricate dynamics, shedding light on the ethical, technical, and societal considerations that shape the future of AI in healthcare.

- **Data Privacy and Security:** As AI processes vast amounts of patient data, data privacy and security emerge as paramount concerns. Safeguarding patient information from breaches and unauthorized access is a critical challenge that demands robust encryption, secure storage practices, and stringent access controls. Striking a balance between data utility for AI-driven insights and preserving patient confidentiality is an ongoing endeavor.
- **Ethical Decision-Making:** The reliance on AI in clinical decision-making raises ethical questions. How much autonomy should AI have in determining treatment options? How are decisions made when AI algorithms and human experts diverge? Ensuring transparency in AI's decision-making processes and defining clear guidelines for when AI can autonomously make decisions are ethical considerations that require careful reflection.
- **Patient-Provider Relationship:** While AI augments healthcare, concerns arise about its impact on the patient-provider relationship. Can AI replace the empathetic connection that human interactions foster? Striking a balance between AI-enabled efficiency and the personalized touch of human care is pivotal to ensure that technology enhances rather than diminishes the patient-provider bond.
- **Bias and Fairness:** AI algorithms are trained on historical data, which may perpetuate biases present in

those datasets. Addressing bias in AI-driven diagnostics and treatment recommendations is a challenge that involves refining algorithms and ensuring diverse representation in training data. Fairness in AI is not only a technical consideration but a moral imperative.

- **Regulation and Oversight:** The rapid pace of AI development outpaces regulatory frameworks. Striking the right balance between fostering innovation and safeguarding patient safety requires adaptive regulations that keep up with evolving AI capabilities. Effective oversight mechanisms ensure that AI-driven technologies meet rigorous standards.

The marriage of AI and healthcare holds transformative potential, offering unparalleled diagnostics, personalized treatments, and expanded access. However, as this section illustrates, the journey towards AI-enhanced healthcare is accompanied by challenges that demand collaborative efforts from healthcare practitioners, policymakers, and technologists. By acknowledging these challenges and seizing the opportunities they present, the healthcare industry can chart a course towards a future where AI-driven innovation harmonizes with ethical considerations, ensuring that patients' welfare remains at the forefront of healthcare's technological evolution.

Conclusion: 3.1. Healthcare: Diagnostics, Personalized Medicine, and Telehealth

The integration of AI into healthcare, spanning diagnostics, personalized medicine, and telehealth, signifies a seismic shift towards more accurate, patient-centric care. As illuminated in this section, AI's implications stretch beyond mere automation—it empowers healthcare professionals to make informed decisions, enriches patient experiences, and democratically extends healthcare access. By embracing the transformative potential of AI and proactively addressing the ethical and technical complexities it presents, the healthcare industry paves the way for an era of medical excellence that merges human expertise with technological innovation.

3.2. Manufacturing: Automation, Predictive Maintenance, and Supply Chain Optimization

The manufacturing sector, a cornerstone of economic progress, is undergoing a monumental upheaval, driven by the transformative potential of Artificial Intelligence (AI). AI's influence reaches across manufacturing, permeating every facet from automation and predictive maintenance to supply chain optimization, thereby shaping a new era of efficiency and adaptability.

3.2.1. Automation: Precision Redefined

The landscape of manufacturing is undergoing a seismic shift, led by the transformative power of Artificial Intelligence (AI). At the forefront of this revolution is the redefinition of precision through AI-driven automation. This section delves into how AI is reshaping the manufacturing process, elevating precision to unprecedented levels and heralding a new era of efficiency and excellence.

3.2.1.1. AI-Powered Precision

In the dynamic landscape of modern manufacturing, a remarkable transformation is underway, and its driving force is the convergence of Artificial Intelligence (AI) and precision. This section delves into the profound impact of AI-powered precision, unveiling how this fusion is redefining manufacturing processes, elevating quality, and ushering in a new era of unparalleled excellence.

- **The Precision Revolution:** Traditionally, precision in manufacturing has been achieved through meticulous human craftsmanship. However, the integration of AI injects an unprecedented level of precision into the equation. AI-powered precision involves the deployment of algorithms that enable machines to execute tasks with accuracy that surpasses human capabilities. These machines navigate intricate movements, measure with microscopic accuracy, and replicate patterns flawlessly, all while maintaining consistent results across countless iterations.

- **Elevating Quality Standards:** The marriage of AI and precision fundamentally transforms the manufacturing landscape by revolutionizing quality standards. Human-based processes inherently carry the potential for variability due to factors like fatigue and human error. AI-powered precision eliminates these variables, leading to a significant reduction in defects and variations. Each product adheres to exact specifications, ensuring an unparalleled level of quality that resonates with consumers and industries alike.

- **Dynamic Adaptation:** The ingenuity of AI-powered precision lies in its adaptability. Manufacturing environments are dynamic, often requiring rapid adjustments to changing demands. AI-equipped machines seamlessly transition between different tasks and product variations, responding swiftly to market fluctuations. This adaptability minimizes downtime, optimizes resource allocation, and enhances operational efficiency, enabling manufacturers to stay ahead in a rapidly evolving landscape.

- **Catalyzing Innovation:** AI-powered precision is not only a conduit for optimizing existing processes but also a catalyst for innovation. By entrusting routine tasks to AI-driven systems, human creative capacity is liberated. Engineers and designers can channel their energy into pushing the boundaries of innovation, exploring new designs, and conceptualizing cutting-edge technologies. AI's precision, combined with human ingenuity, leads to breakthroughs that redefine the realm of what's possible.

- **A Glimpse into the Future:** The fusion of AI and precision is a glimpse into the future of manufacturing. As AI continues to advance, its precision capabilities will become increasingly sophisticated. From micro-scale components to large-scale industrial processes, AI's precision will permeate every facet of manufacturing, redefining quality benchmarks and igniting an era of uncharted possibilities.

AI-powered precision stands as a beacon of transformation in the manufacturing landscape. Its impact resonates beyond simple automation; it's a revolution that embeds unmatched accuracy, enhances quality, and amplifies the potential for innovation. By embracing AI's precision-driven capabilities, the manufacturing sector not only redefines its processes but also paves the way for a future where precision is not just a goal but an integral part of how industries thrive and shape the world.

3.2.1.2. Reduced Variability and Enhanced Quality

In the realm of modern manufacturing, the pursuit of excellence has found a formidable ally in Artificial Intelligence (AI). This section delves into the transformative power of AI in reducing variability and enhancing quality—a tandem that is revolutionizing manufacturing processes, optimizing outputs, and elevating standards to unprecedented heights.

- **The Conundrum of Variability:** Historically, manufacturing processes have been plagued by the inherent variability introduced by human factors. Skill variations, fatigue, and inconsistencies in human judgment can lead to deviations in product quality. AI intervenes as a game-changer by minimizing these variables. AI-powered machines execute tasks with a level of precision and uniformity that transcends human capabilities, resulting in a consistent output that adheres to the highest quality standards.

- **Elevated Quality Benchmarks:** AI's role in reducing variability translates directly into elevating the quality of manufactured products. Each item produced under AI's watchful eye adheres to the exact specifications and tolerances. Defects and inconsistencies are dramatically reduced, and the end result is a higher-quality product that meets or exceeds customer expectations. AI's ability to consistently reproduce desired outcomes has reshaped what quality truly means in the manufacturing landscape.
- **Accurate and Reliable Results:** The combination of AI's analytical prowess and precision execution ensures that each step of the manufacturing process is meticulously orchestrated. Measurements are accurate to the finest detail, and movements are executed with flawless consistency. This level of accuracy significantly reduces the likelihood of defects, rejections, and costly recalls, fostering a reputation for reliability and dependability in the market.
- **Customer Satisfaction Amplified:** In an era where customer expectations are soaring, AI-powered reduction in variability and enhancement of quality play a pivotal role in customer satisfaction. Products that consistently meet high-quality benchmarks lead to increased customer loyalty, positive brand perception, and decreased instances of customer dissatisfaction due to defects or inconsistencies. AI's impact extends beyond the manufacturing floor, resonating directly with end-users.
- **Envisioning a New Standard:** The influence of AI in reducing variability and enhancing quality is redefining industry standards. As AI technology continues to

evolve, the potential for even more refined processes and outputs grows exponentially. Manufacturing sectors across the board are transitioning from merely meeting standards to setting new benchmarks, all thanks to the precision and reliability bestowed by AI.

The synthesis of AI-driven precision and the elimination of variability is a testament to the transformative potential of technology. By ushering in an era of reduced defects, increased reliability, and elevated quality, AI's impact transcends manufacturing floors and permeates consumer experiences. As industries continue to embrace AI's capabilities, the narrative of quality undergoes a profound rewrite, ushering in a future where excellence isn't just a goal—it's the very fabric of manufacturing's evolution.

3.2.1.3. Swift Adaptability

In the dynamic landscape of modern manufacturing, where change is constant and agility is paramount, Artificial Intelligence (AI) emerges as the linchpin of swift adaptability. This section delves into how AI's capabilities facilitate rapid evolution in manufacturing, enabling industries to navigate complexities, embrace innovation, and respond nimbly to shifting demands.

- **Navigating Complex Terrain:** Manufacturing environments are characterized by multifaceted challenges, from fluctuating market demands to intricate supply chain dynamics. AI's swift adaptability equips manufacturers to navigate this complex terrain with unparalleled finesse. AI algorithms analyze data in real-time, enabling instant response to changing conditions. This agility translates into optimized production schedules, resource allocation, and inventory management, all while mitigating risks and maximizing opportunities.

- **Rapid Process Adjustment:** The ability to swiftly adapt processes in response to changing requirements is a hallmark of AI's impact. Traditional manufacturing adjustments could be time-consuming and disruptive, but AI-driven machines can pivot rapidly. Whether it's recalibrating production lines for different product variations or seamlessly integrating new materials, AI ensures that adjustments are executed swiftly and with minimal downtime.

- **Innovation in Overdrive:** AI's swift adaptability doesn't just address current challenges; it also fuels innovation. By automating routine tasks, AI liberates human resources to focus on creative endeavors and problem-solving. Engineers and designers can channel their efforts into pushing boundaries, exploring novel designs, and experimenting with cutting-edge technologies. AI's adaptability supports innovation cycles that are faster, more daring, and aligned with the rapid pace of technological advancement.

- **Meeting Customer Expectations:** In today's fast-paced market, customer demands evolve rapidly. Manufacturers must stay attuned to these changes and deliver products that meet or exceed expectations. AI's swift adaptability ensures that production can flex to accommodate changes in design, features, or specifications. This adaptability fosters customer satisfaction by ensuring that products are aligned with the latest trends and customer preferences.

- **Future-Proofing the Industry:** AI's role in swift adaptability is not merely reactive; it's proactive in future-proofing the manufacturing industry. As AI algorithms continue to learn and evolve, their capacity to anticipate trends and predict future demands improves. Manufacturers armed with AI-driven insights can make informed decisions about what to produce, when to produce, and how to optimize resources for maximum impact.

The infusion of AI's swift adaptability into the manufacturing landscape is akin to providing the industry with a set of responsive, agile wings. This ability to pivot, innovate, and respond to change positions manufacturers at the forefront of progress. As the manufacturing sector embraces AI's adaptability, it becomes a resilient force that navigates the complexities of the modern world, unlocking new heights of efficiency, innovation, and success.

3.2.1.4. Unlocking Innovation

In the tapestry of technological advancement, Artificial Intelligence (AI) stands as a master key, unlocking doors to innovation that were once deemed unreachable. This section delves into how AI's multifaceted capabilities act as a catalyst for pioneering innovation across diverse fields, transcending conventional boundaries and ushering in a new era of creativity and possibility.

- **Breaking Conventional Boundaries:** AI's unique ability to process vast datasets and identify intricate patterns breaks down traditional barriers to innovation. In fields like drug discovery, AI-enabled simulations dramatically accelerate the identification of potential compounds for novel treatments. This capacity to swiftly analyze complex data spurs scientific breakthroughs, from unraveling the mysteries of genetics to predicting climate patterns and simulating astronomical phenomena.

- **Creative Endeavors Reimagined:** AI's role as an innovation catalyst extends even to creative domains traditionally attributed to human ingenuity. Collaborative robots, known as cobots, are reshaping the creative landscape by partnering with human artists and designers. These cobots generate novel insights, offering fresh perspectives on design, artistic expression, and problem-solving. The fusion of AI's analytical prowess and human creativity gives rise to new forms of art, design, and cultural expression.
- **Rethinking Problem-Solving:** AI's analytical abilities are like a prism that refracts complex challenges into solvable components. Industries from engineering to logistics benefit from AI-driven algorithms that optimize processes, resource allocation, and decision-making. AI's ability to process vast amounts of data in real time empowers professionals to make more informed decisions, transforming industries and streamlining operations.
- **Innovations Beyond Imagination:** AI is the harbinger of innovations that extend beyond human imagination. Generative adversarial networks (GANs) can generate remarkably convincing art, music, and text that challenges traditional notions of creativity. AI-driven simulations predict the behavior of complex systems, aiding in disaster preparedness and urban planning. Even in the realm of quantum computing, AI is used to optimize algorithms and decode quantum properties.
- **Symbiotic Future:** AI's role in innovation is not about replacing human creativity but amplifying it. The interplay between AI's analytical prowess and human intuition leads to a symbiotic relationship that propels innovation to new heights. Professionals are freed from mundane tasks, enabling them to focus on higher-order

thinking, novel problem-solving, and pioneering ideation that shapes the future.

AI's innovation potential is boundless, breaking the shackles of convention and opening doors to new vistas of discovery. As this section illustrates, AI's influence extends across industries, from scientific research to creative arts, and from problem-solving to quantum exploration. By embracing AI's capacity to push boundaries, industries and individuals alike embark on a journey of exploration and creativity, shaping a future that harmoniously blends technological innovation and human ingenuity.

Conclusion: 3.2.1. Automation: Precision Redefined

AI-driven automation is rewriting the rules of manufacturing by redefining precision. The fusion of AI's analytical capabilities and automation's mechanical prowess results in an environment where precision is no longer an aspiration but a reality. From reducing variability and enhancing product quality to enabling swift adaptability and fueling innovation, AI-driven automation is reshaping manufacturing processes to unlock levels of precision that were once unimaginable. This precision paves the way for an era of manufacturing excellence that holds promise for industries, economies, and consumers worldwide.

3.2.2. Predictive Maintenance: A New Horizon

In the realm of modern industries, where efficiency and uptime are paramount, the advent of Artificial Intelligence (AI) heralds a new horizon in maintenance practices. This section delves into how AI's predictive maintenance capabilities are revolutionizing traditional approaches, optimizing operations, and minimizing downtime to unprecedented levels.

3.2.2.1. Shifting from Reactive to Proactive

In the realm of industrial maintenance, a transformational shift is underway, powered by the evolution of Artificial Intelligence (AI). This section explores how industries are moving away from reactive maintenance practices and embracing proactive approaches with the aid of AI, revolutionizing the way assets are managed, and operations are optimized.

- **The Legacy of Reactive Maintenance:** For decades, reactive maintenance has been the norm—an approach where equipment is repaired only after it breaks down. This practice often leads to unplanned downtime, increased operational costs, and decreased overall efficiency. Reactive maintenance hinges on responding to failures as they happen, resulting in disruptions that can ripple through the entire production process.
- **AI's Proactive Paradigm:** The emergence of AI-driven predictive maintenance ushers in a proactive paradigm. Instead of waiting for failures to occur, AI algorithms analyze real-time data from sensors embedded in equipment. By monitoring parameters like temperature, vibration, and performance, AI can detect subtle deviations that signify impending issues. This enables maintenance teams to intervene before failure, preventing costly downtime and optimizing operational continuity.
- **Benefits of Proactive Maintenance:** AI's shift from reactive to proactive maintenance offers a plethora of benefits. Unplanned downtime is minimized, leading to increased productivity and reduced operational disruption. Assets operate at peak efficiency, with timely interventions addressing emerging issues. This

optimization extends the lifespan of equipment, maximizing return on investment. Over time, as AI algorithms learn from data, maintenance strategies become increasingly precise and effective.

- **From Repair to Predict and Prevent:** The essence of the transition lies in moving from a repair-oriented mindset to one of prediction and prevention. AI-enabled systems become proficient in identifying patterns that precede failures. This enables maintenance teams to predict when maintenance is needed, optimizing scheduling and resource allocation. Preventive interventions not only avert breakdowns but also enhance equipment longevity and operational reliability.
- **Empowering Data-Driven Decisions:** AI's proactive approach relies on data as its foundation. Real-time data analytics enable informed decisions about maintenance needs. This data-driven decision-making transforms industries from being firefighting reactive scenarios to orchestrators of efficient and smooth operations. By harnessing the power of AI, industries can ensure that every action taken is strategic, optimizing outcomes and resource utilization.

Shifting from reactive to proactive maintenance with the aid of AI represents a fundamental change in industrial practices. This transition is underpinned by data-driven insights, predictive capabilities, and a commitment to operational excellence. As industries embrace this paradigm shift, they harness the full potential of AI to anticipate challenges, optimize operations, and cultivate a culture of proactive efficiency that paves the way for sustainable growth and success.

3.2.2.2. Data-Driven Precision

In the realm of maintenance practices, precision is paramount—a concept that is undergoing a revolutionary transformation thanks to the prowess of Artificial Intelligence (AI). This section delves into how AI's data-driven capabilities are reshaping maintenance strategies, enhancing precision, and ensuring that interventions are both timely and effective.

- **Unveiling Hidden Insights:** Traditional maintenance often relies on fixed schedules that may not align with equipment needs. AI's data-driven precision changes this by analyzing real-time data from sensors embedded in machinery. These sensors capture an array of parameters such as temperature, vibration, and performance. AI algorithms dissect this data, uncovering hidden insights that indicate potential issues. By deciphering these patterns, maintenance teams gain a comprehensive understanding of equipment health.

- **Tailoring Interventions with Accuracy:** Armed with insights from data analysis, AI empowers maintenance teams to tailor interventions with unparalleled accuracy. Instead of generalized maintenance at set intervals, AI enables interventions that are specific to the current state of equipment. This precision ensures that resources are allocated exactly where needed, minimizing unnecessary downtime and costs. Repairs are no longer conducted based on guesswork but are guided by real-time conditions and predictive analysis.

- **Optimizing Resource Allocation:** Data-driven precision transcends traditional resource allocation models. Instead of overhauls or replacements based on a calendar schedule, AI prompts maintenance when indicators suggest it's necessary. This means that resources, whether human labor or spare parts, are allocated optimally, reducing waste and improving overall efficiency. Over time, as AI systems learn from historical data, precision in allocation improves further.

- **Enhancing Decision-Making:** AI's data-driven precision elevates decision-making to a strategic level. Maintenance teams no longer need to rely solely on experience or intuition; instead, they have access to concrete data-backed insights. This empowers them to make informed choices, prioritize interventions, and allocate resources efficiently. The result is a well-orchestrated symphony of maintenance actions that synchronize with the operational rhythm of the entire facility.

- **Future-Proofing through Learning:** AI's data-driven precision is a dynamic process. As systems continuously collect and analyze data, they learn from each interaction. This iterative learning enables AI to refine its predictions and recommendations over time. This self-improvement loop ensures that the precision of interventions constantly evolves, providing an ever more accurate roadmap for maintenance strategies.

Data-driven precision, fueled by AI's capabilities, is a game-changer in the world of maintenance. It ushers in an era where interventions are guided by real-time conditions, predictive insights, and a commitment to resource optimization. As industries embrace data-driven precision, they ensure that their maintenance practices are not just reactive responses, but strategic actions that enhance equipment longevity, operational efficiency, and ultimately, the bottom line.

3.2.2.3. Optimizing Resource Allocation

In the realm of maintenance practices, resource allocation plays a pivotal role in determining operational efficiency. Traditional approaches often lead to suboptimal resource usage, resulting in excessive downtime and unnecessary use of spare parts. This section delves into how Artificial Intelligence (AI) disrupts traditional resource allocation paradigms, ensuring that interventions are conducted with precision, minimizing downtime, and maximizing resource efficiency.

- **Reimagining Maintenance Scheduling:** Conventional maintenance schedules often adhere to fixed intervals, regardless of the actual state of equipment. AI revolutionizes this by analyzing real-time data from sensors embedded in machinery. By monitoring parameters like temperature, vibration, and performance, AI algorithms gain a holistic view of equipment health. This data-driven approach enables maintenance teams to make informed decisions about when and where interventions are required.
- **Precision in Timing and Execution:** AI's data-driven insights empower maintenance teams to allocate resources with precision. Instead of relying on generic schedules, interventions are timed exactly when indications suggest they are needed. This approach optimizes resource allocation, as labor and spare parts are dedicated to specific maintenance tasks, eliminating wasteful expenditure. Moreover, AI's predictive capabilities mean that only necessary interventions are conducted, reducing the strain on resources.
- **Minimizing Downtime, Maximizing Efficiency:** Resource optimization through AI translates to reduced downtime and heightened operational efficiency. Downtime, often associated with maintenance, is minimized as interventions are conducted precisely when required. This not only keeps equipment operational but also enhances overall productivity. Furthermore, the efficient allocation of resources ensures that spare parts are used judiciously, extending their lifespan and reducing operational costs.

- **A Shift to Dynamic Adaptability:** AI's resource optimization isn't static; it's an ongoing learning process. As AI systems gather more data and learn from past interventions, their predictive capabilities improve. This leads to an ever-refining process of resource allocation, where interventions become even more precise and efficient over time. This dynamic adaptability ensures that maintenance strategies are always aligned with the current operational needs.
- **Empowering Strategic Decision-Making:** Resource allocation influenced by AI empowers maintenance teams with strategic decision-making capabilities. Data-backed insights guide decisions about when to perform maintenance, how to allocate labor, and which spare parts to use. This strategic approach ensures that resources are deployed where they can make the most significant impact, both in terms of equipment longevity and operational continuity.

Optimizing resource allocation through AI is a transformational shift in maintenance practices. It introduces an era where maintenance actions are not just conducted reactively, but strategically orchestrated. By embracing AI's ability to analyze real-time data and predict maintenance needs, industries can unlock a new level of operational efficiency, ensuring that resources are utilized optimally and interventions are conducted with surgical precision.

3.2.2.4. Enhancing Operational Efficiency

In the realm of operations, efficiency reigns supreme, and Artificial Intelligence (AI) is emerging as a catalyst for transformative change. This section delves into how AI's predictive maintenance injects a potent dose of efficiency into operational landscapes. From minimizing machinery downtime to iterative refinements of maintenance processes, AI is redefining the very essence of operational excellence.

- **Minimized Downtime, Maximized Availability:** Downtime is the nemesis of productivity, causing disruptions that ripple through operations. AI's predictive maintenance emerges as the knight in shining armor. By analyzing real-time data from sensors embedded in machinery, AI algorithms preemptively identify issues that could lead to breakdowns. As a result, interventions are conducted precisely when needed, minimizing downtime and ensuring that machinery remains operational and available.
- **Iterative Learning for Continuous Improvement:** One of AI's most remarkable attributes is its capacity for learning from historical data. Predictive maintenance leverages this capability to the fullest. As AI algorithms gather more data from past maintenance interventions, they fine-tune their predictions. This iterative learning process enhances the accuracy of maintenance forecasts over time. The result? A system that becomes increasingly adept at identifying potential issues before they escalate, safeguarding operational continuity.
- **Precision in Maintenance Protocols:** AI doesn't just predict; it transforms maintenance practices into precision operations. Traditional approaches often involved a blanket schedule of maintenance, whether needed or not. AI-driven predictions flip the script. Interventions are now tailored to the actual health and condition of equipment, eliminating unnecessary tasks and optimizing resource utilization. This precision extends to the selection of spare parts, as only those required for specific interventions are used, minimizing wastage.

- **Operational Efficiency in Action:** The impact of AI's enhanced operational efficiency is tangible across various industries. Manufacturing plants experience reduced downtime, translating to higher production output. Transportation networks benefit from improved vehicle reliability, ensuring timely services. Energy grids optimize maintenance scheduling to maintain a steady power supply. The ripple effects of operational efficiency extend to all facets of industry, enhancing overall productivity.
- **A Journey Toward Excellence:** AI's role in enhancing operational efficiency is not a one-time endeavor; it's a continuous journey. As AI systems accumulate more data and learn from past interventions, their predictions become more accurate, and their recommendations become more astute. This iterative refinement embodies a commitment to excellence—a commitment to minimizing disruptions, optimizing resources, and elevating operational performance.

AI's infusion into predictive maintenance has a profound impact on operational efficiency. The minimized downtime, iterative learning, and precision it brings to maintenance processes redefine how industries operate. As AI algorithms evolve, their ability to enhance operational excellence evolves with them. By embracing AI's capabilities and adapting to its insights, industries embark on a trajectory of continuous improvement, where operations become not just efficient but truly exceptional.

3.2.2.5. Unleashing Cost Savings

In the economic landscape, the bottom line speaks volumes, and Artificial Intelligence (AI) is rewriting the financial narrative through its predictive maintenance capabilities. This section delves into how AI's predictive maintenance strategies are not only revolutionizing operational efficiency but also unleashing substantial cost savings across industries.

- **A Productivity Boost from Reduced Downtime:** Downtime is the nemesis of productivity, draining resources and stalling operations. AI's predictive maintenance, by preemptively identifying potential issues, significantly curbs downtime. Machinery breakdowns are minimized, ensuring that operations remain smoothly on track. This translates into increased productivity, allowing businesses to maximize output within the same time frame.
- **Enhanced Production Output:** With reduced downtime, production output receives a significant boost. Industries ranging from manufacturing to energy benefit from uninterrupted operations. Manufacturing plants churn out more products, meeting market demand with precision. Energy grids maintain consistent supply levels, avoiding disruptions in power distribution. AI's role as a productivity enhancer translates into tangible financial gains.
- **Minimized Emergency Repair Costs:** Emergency repairs are not only financially draining but also disruptive to operations. AI's predictive prowess tackles this challenge head-on. By identifying potential issues before they escalate into emergencies, AI-driven maintenance interventions become the norm. This proactive approach minimizes the need for costly emergency repairs, freeing up resources for planned maintenance and strategic investments.

- **Precision in Maintenance Interventions:** Planned maintenance, guided by AI's insights, becomes a precision operation. Traditional approaches often lead to overhauls and replacements that might not be necessary. AI's data-driven predictions tailor interventions to the actual condition of equipment, minimizing unnecessary costs. Spare parts are judiciously allocated, minimizing wastage and expenses.
- **The Ripple Effect of Cost Savings:** The economic impact of AI's predictive maintenance extends beyond individual operations. Cost savings cascade through the entire value chain. Suppliers benefit from steady orders and timely deliveries. Customers experience enhanced service reliability, bolstering satisfaction. As operational costs decrease, businesses can allocate resources to research, innovation, and growth strategies.
- **A Resounding Impact on Profitability:** Ultimately, the culmination of reduced downtime, enhanced production, minimized emergency repairs, and precision maintenance interventions translates into substantial cost savings. These savings reverberate through financial statements, boosting profitability and creating a more resilient economic foundation. AI's role as a cost-saving powerhouse propels industries toward sustainable growth and competitive advantage.

AI's predictive maintenance isn't just about efficiency; it's about financial transformation. By curbing downtime, enhancing productivity, minimizing emergency repairs, and optimizing maintenance strategies, AI becomes a catalyst for cost savings. These savings ripple through the entire business ecosystem, reinforcing profitability and fostering economic resilience. As industries harness AI's potential, they unlock a future where financial success aligns seamlessly with operational excellence.

Conclusion: 3.2.2. Predictive Maintenance: A New Horizon

The era of AI-driven predictive maintenance represents a paradigm shift in industrial operations. As elucidated in this section, the transition from reactive to proactive maintenance strategies unleashes a cascade of benefits, from minimized downtime and optimized resource allocation to enhanced operational efficiency and cost savings. With AI as the guiding compass, industries are poised to navigate this new horizon of maintenance excellence, ensuring that the heartbeat of modern operations remains steady and uninterrupted.

3.2.3. Supply Chain Optimization: Agility in Action

The realm of supply chain management is undergoing a remarkable metamorphosis, and at the heart of this evolution is the power of Artificial Intelligence (AI). This section unveils how AI's prowess in data analysis, trend recognition, and real-time response is transforming supply chain optimization, infusing it with unprecedented agility.

3.2.3.1. Harnessing Historical Insights and Market Trends

In the world of supply chain optimization, Artificial Intelligence (AI) embarks on a profound exploration that commences with an in-depth examination of historical data and a meticulous study of market trends. This section unveils how AI algorithms delve into past performance, unearthing intricate patterns that might have eluded human perception. This journey into history serves as the bedrock upon which strategic decisions are built, forming the basis for orchestrating an agile and efficient supply chain.

- **A Deep Dive into Data:** AI's voyage into supply chain optimization involves diving headfirst into a sea of data, where historical records capture the ebb and flow of previous operations. AI algorithms meticulously sift through this trove of data, extracting insights that reveal the rhythm of past successes and challenges. This analysis lays bare the threads of performance, allowing AI to decipher patterns that are vital for informed decision-making.
- **Unveiling Hidden Patterns:** Market trends can be as elusive as they are transformative. Here, AI shines as a beacon of insight, unraveling hidden patterns that lie beneath the surface of raw data. The intricacies of consumer behavior, seasonal fluctuations, and economic shifts become apparent through AI's discerning eye. This revelation empowers businesses to anticipate market dynamics, adjusting their strategies accordingly.
- **The Foundation of Strategy:** AI's historical analysis serves as the cornerstone upon which strategic blueprints are sketched. Armed with insights from the past, businesses can formulate plans that are informed, rational, and forward-looking. The ability to learn from previous victories and setbacks allows organizations to chart a course that maximizes efficiency, minimizes risks, and positions them for success.
- **Guiding the Path to Optimal Inventory Levels:** AI emerges as a visionary guide, leveraging historical insights to navigate the complex terrain of inventory management. By recognizing recurrent trends and patterns, AI possesses the prescience to recommend optimal inventory levels. This informed guidance ensures that businesses neither drown in excess inventory nor find themselves grappling with shortages.

- **A Vision for the Future:** Incorporating AI's historical insights and trend analysis transforms supply chain management from a reactive endeavor into a visionary pursuit. Armed with the wisdom of hindsight and the foresight to anticipate, businesses can steer their operations with confidence. AI's ability to unveil the intricate dance of historical data and market trends elevates supply chain optimization to an art, where strategy is both informed and visionary.

3.2.3.2. The Dance of Demand and Supply

Within the intricate ballet of supply and demand, a remarkable choreographer steps forward: Artificial Intelligence (AI). This section unveils how AI dons the role of the choreographer, deftly orchestrating moves with precision and finesse. Equipped with historical insights and real-time data, AI algorithms take center stage, predicting the delicate fluctuations of demand with uncanny accuracy. This intuitive anticipation empowers businesses to execute a seamless dance between product availability and prudent stock levels.

- **The Dance Unveiled:** In the world of commerce, supply and demand engage in a complex dance, where each move influences the other. Here, AI emerges as the unseen conductor, analyzing historical data and real-time indicators to predict the tempo of this intricate choreography. Through its algorithms, AI discerns patterns that are beyond human perception, deciphering the rhythm of demand ebbs and flows.
- **Predictive Mastery:** AI's predictive prowess is the star of this performance, executing leaps of anticipation that elevate the supply-demand dance to new heights. Armed with insights from past performances, AI predicts demand fluctuations with a level of precision that leaves traditional methods in the wings. This

mastery allows businesses to navigate the delicate balance between keeping products available and avoiding the pitfalls of overstocking.

- **Maintaining Harmony:** Just as a skilled choreographer ensures every move aligns harmoniously, AI maintains equilibrium between demand and availability. The choreography orchestrated by AI ensures that the right products grace the stage precisely when they are needed. This synchronization minimizes shortages that leave customers unsatisfied and overstocking that burdens the business.
- **A Performance of Efficiency:** The dance of supply and demand, guided by AI's choreography, is a performance of efficiency and strategic brilliance. By predicting demand fluctuations, AI enables businesses to allocate resources with agility, fine-tuning production schedules and distribution strategies. The result is a symphony of operational excellence, where the rhythm of supply aligns harmoniously with the cadence of demand.
- **An Ongoing Symphony:** As AI continues to evolve, its role as the choreographer of supply and demand becomes more refined. With access to larger datasets and improved algorithms, AI's dance becomes an ongoing symphony of precision. Through its nuanced understanding of historical patterns and real-time indicators, AI holds the potential to revolutionize the dance of supply and demand, ensuring that businesses maintain their rhythm even amidst dynamic market shifts.

3.2.3.3. Real-Time Adaptability: The AI Advantage

In the realm of supply chain optimization, real-time adaptability stands as AI's secret weapon. This section unveils the dynamic role of real-time data processing in AI's arsenal, revealing how it confers a decisive advantage to businesses. As market dynamics shift and unexpected demands surge forth, AI algorithms respond with a blend of speed and precision that sets them apart. It is in these moments of rapid change that AI demonstrates its unparalleled agility, recalibrating production schedules and refining distribution strategies in the blink of an eye.

- **Seizing the Moment:** In the fast-paced landscape of commerce, opportunities and challenges arise in real-time. This is where AI excels, leveraging its ability to process data instantaneously and glean insights with remarkable accuracy. As sudden shifts in demand unfold, AI algorithms swiftly interpret these signals, providing businesses with the actionable intelligence they need to make informed decisions.
- **Precision Unleashed:** AI's real-time adaptability transcends mere responsiveness; it is a testament to the precision of its algorithms. Armed with up-to-the-moment data, AI fine-tunes every aspect of the supply chain, from adjusting production rates to optimizing inventory levels. This orchestration ensures that resources are allocated with utmost efficiency, minimizing waste and maximizing profit margins.
- **Maintaining the Edge:** In a competitive landscape, the ability to adapt swiftly is a crucial determinant of success. AI's real-time advantage ensures that businesses remain at the forefront of market shifts, avoiding pitfalls and capitalizing on emerging trends. By staying ahead of the curve, businesses harness AI's real-time adaptability to gain a competitive edge that is not merely maintained but consistently sharpened.
- **The Future of Agility:** As technology continues its inexorable advance, AI's real-time adaptability is poised to evolve further. With more sophisticated algorithms

and the integration of larger datasets, AI's responsiveness will become even more finely tuned. The future promises an era where businesses can not only respond rapidly to change but also anticipate and shape market dynamics through AI's real-time insights.

Real-time adaptability is the beating heart of AI's influence on supply chain optimization. By swiftly analyzing data and recalibrating strategies in response to real-time shifts, AI empowers businesses to thrive in an environment of dynamic change. The precision, agility, and strategic advantage conferred by AI's real-time capabilities usher in a new era of supply chain management—one where opportunities are seized and challenges are overcome with unwavering precision.

3.2.3.4. The Quest for Cost Efficiency

In the realm of supply chain optimization, the twin pillars of waste reduction and cost efficiency are elevated to paramount importance. This section illuminates AI's role as a diligent steward of these pillars, harnessing its intricate algorithms to amplify their impact. Through its adept management of inventory levels, production schedules, and operational processes, AI orchestrates a symphony of precision that maximizes cost efficiency and minimizes waste—a harmony that resonates throughout the supply chain ecosystem.

- **Curbing Excess: The AI Solution to Overstocking and Shortages** - One of AI's most impressive feats in the realm of supply chain optimization is its mastery over the seesawing balance between overstocking and shortages. By accurately predicting demand trends and swiftly adapting to market fluctuations, AI eliminates the blunders of excess inventory costs and missed revenue opportunities. This precision dance ensures that products are available when needed, without languishing in excess or leaving customers wanting.

- **Fine-Tuned Symphony: Leaner Processes through AI -** AI's algorithms, akin to a maestro guiding an orchestra, optimize production schedules with impeccable precision. The result is a reduction in operational inefficiencies, as production flows seamlessly in tune with demand. The synergy between AI's insights and the manufacturing process cultivates a leaner, more agile production ecosystem, where resources are allocated judiciously and waste is minimized.

- **A More Cost-Effective Horizon:** As AI's algorithms fine-tune every aspect of the supply chain, from inventory levels to production schedules, a tangible transformation emerges—an ecosystem that operates with heightened cost efficiency. The reduction of waste and the maximization of resources translate into tangible cost savings, bolstering the bottom line and fortifying the financial health of businesses.

- **AI's Ongoing Quest for Excellence:** The pursuit of cost efficiency, guided by AI's algorithms, is an ever-evolving journey. As technology advances and AI's capabilities expand, the quest for economic excellence grows even more potent. With the integration of larger datasets, deeper insights, and more nuanced algorithms, AI's impact on cost efficiency is destined to become more refined, fostering an era where businesses optimize their resources with unprecedented precision.

The pursuit of cost efficiency is a hallmark of supply chain optimization, and AI's algorithms serve as the engine that propels this pursuit forward. By eliminating excesses, minimizing shortages, and fine-tuning production processes, AI empowers businesses to operate within a leaner and more cost-effective ecosystem. As this section illuminates, AI's contribution to cost efficiency is not just a momentary achievement but an ongoing quest that shapes the future of supply chain management.

3.2.3.5. Elevated Customer Satisfaction

In the intricate orchestration of supply chain optimization, the ultimate crescendo is the symphony of customer satisfaction. This section delves into the pivotal role AI plays in composing this melodic journey, where every note resonates with the promise of timely deliveries, product availability, and a seamless experience that resonates long after the final chord.

- **Product Availability: A Prelude to Delight:** AI's orchestration of supply chain optimization starts with the prelude of product availability. By accurately predicting demand patterns and orchestrating real-time adjustments, AI ensures that products are ready when customers seek them. This harmonious synchronization between supply and demand minimizes out-of-stock instances, eliminating customer disappointments and fostering a sense of reliability.
- **Timely Deliveries: The Rhythmic Heartbeat:** The rhythmic heartbeat of customer satisfaction is the timely delivery of products. AI, attuned to market dynamics and operational efficiencies, choreographs the production and distribution processes with precision. As a result, products find their way to customers' doorsteps in sync with their expectations. The timely rhythm set by AI enhances customer experiences, leaving no room for the dissonance of delays.
- **Seamless Experiences: The Melodic Flow:** The seamless flow of customer experiences is where AI's symphony culminates. Through its orchestration of supply chain optimization, AI minimizes disruptions, ensuring that

every interaction, from order placement to delivery, unfolds effortlessly. Customers find their expectations met, if not exceeded, by a process that is smooth, transparent, and hassle-free. This melodic flow leaves a lasting imprint, fostering customer loyalty and positive word-of-mouth.

- **The Resounding Chord of Satisfaction:** As AI conducts the symphony of supply chain optimization, the resounding chord that emerges is elevated customer satisfaction. The harmonious interplay between product availability, timely deliveries, and seamless experiences strikes a chord that resonates with customers. Satisfied customers become advocates, amplifying the harmony of satisfaction as they share their positive experiences, enhancing brand reputation, and fostering a loyal customer base.

- **AI's Ongoing Harmonic Journey:** The journey towards elevated customer satisfaction, guided by AI's precision, is an ongoing evolution. As AI's capabilities expand and algorithms refine, the symphony of supply chain optimization continues to reach new heights. Businesses that embrace AI's conductor-like role in orchestrating customer-centric experiences are poised to stand out in a landscape where satisfaction is the ultimate measure of success.

Elevated customer satisfaction stands as the masterpiece of supply chain optimization, and AI's role as the conductor of this symphony cannot be overstated. By ensuring product availability, orchestrating timely deliveries, and crafting seamless experiences, AI's contribution to customer delight is profound. As businesses embrace this harmony, they are poised to create a symphony of loyalty, advocacy, and enduring success.

Conclusion: 3.2.3. Supply Chain Optimization: Agility in Action

AI's integration into supply chain optimization is a game-changer, unleashing unparalleled agility and efficiency. As this section reveals, AI's ability to analyze historical data, forecast trends, and respond in real-time elevates supply chain management to new heights. By minimizing waste, enhancing cost efficiency, and maximizing customer satisfaction, AI transforms supply chains into dynamic, adaptable ecosystems poised for success in an ever-changing business landscape.

3.2.4. Challenges and Opportunities Ahead

The journey of integrating AI into manufacturing illuminates a path laden with both opportunities and challenges. This section embarks on a voyage through this transformative landscape, where automation's promise of enhanced productivity coexists with the demands of reskilling, investments, and cybersecurity.

3.2.4.1. Automation's Promise and the Workforce Shift

At the core of AI's integration into manufacturing lies a transformative promise: automation. This tantalizing prospect carries the potential to elevate productivity to unparalleled levels, revolutionizing the manufacturing landscape. Yet, this seismic shift towards automation isn't devoid of its ramifications for the workforce, heralding an era of change that necessitates a delicate balance between technological advancement and human expertise.

- **The Rise of the Machines: A New Industrial Epoch:** Automation embodies the marriage of AI with machinery, resulting in an assembly line dance that outperforms human limitations. Tasks once entrusted to human hands now rest in the capable grip of AI-driven machines. The allure of streamlined processes, enhanced precision, and increased output holds the allure of unparalleled efficiency. However, this reconfiguration prompts a question that resonates through the manufacturing halls: What about the human touch?

- **From Hand to AI: Shifting Workforce Dynamics:** The transition towards AI-driven automation sparks a tectonic shift in workforce dynamics. The tasks that machines can now undertake independently were once a hallmark of human labor. As machines assume these roles, workers find themselves at the nexus of change. They must transition from manual operators to AI collaborators, channeling their expertise towards managing and maintaining these automated systems. The need for a human touch isn't negated; it's just recalibrated.
- **Reskilling: Equipping for the Future:** The rise of automation isn't synonymous with sidelining the workforce; rather, it calls for an evolution in skills. A robust reskilling initiative becomes the linchpin of this transition. Equipping workers with the proficiency to navigate AI-driven systems and harness their potential becomes a mission of paramount importance. The workforce's value isn't in performing rote tasks anymore; it's in orchestrating, monitoring, and optimizing the symphony of AI and machinery.
- **Embracing the Evolving Landscape:** The future isn't bleak; it's transformative. The convergence of AI and manufacturing isn't a zero-sum game but a collaborative venture. As AI-driven machines amplify output, the human element brings intuition,

adaptability, and ingenuity. Navigating this shifting landscape requires a commitment to continuous learning, embracing technological change, and recognizing that the partnership between humans and AI is the harmony that will define this new industrial epoch.

Automation's promise in manufacturing isn't just about machines taking center stage—it's about orchestrating a duet between AI and human expertise. Reskilling becomes the bridge that connects the old with the new, allowing workers to evolve alongside technology. In embracing this transformation, manufacturing can elevate its productivity, while individuals can unleash their potential in a landscape where AI amplifies human ingenuity. As automation's melody reverberates through the manufacturing world, the symphony of the future is poised to resonate with the harmonious collaboration of AI and human skill.

3.2.4.2. Investment Imperatives: A Technological Evolution

The marriage of AI and manufacturing isn't a casual dalliance; it's a full-fledged partnership that beckons businesses to make significant investments in technology and infrastructure. The journey towards AI integration is a roadmap of commitment, demanding resources that span from acquisition to innovation. These investment imperatives aren't mere expenditures; they're the stepping stones towards a future where efficiency, productivity, and competitive edge are the rewards.

- **Embracing Cutting-Edge AI Systems:** To embark on the AI-powered voyage, businesses must first invest in cutting-edge AI systems. These technological marvels aren't just additions to the assembly line; they're the conductors of a symphony that harmonizes human expertise with machine precision. Whether it's AI-driven robotics, predictive analytics, or supply chain optimization, these systems become the cornerstones of modern manufacturing.

- **Nurturing Research and Development:** Investment isn't just about acquiring; it's about cultivating innovation. Businesses that sow seeds in research and development reap the rewards of pioneering advancements. These investments fuel breakthroughs that enhance AI's capabilities, refining algorithms, and expanding AI's horizons. The laboratory becomes a playground of possibilities, where the boundaries of technology are pushed, and the potential for disruption is magnified.

- **Building Digital Infrastructure:** The marriage of AI and manufacturing is a digital affair, demanding a robust digital infrastructure. This entails more than just wires and servers; it's about creating an ecosystem where data flows seamlessly, where AI-driven insights are harnessed, and where the fusion of AI and manufacturing doesn't stumble on technical roadblocks. Investments in cybersecurity, data storage, and connectivity become the building blocks of this digital realm.

- **Initial Challenges, Long-Term Gains:** It's not lost that these investment imperatives present challenges. The initial allocation of resources may feel daunting, demanding a reconfiguration of budgets and priorities. However, this short-term discomfort paves the way for long-term gains. The efficiencies unlocked by AI integration—reduced downtime, optimized processes, and informed decision-making—usher in a new era of productivity that justifies the upfront investments.

- **Competitive Advantage: The Grand Reward:** The true payoff of these investments is a competitive advantage that reverberates through the manufacturing landscape. Businesses equipped with AI-driven capabilities become the agile contenders, capable of adapting to market fluctuations, meeting demand spikes, and navigating supply chain complexities with finesse. They're not just keeping up; they're setting the pace.

The integration of AI into manufacturing isn't a mere transaction; it's an evolution. Investment imperatives aren't burdens; they're catalysts that propel businesses into the future. Cutting-edge AI systems, research and development, and digital infrastructure become the cornerstones of this transformation. As businesses navigate the challenges of today, they forge a path towards the gains of tomorrow—a landscape where technological evolution fuels efficiency, productivity, and the coveted competitive edge.

3.2.4.3. Guardians of Cybersecurity: Shielding AI-Enabled Systems

In the symphony of AI's integration into manufacturing, there's an orchestra that plays a vital role—the guardians of cybersecurity. As AI becomes an integral part of operations, it also becomes a potential target for the nefarious players of the digital realm. Thus, the imperative of cybersecurity is elevated to a position of paramount importance. These guardians are tasked with shielding AI-enabled systems, fortifying them against cyber threats that could disrupt operations, compromise data, and tarnish customer trust.

- **The Intricacies of AI Vulnerabilities:** AI-enabled systems, with their intricate algorithms and data-driven decision-making, harbor vulnerabilities that can be exploited by cybercriminals. From data breaches to espionage and intellectual property theft, the spectrum of threats is vast. An AI-powered assembly line may hold trade secrets; a predictive maintenance algorithm may contain valuable insights. These digital gems are enticing to those who seek to exploit them.

- **Proactive Measures for Protection:** Safeguarding AI-enabled systems requires more than just a reactive stance—it demands proactive measures that anticipate threats before they strike. Cybersecurity frameworks must be designed to identify vulnerabilities, shore up defenses, and fortify digital fortresses. Regular vulnerability assessments, intrusion detection systems, and threat intelligence become the armor that shields AI from the digital onslaught.

- **A Robust Defense: Cybersecurity Reinforcement:** The guardians of cybersecurity reinforce the digital bulwark through a multi-pronged approach. Encryption ensures that data remains secure during transmission and storage. Access controls limit the entry points for potential threats, allowing only authorized personnel to interact with AI systems. Intrusion detection systems stand as sentinels, watching for any anomalous activity that could signal an impending attack.

- **Preserving Customer Trust:** Beyond the technicalities, cybersecurity is a custodian of customer trust. As businesses embrace AI-driven systems, customers entrust them with data and rely on the integrity of operations. Breaches not only compromise sensitive information but also erode the foundation of trust that businesses painstakingly build. Ensuring robust cybersecurity is akin to a promise—a commitment to protect customer data and maintain the trust invested in the brand.

- **A Shared Responsibility:** The guardianship of cybersecurity isn't the responsibility of a few—it's a collective effort that involves everyone within the organization. From IT specialists to executives, each individual plays a role in upholding the digital defenses. Employee training and awareness programs are as critical as the deployment of sophisticated cybersecurity tools. As the digital landscape evolves, so must the defenses.

In the era where AI and manufacturing intertwine, the role of cybersecurity isn't a mere technicality—it's a vanguard that protects the sanctity of operations, the privacy of data, and the trust of customers. The guardians of cybersecurity stand as sentinels, unwavering in their commitment to fortify AI-enabled systems against the digital tides. As they rise to this challenge, they ensure that the symphony of AI's integration into manufacturing remains harmonious and secure.

3.2.4.4. Ethical Considerations: Navigating the AI Ethos

In the intricate dance between AI and manufacturing, ethics emerges as the compass that guides decisions beyond the realms of technology. As AI infiltrates manufacturing processes, it carries the potential to shape not only products but the very fabric of society. Ethical considerations become a cornerstone, influencing choices that ripple through workforce dynamics, product quality, and the well-being of communities. Striking a harmonious chord between innovation and ethical responsibility is the key to shaping AI's narrative in manufacturing.

- **The Ripple Effect of AI Choices:** AI's decisions are not confined to algorithms and data—they have tangible consequences that reverberate through human lives. From automating tasks to dictating production schedules, AI wields influence that extends beyond the assembly line. Decisions made by AI can impact the livelihoods of workers, the quality of products, and even the sustainability of the environment. These ripples extend to communities, where the consequences of AI choices can be felt in terms of job stability and economic well-being.

- **The Tug-of-War: Innovation vs. Ethics:** In the quest for technological advancement, the tension between innovation and ethics often emerges. While AI-driven innovations promise efficiency gains, questions arise about the implications for human employment. Automation can lead to job displacement, raising concerns about the livelihoods of workers. Ethical considerations become the fulcrum on which these competing forces balance. Striking the right equilibrium requires a nuanced understanding of both the potential benefits and unintended consequences of AI integration.
- **The Transparency Imperative:** As AI takes on decision-making roles, transparency becomes a moral imperative. Manufacturers must provide visibility into how AI algorithms arrive at conclusions, ensuring that decisions are not opaque enigmas but comprehensible processes. This transparency fosters trust, allowing stakeholders to assess the fairness and ethical implications of AI choices. Openness in AI decision-making is a safeguard against unintended biases and reinforces accountability.
- **The Blueprint for Ethical AI Integration:** Ethical AI integration demands more than just a vague awareness of potential consequences—it requires a structured approach. Clear ethical guidelines and frameworks must be established, reflecting a collective commitment to responsible AI usage. Cross-functional teams comprising technologists, ethicists, and policymakers collaborate to

set ethical boundaries and ensure AI decisions align with shared values.
- **The Path Forward:** The integration of AI into manufacturing is an evolution that transcends technology—it is a journey that shapes societies and defines industries. As AI becomes a manufacturing ally, ethical considerations stand as sentinels, ensuring that the path forward is traversed responsibly. By embracing innovation while upholding ethical principles, manufacturers can navigate the delicate balance between progress and social well-being. In the symphony of AI integration, ethics is the conductor that harmonizes technological brilliance with human values.

Conclusion: 3.2.4. Challenges and Opportunities Ahead

The integration of AI into manufacturing represents a pivotal juncture—a convergence of innovation, opportunity, and challenge. By recognizing the potential of automation while addressing the need for reskilling, investing in technology, fortifying cybersecurity, and embracing ethical considerations, businesses can navigate this terrain with poise. The symphony of AI's transformational melody, when orchestrated with foresight and responsibility, can resonate harmoniously, shaping a future where technology augments human potential and propels manufacturing into a new era of excellence.

Conclusion: 3.2. Manufacturing: Automation, Predictive Maintenance, and Supply Chain Optimization

The presence of AI within the manufacturing realm heralds a transformative era marked by heightened productivity, efficiency, and adaptability. As exemplified by this section, the fusion of automation, predictive maintenance, and supply chain optimization harnesses AI's capabilities to forge a manufacturing ecosystem that's both agile and responsive. By embracing AI's potential and proactively addressing its associated challenges, the manufacturing sector sets the stage for an era where technology and human ingenuity harmonize to redefine the very essence of industrial prowess.

3.3. Finance: Algorithmic Trading, Fraud Detection, and Customer Service

The financial sector is a crucible of data-driven decision-making, where the swiftness of every action can have far-reaching consequences. Enter Artificial Intelligence (AI), a force that has engendered a transformation in finance that is as profound as it is swift. This section explores AI's impact on finance through algorithmic trading, fraud detection, and customer service.

3.3.1. Algorithmic Trading: The Speed of Precision

In the dynamic landscape of finance, where microseconds can make or break fortunes, a new frontier has emerged that harnesses the formidable power of Artificial Intelligence (AI) - algorithmic trading. This cutting-edge technology has ignited a revolution, fundamentally reshaping the very essence of financial operations and ushering in an era of unparalleled precision and speed. In this section, we delve into the intricacies of algorithmic trading, exploring how AI algorithms have transformed the world of finance and redefined the way investments are made.

3.3.1.1. The Evolution of Algorithmic Trading

Algorithmic trading, often referred to as algo trading, represents the culmination of decades of technological advancement and financial innovation. It stands as a testament to the marriage of data science, computer science, and financial expertise. This innovative approach to trading has given rise to trading floors that more closely resemble digital battlegrounds than the traditional image of brokers shouting orders.

➤ **A Historical Perspective**

To appreciate the evolution of algo trading, it's essential to take a historical perspective. The roots of algorithmic trading can be traced back to the early 1970s when financial markets began the shift from open outcry trading to electronic trading platforms. This shift laid the foundation for the automation of trading processes.

The 1980s and 1990s witnessed the development of early algorithmic trading systems. These systems primarily focused on executing large orders efficiently while minimizing market impact. They used basic algorithms to slice large orders into smaller, manageable chunks and execute them over time.

➢ **The Rise of High-Frequency Trading (HFT)**

The true transformation occurred with the advent of high-frequency trading (HFT) in the late 1990s and early 2000s. HFT firms harnessed the power of advanced algorithms, high-speed data feeds, and co-location services to execute trades at unprecedented speeds—often in microseconds or milliseconds. This speed advantage allowed HFT firms to engage in strategies like market-making and statistical arbitrage, where split-second decisions could lead to profits.

The proliferation of electronic exchanges and the availability of historical market data fueled the growth of HFT. These firms invested heavily in cutting-edge technology, including field-programmable gate arrays (FPGAs) and proximity hosting, to gain an edge in speed.

➢ **The Financial Crisis and Regulation**

The 2008 financial crisis brought increased scrutiny to financial markets and algorithmic trading. Regulators and exchanges introduced measures to enhance market stability and transparency. These included circuit breakers, trading halts, and increased oversight of HFT activities.

➢ **Diversification of Algorithmic Strategies**

In the aftermath of the financial crisis, algorithmic trading continued to evolve. Market participants diversified their algorithmic strategies to encompass a broader range of approaches, including:

- **Execution Algorithms:** These algorithms focus on optimizing trade execution, minimizing market impact, and achieving the best possible prices.
- **Smart Order Routing (SOR):** SOR algorithms automatically route orders to multiple trading venues to find the best available prices.
- **Quantitative Strategies:** Algorithmic trading expanded to encompass quantitative strategies based on mathematical models and statistical analysis.
- **Machine Learning and AI:** Recent advancements in machine learning and artificial intelligence have enabled the development of more sophisticated trading algorithms that can adapt to changing market conditions.

➢ The Future of Algorithmic Trading

Looking ahead, the future of algorithmic trading holds promise and challenges. Continued advancements in AI and machine learning are expected to lead to even more adaptive and predictive algorithms. Regulatory developments will continue to shape the landscape, with a focus on market integrity and fairness.

Algorithmic trading will likely continue to play a central role in financial markets, optimizing trading strategies, providing liquidity, and contributing to market efficiency. However, it will also require ongoing monitoring and oversight to ensure that it aligns with regulatory goals and market stability.

In summary, algorithmic trading has come a long way from its origins as a tool for executing large orders efficiently. It has evolved into a multifaceted field encompassing a wide range of strategies and technologies. As technology and data availability continue to advance, the future of algo trading remains dynamic and full of potential.

3.3.1.2. AI at the Core: Deciphering Market Data

At the heart of algorithmic trading lies the utilization of AI algorithms, which represent the culmination of technological prowess and data-driven decision-making. These algorithms possess the capacity to analyze vast streams of market data with unprecedented speed and accuracy, making them indispensable in the realm of modern finance. Let's delve deeper into how AI algorithms decipher market data and the transformative impact they have on trading strategies.

> **Unparalleled Data Processing**

Financial markets are inundated with data. Price movements, trading volumes, news releases, economic indicators, and a multitude of other variables create a data-rich environment where opportunities and risks are constantly emerging. AI algorithms excel in this data-intensive landscape. They ingest and process this information in real-time, an endeavor that surpasses the capabilities of human traders.

> **Pattern Recognition**

One of AI's core strengths in algorithmic trading is its ability to recognize intricate patterns within data. These patterns might be elusive to human observers, buried in the sheer volume of information. AI algorithms, however, can identify subtle correlations and trends that serve as valuable signals for trading decisions.

For instance, AI algorithms can detect the emergence of a technical trading pattern, such as a "head and shoulders" formation, and trigger a trade accordingly. They can also discern sentiment shifts in news articles and social media that might impact stock prices.

> **Risk Management**

AI is not only about seizing opportunities but also about managing risks. Algorithmic trading systems often incorporate risk management algorithms that continuously monitor positions, market conditions, and other variables to assess and mitigate risk. If a predefined risk threshold is breached, these algorithms can automatically execute risk-reduction strategies, such as adjusting positions or executing stop-loss orders.

> **Market Microstructure Analysis**

AI algorithms delve deep into the market microstructure, analyzing order book data, trade execution patterns, and liquidity dynamics. This granular analysis enables them to optimize execution strategies. For instance, they can determine the optimal order placement strategy to minimize transaction costs or reduce market impact.

> **Machine Learning and Adaptive Strategies**

Modern AI algorithms frequently incorporate machine learning techniques, enabling them to adapt and evolve. They can learn from historical data, continuously improving their strategies and adapting to changing market conditions. For instance, in a volatile market, an algorithm might recognize the need for more conservative risk management.

> **Real-Time Decision-Making**

Perhaps the most distinctive aspect of AI in algorithmic trading is its ability to make real-time decisions at speeds unimaginable to humans. In the blink of an eye, AI algorithms process incoming data, assess trading signals, and execute orders. This split-second decision-making is particularly advantageous in high-frequency trading (HFT), where milliseconds can make the difference between profit and loss.

> **The Human-Machine Partnership**

It's important to emphasize that AI in algorithmic trading doesn't replace human traders but augments their capabilities. Human expertise remains crucial for strategy development, risk oversight, and adapting to unforeseen market events. AI serves as a powerful tool in the trader's toolkit, providing insights, automation, and enhanced decision-making capabilities.

In conclusion, AI algorithms are the beating heart of algorithmic trading, enabling the rapid analysis of vast amounts of market data, pattern recognition, risk management, and real-time decision-making. They represent a symbiotic partnership between human intelligence and machine efficiency, ushering in an era of unprecedented precision and speed in the financial markets. As AI technologies continue to advance, their role in algorithmic trading is likely to evolve, offering even more sophisticated and adaptive strategies.

3.3.1.3. The Need for Speed: Milliseconds Matter

In the fast-paced realm of algorithmic trading, the significance of speed cannot be overstated. It's a relentless race where microseconds can make the difference between substantial profits and significant losses. To understand the gravity of this need for speed, let's explore how algorithmic trading leverages the precious commodity of time and why milliseconds matter.

> **The Race Against Time**

Imagine a scenario where an arbitrage opportunity arises, where the same financial asset is trading at slightly different prices on two different exchanges. To capitalize on this opportunity, an algorithmic trader needs to buy the asset on the exchange where it's priced lower and simultaneously sell it on the exchange where it's priced higher. However, these price differences are fleeting, often lasting only for a fraction of a second.

In this scenario, every millisecond counts. The time it takes for the trader's orders to travel from their algorithmic trading system to the exchange's servers, get executed, and confirm the trades can mean the difference between capturing the arbitrage opportunity and missing out.

➤ **Proximity Matters**

One of the strategies employed to gain a competitive edge in this race is proximity. Proximity, in this context, refers to how physically close an algorithmic trader's servers are to the data center of the stock exchange. The principle is simple: the shorter the distance data needs to travel, the faster it can be processed.

To achieve minimal latency, algorithmic traders often co-locate their servers within the same data center as the exchange's servers. This physical proximity ensures that data, including order requests and trade confirmations, traverses the shortest possible distance. Fiber-optic cables, with their near-instantaneous data transmission capabilities, further facilitate this need for speed.

➤ **High-Frequency Trading (HFT)**

The quest for speed reaches its zenith in the domain of high-frequency trading (HFT). HFT firms specialize in executing a large number of trades in extremely short timeframes, often measured in microseconds or even nanoseconds. These firms invest heavily in cutting-edge technology, from high-performance servers to advanced networking equipment, to minimize latency.

HFT strategies, such as market-making and statistical arbitrage, rely on the ability to react to market movements and execute orders with unparalleled speed and precision. For instance, in market-making, HFT firms continuously quote buy and sell prices for financial instruments, aiming to profit from the bid-ask spread. Any delay in their ability to update quotes or execute trades can result in losses.

➤ **Risk Management and Infrastructure**

The need for speed doesn't come without challenges. Algorithmic traders must implement robust risk management systems to prevent catastrophic losses in the event of unexpected market volatility or technology failures. These systems include mechanisms like circuit breakers, position limits, and fail-safes that can pause trading activities.

Furthermore, maintaining and upgrading the technological infrastructure required for high-speed trading is a constant endeavor. It involves not only substantial financial investments but also the expertise to keep systems running smoothly and securely.

➤ **A Balancing Act**

While speed is paramount in algorithmic trading, it's essential to strike a balance between speed and risk. Pursuing excessive speed can expose traders to unintended risks, including operational glitches or market anomalies. Therefore, algorithmic traders must carefully calibrate their strategies, risk controls, and infrastructure to navigate this high-stakes landscape.

In conclusion, the world of algorithmic trading operates in the realm of milliseconds, where the fastest and most technologically advanced players gain a competitive edge. Speed, facilitated by proximity and cutting-edge technology, is crucial for executing trades with precision and seizing fleeting opportunities. However, this need for speed must be tempered with robust risk management and a deep understanding of the intricacies of the financial markets to navigate this fast-paced and high-stakes environment successfully.

3.3.1.4. Optimizing Strategies: Maximizing Returns

Algorithmic trading isn't solely about speed; it's about optimizing trading strategies for maximum returns. These algorithms can execute complex trading strategies, such as arbitrage, market-making, and trend following, with precision. They can identify arbitrage opportunities where price discrepancies exist between different markets and swiftly capitalize on them.

- **Arbitrage:** Arbitrage is a strategy where an algorithm simultaneously buys and sells the same asset in different markets to profit from price discrepancies. For example, if a stock is trading at a lower price on one exchange and at a higher price on another, the algorithm can execute buy orders on the lower-priced exchange and sell orders on the higher-priced one, profiting from the price difference.
- **Market-Making:** Market-making algorithms aim to profit from the bid-ask spread—the difference between the highest price a buyer is willing to pay (bid) and the lowest price a seller is willing to accept (ask). These algorithms continuously place buy and sell orders to capture this spread. They provide liquidity to the market, ensuring that there are always buyers and sellers for a particular asset.
- **Trend Following:** Trend-following algorithms identify and capitalize on trends in asset prices. They analyze historical price data and technical indicators to determine the direction of a trend, such as an uptrend or downtrend. Once a trend is identified, the algorithm executes trades in the

direction of the trend, aiming to profit from price movements.

These trading strategies require not only speed but also sophisticated analysis and decision-making capabilities. Algorithmic trading systems can process vast amounts of data to make split-second trading decisions, optimizing the execution of these strategies.

Furthermore, these algorithms are not limited to a single asset class. They can trade a wide range of financial instruments, including stocks, bonds, currencies, commodities, and derivatives. This versatility allows algorithmic traders to diversify their portfolios and explore opportunities in various markets.

In summary, algorithmic trading combines speed and strategy to maximize returns. These algorithms excel in executing complex trading strategies, enabling traders to capitalize on price discrepancies, provide liquidity, and follow market trends effectively. Their adaptability across different asset classes makes them a powerful tool for modern financial markets.

3.3.1.5. Reshaping the Market: A Digital Transformation

The adoption of algorithmic trading has ushered in a digital transformation that extends far beyond individual trading strategies. It has fundamentally reshaped the architecture and dynamics of financial markets, leading to profound changes in market structure, liquidity, and regulation.

> **Increased Liquidity**

Algorithmic trading has significantly boosted market liquidity, which refers to the ease with which assets can be bought or sold without causing substantial price fluctuations. This increase in liquidity is a direct result of algorithmic traders' ability to swiftly execute large volumes of orders across various assets.

In traditional trading, a large order could move the market significantly, resulting in unfavorable prices for the trader. Algorithmic trading algorithms, on the other hand, are designed to execute large orders with minimal price impact. This not only benefits algorithmic traders but also other market participants, as it reduces the cost of executing trades and enhances overall market efficiency.

> **Tightened Bid-Ask Spreads**

Bid-ask spreads, the difference between the prices at which buyers are willing to purchase an asset (the bid price) and sellers are willing to sell it (the ask price), have also witnessed a transformation due to algorithmic trading.

In highly liquid markets where algorithmic trading is prevalent, bid-ask spreads tend to be narrower. This means that traders can buy and sell assets at prices that are closer to each other, reducing the cost of trading. Tighter spreads benefit both retail and institutional investors, as they result in better execution prices.

> **Market Microstructure Adaptations**

The rise of algorithmic trading has necessitated adaptations in market microstructure—the rules, regulations, and infrastructure governing financial markets. Exchanges and regulatory bodies have had to respond to the rapid evolution of trading practices and technology.

For instance, circuit breakers, mechanisms that temporarily halt trading during extreme market volatility, have been adjusted to account for algorithmic trading's speed and volume. Risk controls and position limits have been introduced to mitigate the potential risks associated with high-frequency trading.

Market surveillance has also evolved to monitor and detect potentially manipulative or disruptive trading behavior, ensuring market integrity in the age of algorithmic trading.

> **Fragmentation and Connectivity**

Algorithmic trading has led to increased market fragmentation, where trading occurs across multiple platforms and venues. This fragmentation can be a double-edged sword. While it enhances competition and offers traders a variety of execution options, it also presents challenges related to market connectivity, data synchronization, and ensuring best execution.

As a result, financial institutions and market participants have had to invest in sophisticated technology infrastructure to maintain connectivity to various trading venues and adapt to the fragmented market landscape.

> **Regulatory Responses**

Regulators have been vigilant in responding to the impact of algorithmic trading on financial markets. They have introduced a range of regulations aimed at promoting market stability, fairness, and investor protection.

Examples of regulatory responses include the introduction of circuit breakers, the implementation of market access controls, and the monitoring of algorithmic trading activity for signs of market manipulation.

The adoption of algorithmic trading has brought about a digital transformation in financial markets that extends well beyond the trading strategies of individual participants. It has increased liquidity, tightened bid-ask spreads, prompted adaptations in market microstructure, led to market fragmentation, and elicited regulatory responses.

While algorithmic trading has ushered in numerous benefits, including enhanced market efficiency and reduced trading costs, it has also posed challenges related to risk management, connectivity, and market integrity. As a result, market participants, exchanges, and regulatory bodies continue to navigate this evolving landscape, striving to strike a balance between innovation and regulation to ensure the long-term stability and integrity of financial markets.

3.3.1.6. Challenges and Controversies: The Human Touch

While algorithmic trading offers tremendous advantages, it's not without challenges and controversies. These challenges highlight the importance of retaining a human touch in financial markets.

➤ **Market Stability and Flash Crashes**

One of the foremost challenges associated with algorithmic trading is the potential impact on market stability. The speed at which algorithms execute trades can sometimes lead to sudden and extreme market movements, known as "flash crashes." These episodes, while typically short-lived, can have significant consequences, including substantial price swings and disruptions.

To mitigate this risk, regulators have introduced circuit breakers and other mechanisms to temporarily halt trading during periods of extreme volatility. However, ensuring the stability of modern markets, characterized by algorithmic trading's high-speed nature, remains an ongoing challenge.

➤ **Fairness and High-Frequency Trading (HFT)**

Questions of fairness have arisen in the context of high-frequency trading (HFT), a subset of algorithmic trading. HFT firms leverage advanced technology and ultra-fast connections to execute trades within milliseconds or microseconds. This speed advantage allows them to engage in strategies like front-running, where they execute orders ahead of slower traders to profit from anticipated price movements.

Critics argue that such practices create an uneven playing field, as HFT firms can gain advantages inaccessible to traditional investors. This has prompted discussions about market fairness, transparency, and the need for safeguards to level the playing field.

> **Lack of Human Oversight**

Algorithmic trading systems are designed to operate autonomously, making decisions based on pre-defined rules and data analysis. While this autonomy is a key feature, it also poses challenges related to accountability and human oversight. In rare cases, algorithmic errors or glitches have led to significant trading losses.

To address this, financial institutions are increasingly emphasizing the importance of human oversight and risk management in algorithmic trading. Ensuring that humans are in control, understand the algorithms they deploy, and can intervene when necessary is essential for maintaining market stability and integrity.

> **Regulatory Complexity**

The rapid evolution of algorithmic trading has posed challenges for regulators. Crafting regulations that strike the right balance between fostering innovation and ensuring market integrity is a complex task. Regulatory bodies must keep pace with technological advancements and market developments to adapt rules effectively.

> **Data Privacy and Security**

Algorithmic trading relies heavily on real-time market data and vast datasets. This raises concerns about data privacy and security. Safeguarding sensitive financial information and preventing data breaches is crucial to maintain trust in the financial system.

Algorithmic trading offers undeniable benefits, such as increased liquidity and reduced trading costs. However, it also presents challenges related to market stability, fairness, human oversight, regulatory complexity, and data security. Addressing these challenges is essential to ensure that financial markets remain transparent, fair, and resilient in the era of algorithmic trading. Balancing the advantages of technology with the need for human control and ethical considerations remains an ongoing task for market participants and regulators alike.

Conclusion: 3.3.1. Algorithmic Trading: The Speed of Precision

In the grand tapestry of technological advancement, algorithmic trading stands at the intersection of AI, data science, and finance. It epitomizes the transformative power of AI, allowing humans to augment their decision-making capabilities with machine-driven precision. As financial markets continue to evolve, algorithmic trading will remain a dynamic force, shaping the future of finance and propelling the industry into uncharted realms of efficiency and accuracy.

3.3.2. Fraud Detection: Unmasking Cyber Threats

In the interconnected realm of digital transactions, where convenience and vulnerability coexist, a vigilant guardian has emerged to safeguard financial integrity - Artificial Intelligence (AI)-driven fraud detection. This technology has elevated the battle against cyber threats to new heights, employing AI's pattern recognition prowess to unmask anomalies lurking within the sea of transactions. With machine learning algorithms at its core, this digital sentry identifies deviations from established patterns, flagging suspicious activities that could signify fraudulent behavior. Beyond preserving monetary value, AI-driven fraud detection reinforces trust in digital financial ecosystems, providing individuals and institutions with a shield against evolving forms of cybercrime.

The Rise of Cyber Threats

As the world becomes increasingly digitized, the volume and complexity of digital transactions have grown exponentially. While this digitization has brought unprecedented convenience, it has also created fertile ground for cybercriminals. These adversaries continuously devise new methods to infiltrate digital systems and exploit vulnerabilities for financial gain.

The Role of AI in Fraud Detection

AI-powered fraud detection has emerged as a formidable ally in this ongoing battle. Here's how it works:

- **Pattern Recognition:** AI algorithms are trained on vast datasets of legitimate transactions. They learn to recognize patterns of normal behavior, considering factors like transaction frequency, location, and typical transaction amounts.

- **Identifying Anomalies:** Once the AI system establishes a baseline for normal behavior, it continuously monitors incoming transactions in real-time. When a transaction deviates significantly from the established patterns, it raises an alert.
- **Machine Learning:** AI-driven fraud detection systems are not static; they evolve. Machine learning algorithms adapt to new patterns of fraudulent behavior as cybercriminals develop more sophisticated techniques.

Types of Fraud Detected

AI-driven fraud detection can identify various types of fraudulent activities, including:

- **Payment Card Fraud:** This involves unauthorized use of credit or debit card information for fraudulent purchases.
- **Identity Theft:** AI can detect when someone attempts to open accounts or make transactions using stolen identity information.
- **Account Takeover:** Cybercriminals may gain access to individuals' accounts through phishing or hacking attempts. AI can detect unusual account activity, such as login attempts from unfamiliar locations.
- **Phishing and Social Engineering:** AI algorithms can analyze email content and user behavior to identify phishing attempts and suspicious communications.

Benefits of AI in Fraud Detection

The adoption of AI in fraud detection offers several advantages:

- **Real-time Detection:** AI can identify fraud in real-time, preventing unauthorized transactions from occurring.
- **Reduced False Positives:** By continuously learning and adapting, AI systems can reduce the number of false

positives, ensuring that legitimate transactions are not unnecessarily flagged.
- **Scalability:** AI can handle vast amounts of data, making it suitable for large-scale financial institutions and online platforms.
- **Adaptability:** AI systems can adapt to evolving threats, staying one step ahead of cybercriminals.

Enhancing Trust in Digital Ecosystems

AI-driven fraud detection plays a pivotal role in preserving trust in digital financial ecosystems. By proactively identifying and mitigating cyber threats, it helps protect both individuals and financial institutions from financial loss and reputational damage.

Conclusion: 3.3.2 Fraud Detection: Unmasking Cyber Threats

In an era marked by digital transactions and cyber threats, AI-driven fraud detection stands as a stalwart guardian of financial integrity. Through pattern recognition and real-time monitoring, it identifies and mitigates fraudulent activities, reinforcing trust in digital financial systems. As cybercriminals continue to evolve, AI-powered fraud detection remains an indispensable tool for safeguarding financial assets and maintaining the security of digital transactions.

3.3.3 Customer Service: Instantaneous Assistance

In the era of instantaneous gratification, where speed and convenience reign supreme, Artificial Intelligence (AI) has revolutionized customer service by delivering real-time solutions. Enter AI-powered chatbots and virtual assistants, the architects of seamless interactions. These digital agents harness the power of Natural Language Processing (NLP) to comprehend and generate human language, enabling instant responses to customer queries and concerns. From troubleshooting technical glitches to furnishing account information, AI-driven customer service offers immediate assistance, ensuring customer satisfaction and engagement in a fast-paced world.

The Evolution of Customer Service

Customer service has come a long way from the days of waiting on hold for a human agent. With the advent of AI, it has evolved into an efficient and responsive system capable of addressing customer needs instantly. Here's how AI-powered customer service works:

- **Natural Language Processing (NLP):** AI-driven customer service relies on NLP, a branch of AI that focuses on the interaction between computers and human language. NLP algorithms enable machines to understand, interpret, and generate human language, both in written and spoken forms.
- **Chatbots and Virtual Assistants:** Chatbots and virtual assistants are the frontline soldiers of AI-driven customer service. They are designed to engage with customers in a conversational manner, just like human agents, but with the advantage of speed and accessibility 24/7.
- **Instantaneous Responses:** AI-powered customer service can provide immediate responses to a wide range of customer inquiries. These inquiries may include product information, troubleshooting assistance, account management, and even complex problem-solving.

- **Multilingual Support:** NLP-powered AI can offer customer service in multiple languages, making it accessible and inclusive for a global customer base.
- **Data Utilization:** AI systems can tap into vast databases of information to provide accurate and up-to-date responses. This data-driven approach ensures that customers receive precise and relevant information.

Benefits of AI in Customer Service

AI-driven customer service brings several benefits to both businesses and customers:

- **Instantaneous Assistance:** Customers no longer have to wait on hold or navigate lengthy automated phone menus. AI responds instantly, improving customer satisfaction.
- **Cost Efficiency:** AI-powered agents can handle a high volume of inquiries simultaneously, reducing the need for a large customer service workforce.
- **Consistency:** AI provides consistent responses, ensuring that customers receive accurate information every time.
- **24/7 Availability:** AI doesn't sleep or take breaks, offering round-the-clock support to customers in different time zones.
- **Scalability:** AI can scale to meet the demands of growing businesses without significant increases in costs.
- **Data Analysis:** AI systems can analyze customer interactions to provide insights that businesses can use to enhance their products and services.

Conclusion: 3.3.3. Customer Service: Instantaneous Assistance

AI-powered customer service is at the forefront of providing instantaneous assistance in a world where speed and convenience are paramount. Through NLP, chatbots, and virtual assistants, AI systems understand and respond to customer inquiries, ensuring satisfaction and engagement. As businesses embrace this technology, they not only enhance their customer service capabilities but also position themselves at the cutting edge of customer-centricity in today's fast-paced world.

3.3.4. Challenges and Opportunities

The integration of Artificial Intelligence (AI) into the financial sector ushers in a realm of both challenges and opportunities. The benefits are immense, yet ethical and operational challenges abound. Here, we delve into the multifaceted landscape of AI in finance:

Opportunities:

- **Enhanced Efficiency:** AI-driven systems in finance can perform tasks at speeds and accuracies unattainable by humans. This translates to enhanced operational efficiency, reduced costs, and quicker decision-making.
- **Data-Driven Insights:** AI can analyze vast datasets to extract valuable insights, aiding in risk assessment, investment decisions, and fraud detection.
- **Personalized Financial Services:** AI enables the creation of personalized financial services, such as tailored investment portfolios and insurance plans, improving customer satisfaction.
- **Automation of Routine Tasks:** Mundane and repetitive tasks, such as data entry and compliance checks, can be

automated, freeing up human employees for more complex and strategic roles.
- **Risk Management:** AI can provide advanced risk management models that assess and mitigate potential financial risks, contributing to overall financial stability.

Challenges:

- **Ethical Concerns:** The use of AI in finance raises ethical questions, especially in areas like algorithmic trading. Concerns about market manipulation, unfair advantages, and the potential for unchecked automation need to be addressed.
- **Transparency and Explainability:** Maintaining transparency and explainability of AI-driven decisions is vital for customer trust and regulatory compliance. AI systems often operate as "black boxes," making it challenging to understand their decision-making processes.
- **Regulatory Hurdles:** The financial industry is heavily regulated, and integrating AI introduces complexities related to compliance with existing and evolving regulations.
- **Cybersecurity Risks:** AI systems can be vulnerable to cyberattacks, making data security and privacy critical concerns.
- **Human-Machine Balance:** Striking the right balance between automation and human expertise is a delicate challenge. Overreliance on AI could diminish the role of human professionals in finance.
- **Bias and Fairness:** AI systems can inherit biases present in training data, leading to unfair outcomes. Ensuring fairness in AI-driven financial decisions is essential.

As finance continues to evolve under the influence of AI, the industry stands at the crossroads of harnessing its potential while navigating these complex challenges. Addressing these challenges and maximizing the opportunities will be instrumental in shaping a responsible and prosperous AI-driven financial sector.

Conclusion: 3.3. Finance: Algorithmic Trading, Fraud Detection, and Customer Service

AI's disruption in the financial sector is nothing short of transformative. Algorithmic trading alters the fundamental dynamics of markets, fraud detection fortifies the cybersecurity arsenal, and AI-powered customer service sets new standards of responsiveness. In the midst of this technological revolution, the finance industry evolves into a realm where the synergy of human insights and AI precision lays the foundation for a resilient, adaptable, and responsive financial landscape. As we journey through the intricacies of AI's impact, the financial sector emerges as a prime example of innovation shaping the future.

3.4. Retail: E-commerce, Recommendation Systems, and Inventory Management

The retail industry, once characterized by traditional brick-and-mortar stores, is undergoing a radical transformation powered by the discerning capabilities of Artificial Intelligence (AI). This section unveils AI's impact on retail through e-commerce, recommendation systems, and inventory management.

3.4.1. E-commerce: The Evolution of Personalization

In the ever-evolving world of retail, the advent of e-commerce is not merely a change in the way products are bought and sold; it represents a paradigm shift in how consumers experience shopping. This transformation is being driven by the remarkable capabilities of Artificial Intelligence (AI), which are breathing new life into e-commerce platforms. Gone are the days of generic online marketplaces. AI is ushering in a new era of personalization, where every click, every search, and every interaction is harnessed to create a tailor-made shopping journey for each individual customer.

At the heart of this evolution is the intricate dance of AI algorithms that meticulously analyze and decipher vast amounts of consumer data. Browsing histories, past purchases, preferences, and demographic information are all fed into the AI engine. This amalgamation of data serves as the artist's palette, allowing AI to craft a canvas of customized product offerings. The outcome is an online storefront that feels less like a marketplace and more like a personal shopping assistant— one that knows your tastes, anticipates your desires, and presents you with options that resonate on a deeply individual level.

Imagine browsing an e-commerce platform where the products seem to speak directly to you. As you explore, the suggestions that populate your screen align perfectly with your preferences, as if the platform were reading your mind. This sense of being understood and catered to creates an unparalleled sense of engagement and connection. The AI-powered e-commerce experience transcends geographical boundaries, bringing a curated selection of products to your fingertips, regardless of where you are in the world.

In this era of AI-driven e-commerce, the mantra is personalization, and it's changing the way consumers shop and engage with brands. The once-impersonal transactional nature of online shopping is evolving into a more intimate, experiential process. The fusion of AI's analytical prowess with the consumer's individuality is giving rise to a retail landscape where every click is an opportunity for a unique and memorable encounter. As we navigate this transformed landscape, we find ourselves not just shopping, but embarking on a journey of discovery that resonates with our preferences, needs, and aspirations.

3.4.2. Recommendation Systems: Navigating the Infinite Aisles

In the vast digital expanse of modern retail, where countless products populate the virtual shelves, finding what you're looking for can sometimes feel like searching for a needle in a haystack. This is where the magic of Artificial Intelligence (AI) comes into play, reshaping the retail landscape through sophisticated recommendation systems that serve as your guiding compass.

Gone are the days of generic, one-size-fits-all product recommendations. Today's AI-driven recommendation systems are like skilled curators, sifting through mountains of data to offer suggestions that align perfectly with your tastes and preferences. Behind the scenes, complex algorithms analyze your browsing history, previous purchases, and even the choices of shoppers with similar profiles. These algorithms become the maestros of personalization, uncovering hidden patterns and connections between products that might elude human observation.

Consider the experience of browsing an online marketplace, where each click, hover, and scroll is being noted by the AI. As you explore different categories and products, the recommendation engine is working tirelessly to piece together the puzzle of your shopping journey. It understands not just what you're interested in at the moment, but also what you might be interested in next. The result is a cascade of suggestions that appear almost like they've been plucked from your thoughts—products that resonate with your preferences, align with your style, and cater to your needs.

These recommendations guide you through the infinite aisles of the digital marketplace, making the shopping experience less overwhelming and more enjoyable. You no longer have to sift through pages of products; the AI has already done that for you, presenting options that are both relevant and appealing. This level of personalization elevates the shopping journey from transactional to experiential. It feels like having a knowledgeable shopping companion who knows your preferences better than you do yourself.

In the realm of AI-powered recommendation systems, choice and serendipity coexist. While these systems guide you towards products you're likely to purchase, they also have the power to introduce you to items you might not have considered otherwise. This fusion of predictability and surprise adds an element of excitement to the shopping experience, making each interaction with the platform a delightful discovery.

As we traverse the landscape of AI's influence on retail, the recommendation system stands as a testament to technology's ability to understand, predict, and enhance human experiences.

It's a glimpse into a future where shopping isn't just about acquiring products; it's about embarking on a curated journey that reflects your unique preferences and aspirations.

3.4.3. AI-driven Chatbots: Instantaneous Retail Concierge

In the bustling world of modern retail, where speed and convenience are paramount, AI-driven chatbots have emerged as the ultimate retail concierges. These virtual assistants, powered by Artificial Intelligence (AI), have revolutionized the way customers interact with brands, offering instant gratification and personalized guidance at every step of the shopping journey.

Imagine entering a busy retail store, but instead of searching for a human assistant, you're met with an AI-powered chatbot ready to assist you. These digital helpers are equipped with Natural Language Processing (NLP) capabilities, allowing them to understand and generate human language. They can seamlessly comprehend your inquiries, respond to your concerns, and provide real-time information about products and services.

When you visit an online store, a chatbot might pop up in the corner, greeting you like a friendly sales associate. It might ask if you need help finding a specific item, offer recommendations based on your preferences, or guide you through the checkout process. And just like a skilled concierge, the chatbot is available 24/7, ensuring that you receive assistance whenever you need it, without any waiting time.

These AI-driven chatbots bring the immediacy of an in-store shopping experience to the digital realm. They bridge the gap between customers and brands, offering a direct channel for communication that feels personal and human-like. Whether you're seeking information about product features, checking on an order status, or troubleshooting an issue, the chatbot is there to assist with accuracy and efficiency.

But the magic doesn't stop there. These chatbots are also adept at remembering your previous interactions, creating a sense of continuity in your conversations. They can recall your purchase history, preferences, and even recommend products based on your past choices. This level of personalization not only enhances the customer experience but also fosters a stronger sense of brand loyalty.

AI-driven chatbots aren't just limited to providing information; they can also facilitate transactions. Imagine being able to place an order, make a reservation, or even track a delivery all through a simple chat interface. The convenience of such interactions is unparalleled, especially in a world where time is a precious commodity.

As we venture deeper into the realm of AI's influence on retail, chatbots emerge as a shining example of technology's ability to enhance human interactions. They're not just tools for efficiency; they're companions that offer real-time guidance, tailored suggestions, and instant assistance—all at the touch of a button. Through the lens of AI-driven chatbots, the future of retail is one where customer service transcends transactional exchanges and evolves into meaningful conversations.

3.4.4. Inventory Management: Orchestrating Efficiency

In the intricate dance of retail operations, where supply meets demand, the role of AI-driven inventory management emerges as the master orchestrator of efficiency. This transformative technology has revolutionized the way retailers manage their stock, ensuring products are available to customers precisely when and where they are needed.

Traditionally, inventory management was a delicate balancing act, prone to errors and uncertainties. Retailers grappled with the challenges of overstocking, which tied up capital and led to wastage, or understocking, which resulted in lost sales opportunities and frustrated customers. Enter AI-driven inventory management, a solution that harnesses the power of data and algorithms to optimize stock levels with unparalleled precision.

At the heart of AI-driven inventory management lies a web of algorithms that analyze a multitude of variables. These algorithms process historical sales data, market trends, seasonal fluctuations, and even external factors like weather patterns or economic indicators. By examining these diverse data points, AI systems can predict consumer demand with remarkable accuracy.

Imagine a retail scenario where the AI system anticipates the surge in demand for umbrellas as a storm approaches, or the increase in sunscreen sales as temperatures rise. These insights enable retailers to adjust their stock levels in advance, preventing the pitfalls of overstocking or the disappointment of empty shelves.

Furthermore, AI-driven inventory management operates in real-time, constantly adapting to changing conditions. If a sudden trend emerges—whether it's a viral social media post or a celebrity endorsement—AI algorithms can swiftly adjust inventory levels to meet the newfound demand. This agility ensures that retailers remain responsive to market dynamics and customer preferences.

The benefits of AI-driven inventory management extend beyond just avoiding stockouts and excess inventory. By optimizing stock levels, retailers reduce storage costs and minimize waste. Capital that was once tied up in excess inventory can now be allocated more strategically. The result is a leaner, more efficient supply chain that translates to improved bottom-line profitability.

Moreover, the positive impact on customer satisfaction is undeniable. With AI-powered inventory management, retailers can fulfill orders promptly, preventing customers from leaving empty-handed or seeking alternatives elsewhere. This not only enhances the shopping experience but also fosters brand loyalty and repeat business.

As we navigate the landscape of modern retail, AI-driven inventory management emerges as a critical enabler of efficiency and customer satisfaction. By harnessing the power of data and algorithms, retailers can transform the supply chain into a well-orchestrated symphony, where products seamlessly flow from manufacturers to consumers, meeting demand with precision and elegance.

3.4.5. Challenges and Opportunities

While AI's integration into the retail industry offers a wealth of opportunities, it also presents a set of challenges that businesses must navigate in order to reap its benefits fully.

- **Data Privacy and Consumer Consent:** The personalized experiences enabled by AI rely on customer data. However, the collection and utilization of this data raise concerns about data privacy and security. Striking a balance between offering tailored experiences and respecting user privacy is a challenge that retailers must address. Ensuring transparent data collection practices and obtaining explicit consent from consumers become crucial steps in building trust.

- **Ethical Considerations:** AI-driven recommendation systems and personalization can lead to filter bubbles, where consumers are exposed only to content that aligns with their existing preferences. This can limit exposure to diverse perspectives and contribute to echo chambers. Retailers need to design AI systems that balance personalized recommendations with serendipitous discovery, promoting a more well-rounded shopping experience.
- **Investment and Implementation:** Integrating AI into retail operations requires investments in technology, infrastructure, and talent. This can be a barrier for smaller businesses or those with limited resources. Retailers must carefully consider their AI strategy, weighing the potential benefits against the initial costs and ensuring a seamless integration across platforms.
- **Human-AI Collaboration:** While AI-driven chatbots enhance customer interactions, they cannot replace the human touch entirely. Striking the right balance between automated responses and human intervention is essential to maintain the quality of customer service. Training staff to work alongside AI systems effectively becomes an opportunity to create a harmonious synergy between human expertise and AI capabilities.
- **Unintended Consequences:** AI-driven decisions can have unintended consequences. For instance, relying solely on algorithmic trading can lead to market instability, as seen in instances of flash crashes. Retailers must anticipate and mitigate potential negative outcomes of AI systems and have mechanisms in place to intervene when needed.

- **Continuous Learning and Adaptation:** AI algorithms require continuous learning and adaptation to remain effective. Market trends, consumer preferences, and external factors are ever-changing. Retailers need to invest in ongoing training and updates for their AI systems to ensure they remain accurate and relevant.

In the face of these challenges, retailers also have the opportunity to reshape the industry through AI:

- **Enhanced Customer Experience:** AI-driven personalization, recommendation systems, and chatbots enable retailers to offer unparalleled customer experiences. By understanding and anticipating customer needs, retailers can forge deeper connections and foster brand loyalty.
- **Efficiency and Optimization:** AI-powered inventory management and supply chain optimization streamline operations, reducing waste, and minimizing costs. Retailers can achieve leaner processes that improve operational efficiency and drive profitability.
- **Global Reach:** E-commerce platforms empowered by AI can transcend geographical boundaries. Retailers can tap into global markets and offer products and services to customers around the world, expanding their reach and potential customer base.
- **Innovation and Creativity:** AI-driven insights can inform retailers about emerging trends and consumer preferences. This information can spark innovation in product development and marketing strategies, enabling retailers to stay ahead of the competition.
- **Reskilling and Upskilling:** The integration of AI necessitates a skilled workforce capable of operating and managing AI-driven systems. Retailers have the opportunity to invest in reskilling and upskilling

programs, ensuring that employees remain relevant in a technology-driven environment.

In conclusion, AI's disruption of the retail industry is a transformative journey filled with both challenges and opportunities. By navigating these challenges and embracing the potential, retailers can reshape the way they engage with customers, manage their operations, and create a retail landscape that seamlessly blends human creativity with AI precision.

Conclusion: 3.4. Retail: E-commerce, Recommendation Systems, and Inventory Management

The retail landscape is undergoing a profound metamorphosis, and AI is the catalyst propelling this transformation. E-commerce evolves into a realm of personalized journeys, recommendation systems redefine how we discover products, AI-driven chatbots revolutionize customer interactions, and inventory management attains unprecedented levels of efficiency. Beyond mere transactions, shopping becomes an art of engagement, where the fusion of human ingenuity and AI precision creates a future where the boundaries of shopping are redefined and the customer experience is elevated to new heights.

3.5. Agriculture: Precision Farming, Drone Technology, and Crop Monitoring

Agriculture, the bedrock of sustenance, is undergoing a profound metamorphosis through the transformative capabilities of Artificial Intelligence (AI). This section illuminates AI's role in agriculture through precision farming, drone technology, and crop monitoring.

3.5.1. Precision Farming: Cultivating Efficiency

In the ever-evolving landscape of agriculture, precision farming emerges as a beacon of transformation driven by the fusion of Artificial Intelligence (AI) and the Earth's natural resources. Here, we dive deeper into the intricate symphony of precision farming:

➤ **The Complexity of Agriculture: A Multifaceted Challenge**

Agriculture is a multifaceted endeavor, with a tapestry of soil conditions, weather patterns, and crop health intricately woven together. Managing these variables traditionally required extensive manual labor and often resulted in inefficiencies, resource wastage, and environmental impact.

➤ **AI's Virtuoso Role: Orchestrating Efficiency**

Enter AI, the virtuoso conductor in the orchestra of precision farming. AI leverages real-time data streams from sensors and combines them with historical and environmental data to gain a comprehensive understanding of the farming ecosystem.

➤ **Precision Resource Allocation: Nurturing Crops with Care**

AI algorithms take this understanding and transform it into actionable insights. They guide the dispensation of vital resources—water, fertilizers, and pesticides—in precise proportions. No drop of water is wasted, no nutrient is overused, and no harmful chemical is applied unnecessarily. It's the epitome of resource efficiency.

➤ **Enhanced Crop Yields: Maximizing Productivity**

This harmonization of resources results in a symphony of enhanced crop yields. Plants receive exactly what they need, precisely when they need it. This not only increases productivity but also reduces operational costs for farmers.

➢ **Environmental Stewardship: Respecting the Ecosystem**

Perhaps most importantly, precision farming practices respect the delicate balance of our ecosystem. By minimizing resource wastage and reducing the use of harmful chemicals, AI-driven precision farming contributes to sustainable agriculture.

➢ **A Paradigm of Efficiency and Sustainability**

Precision farming, guided by AI, represents a new paradigm in agriculture—one that resonates with efficiency, productivity, and environmental stewardship. It is a testament to how technology can revolutionize age-old practices, ensuring that we can feed a growing global population while safeguarding our planet's resources.

3.5.2. Drone Technology: Aerial Insights

In the vast expanses of agriculture, a new guardian emerges, one equipped not with a shield but with wings—AI-driven drones. These aerial sentinels offer a perspective that was once reserved for birds and pilots, but their capabilities extend far beyond mere observation.

➢ **The Eyes in the Sky: High-Resolution Imagery**

Outfitted with advanced cameras and sensors, AI-driven drones capture breathtaking high-resolution imagery of sprawling fields and undulating landscapes. They transform these expansive agricultural canvases into intricate mosaics of insight. But what truly sets them apart is not just their ability to capture images, but their capacity to interpret them.

➢ AI's Analytical Prowess: Unraveling Hidden Insights

AI algorithms take the captured imagery and meticulously analyze it. They become the modern-day detectives of agriculture, unveiling hidden tales within these images. These algorithms can identify signs of disease, infestations, nutrient deficiencies, and other crop health indicators that often elude human perception.

➢ Targeted Precision: Intervention Where Needed

With this newfound intelligence in hand, farmers can take precisely targeted actions. They intervene where it's needed most, sparing healthy crops from unnecessary treatments. This not only conserves resources but also reduces the environmental impact of farming. It's a win-win for both productivity and sustainability.

➢ Sustainability in Action: Treading Lightly on Earth

Drones, guided by AI, epitomize a sustainable approach to farming. By mitigating the need for indiscriminate pesticide or fertilizer use, they reduce the ecological footprint of agriculture. They become the aerial guardians of a future where farming not only feeds a growing population but also treads lightly on the Earth.

➢ Agriculture Elevated: The Future of Farming

In essence, drone technology in agriculture elevates farming to new heights. It combines the power of AI's analytical prowess with the versatility of aerial perspectives. It offers a glimpse into a future where technology not only meets the needs of the present but also ensures a sustainable and prosperous future for agriculture.

3.5.3. Crop Monitoring Systems: Insights from Above

In the vast expanse of agricultural landscapes, a silent sentinel stands vigilant—a network of AI-driven crop monitoring systems that operates as the all-seeing eye of farming. These systems weave together data from satellites orbiting high above, ground-based sensors nestled in the soil, and aerial drones gracefully gliding through the skies. Together, they create a digital tapestry that unveils the intricacies of crop health, growth, and the encompassing environmental conditions.

➢ **AI Algorithms: The Intellectual Powerhouses**

At the heart of this network lie AI algorithms, the intellectual powerhouses tirelessly processing this wealth of data with unparalleled efficiency. These algorithms are akin to the wise guardians of agriculture, perpetually observant and unwavering in their duties.

➢ **Detecting Subtle Signs: Unveiling Threats**

With keen eyes, they spot subtle shifts in plant physiology that forewarn of impending diseases or nutrient deficiencies. These early warning signs, often escaping the human eye, empower farmers to take timely and effective action.

➢ **Predicting Yield: The Prophetic Insight**

Yet, these systems offer more than just observation; they possess a prophetic quality. By predicting potential yield fluctuations based on their data, they provide farmers with a glimpse into the future. This foresight allows for informed decisions and future planning.

➢ **Optimizing Resources: Precision Agriculture**

Perhaps their most significant contribution lies in precision farming. These systems can prescribe precisely tailored irrigation schedules based on real-time soil moisture levels. This ensures the judicious and efficient use of water, a vital and finite resource.

> **From Conjecture to Precision: A New Dawn for Agriculture**

In essence, these AI-driven crop monitoring systems herald a transformation in agriculture. They shift the paradigm from conjecture to precision. Through early intervention, maximized yield potential, and the conservation of invaluable resources, they epitomize the potential of AI in agriculture. This is the harmonious fusion of technology and nature, working in concert to ensure bounteous harvests while safeguarding the environment. It is a new era for agriculture, where technology meets the timeless art of farming, with a resolute focus on efficiency, sustainability, and abundance.

3.5.4. Challenges and Opportunities

While the integration of AI in agriculture promises a revolutionary leap forward, it is accompanied by a set of challenges and opportunities that warrant careful consideration.

Challenges:

- **Data Security and Privacy:** The digitization of sensitive agricultural data raises concerns about data security and privacy. Ensuring that data collected from farms, drones, and sensors is protected from unauthorized access is crucial to maintain farmers' trust.
- **Access and Education:** For AI to truly benefit farmers, access to technology and adequate training is

imperative. Bridging the digital divide and providing training on AI-powered systems will empower farmers to harness the technology effectively.
- **Ethical Considerations:** As AI becomes deeply integrated into agricultural practices, ethical dilemmas may arise. Balancing the benefits of increased productivity with potential environmental and societal impacts will require careful deliberation.
- **Cost and Affordability:** While AI technologies offer long-term benefits, their upfront costs can be a barrier for small and resource-constrained farmers. Efforts to make AI solutions affordable and accessible will be crucial for broad adoption.

Opportunities:

- **Sustainable Practices:** AI-driven precision farming enables efficient resource allocation, reducing waste and minimizing the environmental impact of agricultural activities. This aligns with the growing demand for sustainable agricultural practices.
- **Enhanced Productivity:** By providing insights into crop health, disease prevention, and optimal resource usage, AI can significantly enhance agricultural productivity. This is particularly important as the global population continues to grow.
- **Yield Prediction:** AI's predictive capabilities can help farmers forecast crop yields more accurately. This, in turn, aids in planning harvesting, storage, and distribution activities more effectively.
- **Disease Detection:** AI-powered systems can detect early signs of disease outbreaks, allowing farmers to take proactive measures and prevent widespread losses. This reduces the reliance on chemical interventions.

- **Global Food Security:** AI's potential to improve crop yields and optimize resource usage contributes to global food security. As demand for food increases, AI can play a pivotal role in meeting this challenge.

In navigating these challenges and seizing opportunities, the agricultural industry has a unique chance to embrace AI's transformative potential. By fostering a collaborative approach among stakeholders, including farmers, technology providers, and policymakers, the agricultural landscape can be shaped in a way that promotes sustainability, efficiency, and equitable access to technological advancements.

Conclusion: 3.5. Agriculture: Precision Farming, Drone Technology, and Crop Monitoring

The amalgamation of AI and agriculture is not just a technological advancement; it's a reimagining of how we nourish the planet. Precision farming optimizes resource utilization, drone technology offers aerial insights, and crop monitoring systems predict and prevent losses. This transformation is not only about increased productivity—it's about sustainable practices, reduced ecological impact, and the preservation of Earth's resources. As we navigate this intersection of technology and nature, the promise of AI in agriculture beckons a future where innovation aligns with stewardship, securing sustenance for generations to come.

3.6. Education: Personalized Learning, Virtual Classrooms, and Educational AI Tools

The landscape of education, marked by its timeless pursuit of knowledge, is undergoing a renaissance powered by the transformative capabilities of Artificial Intelligence (AI). This section delves into AI's impact on education through personalized learning, virtual classrooms, and innovative educational tools.

3.6.1. Personalized Learning: Nurturing Individual Growth

Traditional education, often characterized by a one-size-fits-all approach, is undergoing a profound transformation, largely propelled by the intervention of Artificial Intelligence (AI). In this new era of education, adaptive learning platforms, powered by AI, are at the forefront of change. They are revolutionizing the educational landscape by redefining the way students learn.

➤ **Tailoring Education to Unique Needs**

Adaptive learning platforms are like educational chameleons. They have the extraordinary ability to assess the progress of each student, understand their individual learning style, and gauge their pace of learning. With this information, AI algorithms craft a bespoke educational experience for each student. It's like having a personal tutor who knows you inside out.

➤ **Unraveling Complex Learning Patterns**

The magic of AI lies in its ability to decipher the most intricate of learning patterns. It can identify a student's strengths, recognize areas that need improvement, and even predict future stumbling blocks. Armed with this insight, the AI system curates a curriculum that precisely targets the student's unique needs.

➤ **Beyond Comprehension: Fostering Motivation**

But the impact of AI-driven personalized learning extends far beyond improved comprehension and retention. It touches the very heart of motivation. When students engage with content that aligns with their personal preferences and aptitudes, they become more motivated, more eager to learn. Learning ceases to be a chore and becomes a thrilling journey of self-discovery.

> **The Promise of Personalized Learning**

In essence, AI-powered personalized learning is ushering in a new era of education—one where every student can truly shine. It's a world where the potential for growth knows no bounds, where education is not a rigid structure but a flexible, adaptable, and deeply personal experience. The promise of personalized learning, driven by AI, is nothing short of the nurturing of individual growth, a reimagining of education for the better.

3.6.2 Virtual Classrooms: Borderless Learning Experiences

Artificial Intelligence (AI) is erasing the limitations of geographical boundaries in education with the emergence of virtual classrooms. These dynamic and innovative settings enable seamless real-time interaction between students and educators, regardless of their physical locations. Underpinned by AI algorithms, virtual classrooms amplify engagement by evaluating student participation and delivering immediate feedback. This synergy results in an educational experience that transcends traditional borders, fostering collaborative learning and cross-cultural exchanges. This inclusive approach to education embraces a variety of perspectives, broadening horizons and enriching the overall learning voyage.

3.6.3 Educational AI Tools: Engaging Innovation

Artificial Intelligence (AI) is erasing the limitations of geographical boundaries in education with the emergence of virtual classrooms. These dynamic and innovative settings enable seamless real-time interaction between students and educators, regardless of their physical locations. Underpinned by AI algorithms, virtual classrooms amplify engagement by evaluating student participation and delivering immediate feedback. This synergy results in an educational experience that transcends traditional borders, fostering collaborative learning and cross-cultural exchanges.

➤ Breaking Down Geographic Barriers

Virtual classrooms are essentially a digital bridge connecting students and educators from around the world. Regardless of where they are located, students can access world-class education, interact with expert instructors, and collaborate with peers who bring diverse perspectives to the virtual table. AI ensures that the learning experience is tailored to each student, adapting to their unique needs and pacing.

➤ The Power of Real-Time Engagement

What sets virtual classrooms apart is the real-time engagement they offer. AI algorithms track student participation, assess their understanding of the material, and provide instant feedback. This feedback loop empowers students to grasp complex concepts more effectively and allows educators to adjust their teaching methods in real time, ensuring that no student is left behind.

➤ Cultivating Collaboration and Cross-Cultural Understanding

One of the most exciting aspects of virtual classrooms is their potential to foster collaboration and cross-cultural exchanges. Students from different parts of the world come together to learn, share ideas, and work on projects. This not only broadens their horizons but also enriches the overall learning voyage. It's a glimpse into a future where education is truly global, where knowledge knows no borders.

> **An Inclusive Approach to Education**

In essence, virtual classrooms driven by AI promote an inclusive approach to education. They democratize access to quality learning, making it available to a wider audience. They celebrate diversity, encouraging students to appreciate and learn from different cultures and perspectives. They break down the barriers that once confined education to physical spaces. Virtual classrooms, underpinned by AI, are a testament to the power of technology to transform and enrich the learning experience, making education more accessible, engaging, and global than ever before.

3.6.4 Challenges and Opportunities

The integration of Artificial Intelligence (AI) into education brings forth a realm of possibilities along with notable challenges. The potential for AI to elevate learning experiences and outcomes is significant, but it also sparks ethical considerations.

> **Harmonizing AI and Human Educators**

One of the key challenges in the era of AI-driven education is finding a harmonious equilibrium between AI tools and human educators. While AI can automate administrative tasks, provide personalized learning experiences, and offer immediate feedback, the essential human element in education, such as mentorship, guidance, and emotional support, must not be overshadowed. The challenge lies in creating a symbiotic relationship where AI complements human educators, freeing them from mundane tasks and enabling them to focus on fostering critical thinking, creativity, and emotional intelligence in students.

➤ Privacy Concerns and Data Management

The collection and analysis of student data for personalized learning introduce privacy concerns that necessitate careful management. AI-driven educational systems thrive on data, ranging from students' learning patterns to their preferences and strengths. Safeguarding this data against breaches and ensuring that it is used responsibly and transparently are paramount. Striking the right balance between data-driven personalization and privacy protection is an ongoing challenge in the AI-enhanced educational landscape.

➤ Equitable Access to AI-Enhanced Educatio

Another crucial challenge is addressing the digital divide and ensuring equitable access to AI-driven educational tools. Not all students have the same level of access to technology and the internet, creating disparities in their ability to benefit from AI-enhanced learning experiences. Bridging this gap is essential to ensure that all students, regardless of their socioeconomic background, have equal opportunities for enriched learning experiences. This requires concerted efforts from educational institutions, policymakers, and technology providers to make AI-powered resources accessible to all.

➤ A Holistic and Equitable Educational Landscape

As education journeys into an AI-enabled future, striking the balance between the opportunities AI offers and the challenges it presents becomes pivotal for creating a holistic and equitable educational landscape. It involves not only harnessing the potential of AI to enhance learning but also addressing ethical concerns, safeguarding privacy, and ensuring that AI is a tool that empowers both educators and learners without leaving anyone behind. It's a path towards an educational ecosystem where technology and humanity work hand in hand to nurture the next generation of thinkers, innovators, and problem solvers.

Conclusion: 3.6. Education: Personalized Learning, Virtual Classrooms, and Educational AI Tools

AI's influence on education is not a mere digitization—it's a transformation that cultivates individual growth, transcends geographical boundaries, and introduces innovation into learning. Personalized learning experiences, virtual classrooms, and educational AI tools foster engagement, collaboration, and empowerment. As we navigate this educational renaissance, the synergy between AI and human educators crafts a future where learning is not just about imparting knowledge but igniting curiosity, nurturing creativity, and preparing individuals to thrive in a rapidly evolving world.

Conclusion: Chapter 3: AI's Disruption across Industries

AI's disruption across these diverse industries underscores its pervasive impact, transcending boundaries and reshaping established practices. As the following chapters delve into the changing job landscape and the skills demanded by an AI-augmented world, remember that these industry-specific transformations reflect a broader revolution—a shift towards a future where AI and human collaboration redefine what is possible.

Chapter 4: Shifting Job Landscapes

The advent of the AI era has ushered in a wave of transformative changes in the realm of employment. This chapter delves into the intricate impacts of AI on the job landscape, encompassing displacement, augmentation, and the creation of new roles. By dissecting job categories that stand at risk, those poised for expansion, and presenting case studies of industries that have undergone substantial shifts, we uncover the multifaceted nature of AI's influence on jobs.

4.1. AI's Impact on Jobs: A Complex Interplay of Displacement, Augmentation, and Creation

The introduction of AI into the job market has set the stage for a multifaceted transformation that involves a delicate interplay between displacement, augmentation, and creation of roles. This chapter delves into the intricate dynamics of AI's influence on jobs, unraveling how these three distinct forces collectively shape the ever-evolving landscape of employment.

4.1.1. Displacement: AI-powered automation has the potential to reshape industries by rendering certain tasks obsolete. Routine and repetitive tasks, which were once the cornerstone of many jobs, now face the prospect of being efficiently carried out by AI-driven systems. Manual labor, data entry, and administrative tasks are particularly vulnerable to this form of displacement. While this may raise concerns about job loss, it also prompts a fundamental shift in how humans engage with work, encouraging a focus on roles that require creativity, critical thinking, and emotional intelligence.

4.1.2. Augmentation: Contrary to concerns of complete job displacement, AI also holds the promise of augmenting human capabilities. This augmentation occurs when AI collaborates with humans, enhancing their skills and enabling them to perform tasks more effectively. For example, AI-powered analytics tools can process vast amounts of data, allowing human professionals to make more informed decisions. In healthcare, AI assists doctors in diagnosing complex conditions by analyzing medical images. This symbiotic relationship between AI and humans results in improved productivity and enriched problem-solving capacities.

4.1.3. Creation: The integration of AI generates an entirely new realm of job opportunities that did not exist before. As AI technologies advance, the demand for professionals specializing in AI programming, machine learning, and data analysis continues to grow. Ethical oversight roles emerge to ensure the responsible deployment of AI systems, while AI-driven creativity gives rise to positions in fields such as content generation and digital design. This creation of new roles not only meets the demands of evolving technology but also fosters the exploration of uncharted professional territories.

The intricate dance of displacement, augmentation, and creation underscores the transformative nature of AI's impact on jobs. As we navigate this paradigm shift, it becomes evident that AI's role in the job landscape extends beyond mere replacement—it redefines how humans engage with work, fosters collaboration between technology and human intellect, and opens doors to unprecedented opportunities. This chapter traverses the dimensions of displacement, augmentation, and creation to provide a comprehensive understanding of the intricate web of changes brought about by AI's integration into the workforce.

4.2. Job Categories Vulnerable to Transformation: Routine Tasks, Manual Labor, Data Entry

In the wake of the AI revolution, certain job categories are particularly vulnerable to transformation due to the increased automation and efficiency AI technologies bring. This section sheds light on three key job categories that are susceptible to significant changes as AI continues to reshape the job landscape.

4.2.1. Routine Tasks: Jobs that center around repetitive and routine tasks are at risk of being automated by AI. These tasks, often characterized by their predictability and lack of creativity, can be efficiently carried out by AI-powered systems. For example, data processing, basic customer inquiries, and administrative duties are tasks that AI algorithms can handle with precision, freeing up human workers to focus on more strategic and complex responsibilities.

4.2.2. Manual Labor: The realm of manual labor is undergoing a transformation as AI-powered machines and robots take over physical tasks. Industries like manufacturing, agriculture, and logistics are witnessing the integration of robotic systems that can handle tasks like assembly, packaging, and even harvesting. While this shift may lead to job displacement in traditional manual labor roles, it also presents opportunities for upskilling and reskilling to manage and maintain these automated systems.

4.2.3. Data Entry: Jobs that involve data entry and processing are also prone to transformation through AI. AI algorithms are adept at handling large volumes of data with speed and accuracy, significantly reducing the need for manual data entry. By automating data extraction, data cleaning, and basic analysis, AI streamlines processes and minimizes human error. While this may lead to reduced demand for traditional data entry roles, it also opens doors for individuals to engage in more value-added data analysis and interpretation.

As AI continues to evolve, these vulnerable job categories prompt a shift in the workforce's skillset. While automation may lead to job displacement in some areas, it also calls for a strategic approach to reskilling and upskilling. The transformation of routine tasks, manual labor, and data entry roles paves the way for the workforce to embrace roles that require creativity, critical thinking, and expertise in AI-driven technologies.

4.3. Job Categories on the Cusp of Expansion: AI Programming, Data Analysis, Ethical Oversight

In the rapidly evolving job landscape shaped by AI, certain categories are poised for significant expansion, reflecting the growing demands of a technology-driven world. This section delves into three pivotal job categories that stand on the cusp of expansion, playing integral roles in harnessing the potential of AI while addressing its ethical considerations.

4.3.1. AI Programming: As AI technologies become more intricate and sophisticated, the demand for skilled professionals in AI programming is soaring. These individuals serve as the architects of AI systems, designing algorithms that power machine learning, natural language processing, and computer vision. Their expertise is essential in crafting AI solutions that align with specific needs, whether it's optimizing supply chains, enhancing customer experiences, or predicting market trends. AI programmers bridge the gap between technological innovation and real-world applications, paving the way for AI's integration across industries.

4.3.2. Data Analysis: In an era where data is hailed as the new currency, the role of data analysts has become paramount. These experts possess the ability to extract meaningful insights from vast and complex datasets, driving informed decision-making. As AI generates enormous amounts of data, data analysts play a crucial role in interpreting this information, identifying trends, and deriving actionable intelligence. From healthcare to finance, their contributions span industries, aiding in the development of strategies, refining business models, and unveiling opportunities hidden within the data.

4.3.3. Ethical Oversight: With the power of AI comes the responsibility to ensure its ethical and responsible deployment. Ethical oversight roles are emerging to monitor AI systems and algorithms, safeguarding against biases, discrimination, and potential harm to society. These professionals develop guidelines and frameworks that guide the ethical use of AI, ensuring fairness, transparency, and accountability. Their work is pivotal in maintaining trust in AI-driven systems and mitigating unintended consequences, ultimately shaping the ethical foundations of AI's integration into various domains.

These expanding job categories epitomize the evolution of the workforce in the AI era. AI programming, data analysis, and ethical oversight collectively underscore the fusion of human expertise and technological advancement. As industries adapt to AI-driven changes, these roles provide the compass for responsible innovation, data-driven decision-making, and the ethical considerations that underpin AI's transformative potential.

4.4. Unveiling Industry Case Studies Exhibiting Profound Job Transformations

Examining real-world case studies in various industries reveals the profound impact of AI on job landscapes, showcasing the transformative power of technology in reshaping traditional roles and creating new opportunities. Here are a few industry case studies that illustrate these shifts:

4.4.1. Manufacturing: The manufacturing sector has experienced a significant evolution due to AI-driven automation. Traditional manual labor roles on assembly lines have given way to supervisory roles that oversee and maintain automated systems. Workers now require skills in programming, robotics, and system troubleshooting. This shift highlights the need for a workforce that can adapt to the changing technological landscape.

4.4.2. Retail: The rise of e-commerce and AI-powered customer service has redefined the retail industry. Traditional brick-and-mortar roles are being replaced by positions in online operations, digital marketing, and customer experience management. Retail employees now need skills in managing online platforms, analyzing consumer data, and providing personalized online shopping experiences.

4.4.3. Healthcare: The healthcare industry has seen the emergence of AI-powered diagnostic tools and telehealth platforms. While traditional diagnostic roles remain vital, medical professionals are also required to collaborate with AI systems to interpret results and make informed decisions. Additionally, the integration of telehealth has created new roles in virtual care management, necessitating expertise in remote patient monitoring and digital communication.

4.4.4. Finance: In the finance sector, AI has led to a shift in roles related to data analysis and risk assessment. Traditional roles in data entry and basic analysis have been replaced by positions that require expertise in AI programming, algorithm development, and machine learning. Professionals skilled in understanding and implementing AI algorithms are in high demand to drive more accurate financial predictions and decision-making.

These case studies underscore the need for adaptability and continuous learning in a rapidly changing job landscape. While certain roles may be transformed or even displaced by AI, new opportunities emerge that demand expertise in AI-related technologies and the ability to work alongside AI systems. As industries embrace automation and innovation, the workforce's ability to evolve and embrace these changes becomes a critical factor in shaping the future of jobs.

4.5. Confronting Workforce Challenges and Embracing Opportunities

The dynamic evolution of the job landscape presents a rich fabric woven with both challenges and opportunities. The rapid advancement of technology, particularly AI, demands a workforce that possesses adaptable skills capable of transcending specific job roles. In response to this need, education and training programs play a pivotal role in equipping individuals with the proficiencies required to navigate industries that are increasingly augmented by AI technologies.

4.5.1. Adaptable Skills for AI-Augmented Industries: The ongoing fusion of AI into various sectors underscores the importance of cultivating versatile skills. These skills go beyond traditional job descriptions, encompassing traits such as problem-solving, critical thinking, and adaptability. As job roles evolve and blend with AI technologies, professionals who possess these adaptable skills are better equipped to pivot and succeed in a rapidly changing work environment.

4.5.2. Education and Upskilling: Amid the evolution of the job landscape, education and upskilling initiatives are paramount. These programs empower individuals with the knowledge and tools needed to harness AI's potential. By offering relevant courses, workshops, and training, educational institutions and organizations ensure that the workforce remains competitive and agile, capable of embracing new roles and adapting to technological shifts.

4.5.3. Ethical Oversight and Governance: The integration of AI into various industries raises ethical considerations that require careful navigation. As AI technologies interact with society in profound ways, it becomes essential to establish responsible oversight and governance mechanisms. Ensuring that AI systems operate transparently, ethically, and equitably becomes a cornerstone of maintaining public trust and ensuring that the benefits of AI are realized without unintended negative consequences.

In this ever-evolving landscape, the workforce is not just a passive recipient of change; it's an active participant in shaping the future of work. By cultivating adaptable skills, embracing continuous education, and championing ethical AI implementation, individuals and industries can collectively harness the opportunities presented by AI's disruptive influence. As AI becomes a ubiquitous part of the working world, the workforce's ability to confront challenges and seize opportunities will define its capacity to thrive and innovate.

Conclusion: Chapter 4: Shifting Job Landscapes

The interplay between AI and jobs unfolds as an evolution, not a mere replacement. While AI-driven automation may lead to role displacement, it simultaneously lays the foundation for new avenues and the amplification of human capacities. This chapter traverses the shifting job landscape, emphasizing the indispensability of reskilling, upskilling, and embracing the symbiotic relationship between humans and AI. As industries metamorphose, the ability of the workforce to adapt and flourish stands as the cornerstone of a prosperous and innovative future.

Chapter 5: Skills for the AI Era: Navigating the Evolving Landscape

In a world transformed by the integration of Artificial Intelligence (AI), the demand for skills has undergone a seismic shift. This chapter delves into the dynamic skillset essential for thriving in the AI era. It explores the delicate balance between soft skills and technical competencies, delving into the transformation of creativity, critical thinking, and emotional intelligence. As the landscape of work evolves, reskilling and upskilling become essential strategies, and emerging technical proficiencies come to the forefront.

5.1. The Interplay of Soft and Technical Skills: A New Hierarchy

In the age defined by the integration of Artificial Intelligence (AI), the established emphasis on technical skills is undergoing a transformative shift. Soft skills have risen to prominence as pivotal factors in distinguishing professionals. Within this paradigm, creativity emerges as a leading force. AI's mastery over repetitive tasks liberates human cognitive resources, enabling the exploration of novel concepts and ingenious solutions. As AI-generated insights permeate decision-making processes, critical thinking assumes greater significance, demanding the nuanced interpretation, contextualization, and strategic application of these insights. Simultaneously, emotional intelligence takes the spotlight as a cornerstone of success. In a world increasingly shaped by digital interactions, the ability to navigate human connections, engage in ethical decision-making, and foster empathetic engagement becomes imperative. The interplay between these soft skills and technical competencies becomes the compass guiding individuals through the intricate terrain of the AI era.

5.1.1. Creativity in the AI Era

One of the standout skills in the AI era is creativity. As AI excels in automating routine tasks and generating data-driven insights, it liberates human cognitive resources for creative endeavors. Professionals are encouraged to explore novel concepts, devise ingenious solutions, and think beyond conventional boundaries. In a world where AI can generate ideas and optimize processes, human creativity becomes a driving force for innovation and problem-solving.

5.1.2. Critical Thinking: Navigating AI Insights

While AI can provide valuable insights, critical thinking is essential for navigating the nuances of AI-generated information. It involves the skill of interpreting data, contextualizing insights, and strategically applying them to real-world scenarios. Critical thinkers can discern the relevance and reliability of AI-generated recommendations, making them invaluable decision-makers in AI-enhanced environments.

5.1.3. Emotional Intelligence: Nurturing Human Connections

In an increasingly digitized world, emotional intelligence takes center stage. This skill involves understanding and managing emotions, both in oneself and others. It's crucial for effective communication, collaboration, and leadership, especially in a landscape where human interactions occur in digital spaces. Professionals with high emotional intelligence can foster empathetic engagement, ethical decision-making, and meaningful relationships in the AI era.

5.1.4. The Interplay of Soft and Technical Skills

The interplay between these soft skills and technical competencies becomes a compass for navigating the AI era. While technical skills remain essential, they are enhanced by creativity, critical thinking, and emotional intelligence. Professionals who can harness the power of AI while applying these soft skills are poised to excel in the intricate terrain of the AI-driven world. It's a paradigm shift where human abilities complement AI capabilities, resulting in more innovative, empathetic, and ethically grounded professionals.

5.2. Reskilling and Upskilling: Lifelong Learning Redefined

In the relentless march of AI advancement, the conventional notion of learning has undergone a seismic shift. Reskilling and upskilling have risen as paramount imperatives, heralding a new era of perpetual education. Reskilling entails the agile adaptation of existing skills to seamlessly meld with new roles and demands. Upskilling, in contrast, is the pursuit of novel proficiencies that align with the evolving technological landscape. This culture of relentless learning has become the bedrock of professional growth and adaptability, ensuring that individuals not only weather the storm of technological change but thrive within its transformative currents.

5.2.1. Reskilling: Adapting to the Shifting Landscape

Reskilling represents a fundamental shift in how individuals approach their careers. It involves the agile adaptation of existing skills to meet the demands of evolving job roles and industries. In a world where AI and automation can change the nature of work rapidly, reskilling is a proactive strategy for staying relevant. It means learning new tools, technologies, and approaches to remain effective in one's profession. For example, a marketing professional might reskill by learning data analytics to stay competitive in a data-driven marketing landscape.

5.2.2. Upskilling: Embracing New Proficiencies

Upskilling complements reskilling by encouraging individuals to pursue entirely new proficiencies that align with the evolving technological landscape. This isn't merely about adapting existing skills but actively seeking out novel knowledge and capabilities. For instance, someone in a traditional manufacturing role might upskill by learning how to operate and troubleshoot advanced robotics and automation systems, preparing for the future of manufacturing.

5.2.3. A Culture of Lifelong Learning

Both reskilling and upskilling are underpinned by a culture of lifelong learning. This culture recognizes that learning doesn't end with formal education but is a continuous and evolving process. It's a mindset that embraces the idea that to thrive in an AI-driven world, individuals must commit to ongoing education and skill development throughout their careers. This approach ensures that professionals not only adapt to technological change but harness it to their advantage.

5.2.4. Professional Growth and Adaptability

The combination of reskilling, upskilling, and a commitment to lifelong learning forms the bedrock of professional growth and adaptability. It equips individuals with the tools to not only weather the storm of technological change but to thrive within its transformative currents. In a rapidly evolving job market, those who embrace reskilling and upskilling as integral parts of their career journey are better prepared to seize opportunities, navigate challenges, and remain valuable contributors to their industries.

5.3. Emerging Technical Proficiencies: Building AI Foundations

In the evolving landscape of AI, technical proficiencies serve as the bedrock for professional success. AI programming takes center stage as the fundamental framework for crafting, refining, and sustaining AI systems that seamlessly align with human requirements. Proficiency in data science becomes the key to unlocking the transformative potential of AI-generated insights, converting raw data into actionable knowledge that guides strategic decision-making. In an age where the scope of AI's impact continues to expand, the importance of cybersecurity surges forward, becoming the guardian that shields AI-driven systems from potential vulnerabilities, ensuring their robustness and safeguarding the integrity of critical operations.

5.3.1. AI Programming: Crafting the Future

AI programming is at the heart of creating and nurturing AI systems. It involves developing the software, algorithms, and neural networks that power AI applications. Professionals proficient in AI programming have the skills to design AI solutions that can understand natural language, recognize patterns in data, make predictions, and even interact with users in human-like ways. As AI continues to permeate various industries, AI programming is an essential technical proficiency for those who want to shape the future of technology.

5.3.2. Data Science: Turning Data into Knowledge

Data science is the bridge between raw data and actionable insights. It encompasses skills in data analysis, machine learning, and statistical modeling. Data scientists are adept at collecting, cleaning, and interpreting data to extract valuable information. In the AI-driven world, data science is invaluable for organizations looking to make data-driven decisions, optimize processes, and gain a competitive edge. Proficiency in data science enables professionals to unlock the full potential of AI-generated insights and drive innovation.

5.3.3. Cybersecurity: Safeguarding AI Systems

As AI systems become more integrated into critical infrastructure and daily life, the importance of cybersecurity surges. Cybersecurity professionals play a crucial role in protecting AI-driven systems from potential vulnerabilities, threats, and attacks. They are responsible for ensuring the confidentiality, integrity, and availability of data and AI models. With the increasing reliance on AI for decision-making, cybersecurity proficiency is vital for safeguarding the trust and integrity of AI systems.

5.3.4. A Foundation for Professional Success

Proficiency in AI programming, data science, and cybersecurity forms a solid foundation for professional success in the AI-driven landscape. These technical skills empower individuals to not only create and implement AI solutions but also to ensure their security and reliability. As AI continues to evolve and expand its reach across industries, these emerging technical proficiencies become increasingly essential for professionals looking to thrive in the transformative age of AI.

5.4. Educational Institutions and Corporate Training: Guiding Skill Evolution

In the era of AI, the pivotal role of educational institutions and corporate training programs comes to the forefront. These institutions act as the architects of preparedness, equipping individuals with the requisite skills to thrive in this transformative landscape. Educational curricula must undergo a profound shift, embracing a multidisciplinary approach that blends technical expertise with essential soft skills such as effective communication, adaptability in the face of change, and the art of collaborative teamwork. Concurrently, corporate training initiatives gain significance as they facilitate the reskilling and upskilling of employees. These initiatives ensure that the workforce remains a valuable asset, capable of navigating and contributing effectively to industries that are undergoing rapid and profound shifts.

5.4.1. Educational Institutions: Fostering the Future Workforce

Educational institutions play a fundamental role in shaping the future workforce. They are tasked with preparing students for careers in a world where AI and automation are becoming increasingly prevalent. This requires a shift in educational curricula to incorporate technical skills such as AI programming and data science, as well as a strong emphasis on soft skills. Effective communication, critical thinking, adaptability, and collaboration are essential for individuals to thrive in the AI-driven landscape. Educational institutions must create holistic programs that not only teach technical competencies but also nurture creativity and emotional intelligence.

5.4.2. Corporate Training: Empowering the Existing Workforce

The rapid pace of technological change demands that the existing workforce continuously update their skills. Corporate training programs are essential for facilitating this reskilling and upskilling process. These initiatives ensure that employees remain competitive and relevant in their respective fields. Corporate training can encompass a wide range of topics, from AI and data analysis to cybersecurity and soft skills development. By investing in the growth and development of their employees, organizations not only future-proof their workforce but also enhance their overall productivity and competitiveness.

5.4.3. The Synergy Between Education and Corporate Training

There is a growing synergy between educational institutions and corporate training programs. Educational institutions can partner with businesses to tailor their curricula to the specific needs of industries. This collaboration ensures that graduates possess the skills that employers are looking for in the AI-driven job market. Additionally, businesses can provide ongoing training and development opportunities for their employees through partnerships with educational institutions or by offering in-house training programs. This symbiotic relationship between education and industry is crucial for bridging the skills gap and fostering a workforce that is well-prepared for the challenges and opportunities of the AI era.

5.4.4. A Collective Effort for Skill Evolution

Preparing individuals and the workforce for the AI era is a collective effort that involves educational institutions, businesses, and individuals themselves. It requires a commitment to lifelong learning and a recognition of the evolving nature of skills. By embracing this mindset and investing in education and training, we can ensure that AI becomes a force for empowerment rather than a source of disruption. Educational institutions and corporate training programs are the guiding lights on this transformative journey, illuminating the path to skill evolution and a brighter future in the AI-driven world.

5.5. Challenges and Opportunities in Skill Development

Amidst the transformative potential of skill development, a landscape of both challenges and opportunities unfolds. The breakneck pace of technological advancement demands educational systems that can pivot swiftly, updating curricula to keep up with the latest industry trends and technological shifts. Access to high-quality education and training becomes an essential cornerstone to ensure that the benefits of skill development are universally accessible and do not exacerbate existing societal inequalities.

5.5.1. The Challenge of Rapid Technological Advancement

One of the primary challenges in skill development is the unprecedented speed at which technology is advancing. The skills that are in demand today may become obsolete in just a few years. Educational systems and training programs must be agile and responsive, capable of adjusting their curricula and content to align with the evolving needs of the job market. This requires collaboration between educational institutions, businesses, and policymakers to create flexible and up-to-date learning pathways.

5.5.2. Ensuring Equal Access to Skill Development

Access to high-quality education and training is another critical challenge. In an era where skills are at a premium, it's essential to ensure that everyone, regardless of their background or socioeconomic status, has equal opportunities to develop the skills they need to succeed. This means addressing issues of affordability, accessibility, and inclusivity in education and training programs. Bridging the digital divide and providing resources to underserved communities are essential steps in this direction.

5.5.3. The Proactive Approach to Learning

On the flip side, the rapid evolution of the job market also presents significant opportunities for individuals who are proactive about their learning. Embracing a growth mindset and taking ownership of one's professional development empower individuals to thrive in this dynamic environment. Online courses, self-directed learning, and access to vast educational resources through the internet make it easier than ever for individuals to acquire new skills and stay competitive in their fields.

5.5.4. The Synergy of Education, Corporate Training, and Individual Drive

The synergy between educational institutions, corporate training programs, and individuals' drive to continuously learn creates a harmonious ecosystem that propels success in the era defined by constant evolution. Educational institutions and businesses can work together to ensure that the skills being taught align with industry needs. Corporate training programs can complement formal education by providing employees with specific, job-relevant skills. Meanwhile, individuals who embrace lifelong learning and adaptability are better positioned to seize opportunities in the ever-changing job market.

5.5.5. A Call for Collaboration and Innovation

Addressing the challenges and capitalizing on the opportunities in skill development requires collaboration and innovation at all levels of society. Educational institutions must be willing to adapt, businesses should invest in their workforce, and individuals need to embrace continuous learning. Policymakers also have a role to play in creating an environment that fosters skill development and provides support to those who need it most. By working together, we can navigate the challenges and unlock the vast potential that skill development offers in the AI-driven era.

Conclusion: Chapter 5: Skills for the AI Era: Navigating the Evolving Landscape

As the AI era unfolds, the focus transitions from static skills to dynamic competencies that empower individuals to navigate uncharted waters. The fusion of technical skills with creativity, critical thinking, and emotional intelligence becomes the formula for success. Reskilling, upskilling, and a dedication to lifelong learning become essential strategies in a landscape defined by constant evolution. In this journey, educational institutions and corporations emerge as collaborative partners in cultivating an adaptable and innovative workforce, laying the foundation for a future where human potential and AI capabilities synergize to shape a remarkable tomorrow.

Chapter 6: The Human-AI Collaboration

In an era where the harmonious interplay of human intellect and technological prowess defines progress, the collaboration between humans and Artificial Intelligence (AI) takes center stage. This chapter delves into the intricate and dynamic dance between AI and human ingenuity, emphasizing the pivotal role of AI as a tool that enhances human capabilities rather than replacing them. It explores the multifaceted facets of successful human-AI collaboration across diverse domains and navigates the ethical considerations that underpin this powerful partnership.

6.1. AI as an Amplifier of Human Potential, Not a Replacement

In the landscape of AI, the role of technology is not to replace human capabilities but to act as a catalyst that amplifies human potential. AI's emergence does not signify the usurpation of human involvement, but rather a profound transformation in how humans collaborate with technology. Here, we delve deeper into this concept and explore the implications of this symbiotic relationship between humans and AI.

6.1.1. AI as an Enhancer, Not a Substitute

AI serves as an enhancer, a tool that liberates individuals from routine and mundane tasks, allowing them to channel their energies towards more creative, strategic, and empathetic endeavors. This fundamental shift in the nature of work is crucial to understand. Rather than fearing AI as a threat to job security, individuals can embrace it as a means to augment their capabilities. For example, in industries where data analysis is paramount, AI can swiftly process vast datasets, providing insights that would be impossible for a human to achieve in the same timeframe. This allows professionals to make more informed decisions and focus on the strategic implications of the data.

6.1.2. Liberating Human Creativity

One of the most remarkable aspects of AI's role as an amplifier of human potential is its ability to liberate human creativity. As AI handles repetitive, data-driven tasks, individuals are freed from the drudgery of these activities. This newfound freedom enables them to explore novel concepts, experiment with innovative solutions, and engage in creative endeavors that were previously hindered by time-consuming tasks. For instance, in the field of content creation, AI can generate initial drafts of articles or reports, allowing human writers to refine and infuse them with creativity and style.

6.1.3. Enhancing Strategic Thinking

AI also plays a pivotal role in enhancing strategic thinking. Its data processing capabilities are unmatched, enabling it to analyze historical trends, identify emerging patterns, and predict future developments with remarkable accuracy. In fields such as finance, healthcare, and marketing, this ability is invaluable. Professionals can leverage AI-generated insights to make strategic decisions that have a profound impact on their organizations. This synergy between AI and human strategic thinking opens up new avenues for innovation and growth.

6.1.4. Fostering Empathetic Engagement

While AI excels at data analysis and automation, it lacks the essential human qualities of empathy and emotional intelligence. This is where humans continue to shine. In roles that require compassion, understanding, and ethical judgment, humans are irreplaceable. AI can support these roles by handling administrative tasks, allowing human professionals to focus on building meaningful relationships and providing personalized care and support.

6.1.5. A Collaborative Harmony

The result of this symbiotic partnership between humans and AI is a collaborative harmony where technology and human ingenuity coalesce. It's a future where the boundaries of innovation are pushed, and new vistas of what can be achieved emerge. Instead of fearing AI as a threat, individuals and organizations can embrace it as a powerful ally in their quest for progress, productivity, and innovation. The AI-augmented future is one where human potential knows no bounds, and the possibilities are limited only by our imagination.

6.2. Examples of Successful Human-AI Collaboration in Various Fields

The realm of human-AI collaboration is brimming with diverse and successful instances across various fields, showcasing the transformative potential of this partnership.

1. Healthcare: Radiology with AI Assistance

In healthcare, AI collaborates with radiologists to enhance diagnostic accuracy. AI algorithms analyze medical images, such as X-rays and MRIs, to identify patterns and anomalies that might be difficult for humans to detect. Radiologists then combine their clinical expertise and intuition with AI-generated insights to make more informed and accurate diagnoses.

2. Astronomy: Data Analysis with AI Algorithms

In astronomy, AI algorithms sift through massive datasets collected by telescopes to identify celestial phenomena. The vast amount of data would be overwhelming for humans to analyze manually. AI identifies potential objects of interest, such as new stars or galaxies, allowing astronomers to focus their attention and resources on further exploration.

3. Creative Arts: Collaborative Art Generation

AI-generated art has become a collaborative tool in creative domains. Artists use AI algorithms to generate unique visual and auditory experiences that serve as inspiration for their work. Musicians compose music with AI-generated melodies, while visual artists incorporate AI-generated designs into their pieces. This collaboration between human creativity and AI innovation produces novel and captivating forms of artistic expression.

4. Finance: AI-Driven Investment Strategies

In finance, AI collaborates with investment professionals to optimize trading strategies. AI algorithms analyze vast amounts of market data, identifying trends and patterns that influence investment decisions. While human experts provide domain knowledge and intuition, AI assists in making data-driven predictions that can inform more informed and timely investment choices.

5. Manufacturing: AI-Enhanced Quality Control

Manufacturing benefits from AI-powered quality control. Robots equipped with AI vision systems inspect products for defects, ensuring consistent quality standards. Human technicians collaborate with these AI systems to fine-tune their algorithms and address complex or nuanced issues that require human judgment.

These examples underline the collaborative nature of AI integration, where technology augments human capabilities to achieve outcomes that are more accurate, efficient, and innovative. The synergy between human expertise and AI capabilities creates a partnership that surpasses what either can achieve in isolation.

6.3. Ethical Considerations: Bias, Privacy, and Responsible AI Development

As the collaboration between humans and AI deepens, ethical considerations become increasingly significant. These considerations encompass various aspects of AI development and deployment, ensuring that the partnership remains responsible and equitable.

1. Bias in AI Algorithms: AI algorithms can inadvertently inherit biases present in the data used to train them. This bias can lead to unfair and discriminatory outcomes, affecting decisions related to hiring, lending, and more. Ethical AI development requires continuous monitoring and mitigation of bias to ensure that AI systems provide equitable results across diverse populations.

2. Privacy Concerns: AI's integration often involves the processing of personal data. This raises concerns about the privacy and security of individuals' information. Striking a balance between AI's capabilities and individuals' privacy rights is essential. Transparency about data usage, informed consent, and robust data protection measures are crucial to building and maintaining trust.

3. Responsible AI Development: The development of AI systems should adhere to ethical standards. Responsible AI development involves transparency in algorithms and decision-making processes. AI should be designed to provide explanations for its decisions (explainable AI) to ensure accountability and foster trust among users.

4. Human Oversight and Control: The collaboration between humans and AI should always ensure that humans retain oversight and control. Automated decisions should be subject to human review, especially in critical domains such as healthcare and finance. This helps prevent undue reliance on AI systems and maintains human accountability.

5. Economic Disruptions: While AI can lead to enhanced efficiency, it can also lead to job displacement. Ethical considerations involve not only ensuring a smooth transition for displaced workers through reskilling and upskilling programs but also addressing broader economic implications of these disruptions.

6. Transparency and Accountability: Organizations that deploy AI systems have a responsibility to be transparent about their use and potential impact. Clear guidelines, protocols, and accountability mechanisms should be in place to address any unintended consequences of AI-powered decisions.

7. Societal Impact: The impact of AI extends to society at large. As AI-driven systems influence various aspects of life, from healthcare to transportation, ethical considerations encompass societal well-being. Ensuring that AI is developed and used in ways that benefit humanity is a paramount ethical concern.

Addressing these ethical considerations requires collaboration between stakeholders, including AI developers, policymakers, industry leaders, and ethicists. A collective effort is needed to establish frameworks that uphold the responsible and ethical deployment of AI, fostering a harmonious partnership between humans and technology that prioritizes fairness, transparency, and human well-being.

Conclusion: Chapter 6: The Human-AI Collaboration

The trajectory of AI's evolution charts a course where machines and humans coexist harmoniously, their synergy magnifying the potential for progress. The collaborative symphony between humans and AI resounds with notes of creativity, innovation, and advancement. Instances of triumphant human-AI partnerships exemplify the transformative power of this alliance, transcending boundaries from healthcare to the realm of arts. Yet, this journey is fraught with ethical considerations—combating bias, preserving privacy, and steering AI's development responsibly. As we traverse this path, the fusion of human ingenuity and AI precision unveils a future where the peaks of human imagination find resonance in the depths of technological brilliance.

Chapter 7: Navigating Ethical and Societal Challenges

As Artificial Intelligence (AI) accelerates into new frontiers, the intricate landscape of ethical and societal challenges emerges as a focal point of consideration. This chapter delves deeply into the imperative of AI ethics, exploring the principles of fairness, transparency, and accountability that underpin the responsible deployment of AI. Moreover, it delves into strategies to address the potential disruption in job markets caused by the ascent of AI, including Universal Basic Income, retraining initiatives, and robust social safety nets. Additionally, the chapter delves into the profound cultural and societal implications of AI's influence, reshaping not only work and leisure dynamics but also the very essence of human identity.

7.1. Upholding Ethical AI: Fairness, Transparency, and Accountability

As Artificial Intelligence (AI) takes on an increasingly prominent role in our lives, the importance of ethical considerations cannot be overstated. The integration of AI into various aspects of society, from decision-making algorithms to autonomous systems, demands a foundation built on fairness, transparency, and accountability.

7.1.1. Fairness: Ensuring fairness in AI systems is crucial to prevent biased outcomes that perpetuate discrimination. AI algorithms learn from data, and if that data contains biases, it can lead to unfair or discriminatory results. Recognizing this, AI developers must strive to identify and mitigate biases in training data and algorithms. A commitment to fairness involves constant monitoring, auditing, and refinement of AI models to eliminate unjust disparities in their outputs.

7.1.2. Transparency: The complexity of AI algorithms can make it difficult to understand how decisions are reached. Transparency entails making AI systems more interpretable and explainable to both experts and the general public. This not only fosters trust but also enables users to comprehend the rationale behind AI-generated recommendations or decisions. Researchers are actively exploring methods to create "explainable AI" to bridge the gap between the seemingly inscrutable inner workings of AI models and human comprehension.

7.1.3. Accountability: Just as humans are held accountable for their actions, the creators and operators of AI systems must also be accountable for the outcomes of their creations. Accountability involves taking responsibility for the ethical, social, and economic consequences of AI systems. It's essential to establish clear lines of responsibility and establish mechanisms to rectify any unintended negative impacts. Ethical guidelines and frameworks for AI development can provide a roadmap for ensuring accountability throughout the AI lifecycle.

In an era where AI can influence everything from hiring decisions to medical diagnoses, upholding fairness, transparency, and accountability in AI is not just a matter of technological optimization, but a moral imperative. By integrating these principles into AI development, we can foster a more just, transparent, and responsible AI landscape that aligns with human values and societal well-being.

7.2. Mitigating Job Displacement: Universal Basic Income, Reskilling, and Social Safety Nets

As Artificial Intelligence (AI) continues to advance, concerns about job displacement due to automation have become more pronounced. To address the potential impacts on employment and livelihoods, several strategies have been proposed to ensure a smooth transition for the workforce.

7.2.1. Universal Basic Income (UBI): UBI is a concept that involves providing all citizens with a regular, unconditional cash payment to cover their basic needs. This approach aims to alleviate the financial stress caused by job displacement and shifts in the job market. UBI ensures that individuals have a safety net to rely on, regardless of their employment status. By providing a steady income floor, UBI supports economic stability and empowers individuals to pursue new opportunities or reskilling without the fear of financial insecurity.

7.2.1.1. Cushioning the Impact of Disruption

In a world where technological advancements are reshaping industries and altering the nature of work, Universal Basic

Income (UBI) emerges as a powerful tool to cushion the impact of disruption. As jobs evolve and traditional employment patterns shift, UBI serves as a safety net that mitigates the financial stress faced by individuals during transitional phases.

- **Adapting to Technological Change:** The rapid pace of technological advancements can lead to job displacement and uncertainty. Automation and AI-driven transformations may render certain jobs obsolete. UBI acts as a buffer against such disruptions, ensuring that individuals can navigate these changes without falling into financial hardship.
- **Job Transitions and Retraining:** UBI supports individuals as they transition between jobs or pursue retraining initiatives. In a dynamic job market, career shifts and the acquisition of new skills become essential for staying relevant. UBI provides a stable income that allows individuals to focus on reskilling without the pressure of immediate financial obligations.
- **Promoting Dignity and Security:** One of the core principles of UBI is to provide individuals with a steady income floor that covers their basic needs. This financial security promotes dignity, as individuals are not forced into survival-mode decision-making. UBI ensures that individuals can maintain their quality of life during periods of disruption.
- **Encouraging Entrepreneurship and Innovation:** The cushioning effect of UBI extends to entrepreneurship and innovation. Individuals who have an innovative idea or entrepreneurial vision may hesitate to pursue it due to the financial risks involved. UBI provides them with the confidence to take calculated risks, explore new opportunities, and contribute to economic growth.
- **Supporting Economic Flexibility:** UBI enables individuals to make choices that align with their

aspirations and goals, rather than being solely dictated by immediate financial needs. This economic flexibility empowers individuals to explore unconventional career paths, creative pursuits, and community engagements.

As technological advancements reshape industries and careers, Universal Basic Income (UBI) emerges as a mechanism to cushion the impact of disruption. UBI provides a safety net that eases the financial stress faced by individuals during times of job displacement and career transitions. By offering security, dignity, and the freedom to pursue new opportunities, UBI contributes to a more resilient and adaptive workforce in the face of technological change.

7.2.1.2. Unleashing Economic Freedom

Universal Basic Income (UBI) has the transformative potential to reshape the dynamics of work and income, offering individuals newfound economic freedom and opportunities for exploration. By providing a regular unconditional cash payment to all citizens, UBI liberates individuals from the traditional dependence on employment as the sole source of income. This liberation carries a range of implications for both individuals and society at large.

- **Redefined Work and Income Relationship:** UBI challenges the traditional notion that work is the primary means of earning a livelihood. With a guaranteed income floor, individuals are free to pursue a variety of activities beyond traditional employment. This redefines the relationship between work and income, offering the freedom to engage in work that aligns with personal passions, interests, and skills.
- **Entrepreneurship and Innovation:** The economic security offered by UBI encourages entrepreneurial endeavors. Individuals have the financial stability to

take calculated risks and start their own businesses without the fear of financial ruin. This fosters a culture of innovation and creativity, as aspiring entrepreneurs can dedicate time and resources to developing new ideas, products, and services.

- **Skill Development and Upskilling:** UBI enables individuals to invest in their own skill development and education. With the pressure of meeting basic needs alleviated, people can pursue training, education, and upskilling to enhance their employability and adapt to changing job requirements. This leads to a more skilled and adaptable workforce, better equipped to thrive in a rapidly evolving job market.
- **Exploration of Non-Traditional Work Models:** The economic freedom provided by UBI encourages the exploration of non-traditional work models. Freelancing, gig work, and part-time employment become more viable options, as individuals are not solely reliant on these forms of income for survival. This flexibility supports diverse work arrangements and accommodates the evolving preferences of the modern workforce.
- **Cultural and Social Impact:** UBI can have profound cultural and social implications. It challenges societal norms that equate one's worth with their employment status. This shift in mindset can lead to a more inclusive and empathetic society, where individuals are valued for their contributions beyond conventional jobs. UBI can also reduce stigma associated with unemployment and offer a safety net for vulnerable populations.

Universal Basic Income offers more than just financial security—it redefines how individuals perceive work, income, and their relationship to society. By liberating individuals from the immediate pressures of meeting basic needs, UBI opens doors to entrepreneurship, skill development, and creative pursuits. As societies explore the potential of UBI, they embark on a journey towards economic empowerment, innovation, and a reimagined understanding of human potential.

7.2.1.3. Fostering Innovation and Entrepreneurship

Universal Basic Income (UBI) acts as a catalyst for fostering innovation and entrepreneurship by removing the financial barriers that often deter individuals from pursuing their ideas and ventures. This financial safety net creates an environment that encourages risk-taking, experimentation, and the exploration of new opportunities.

- **Eliminating Financial Barriers:** Traditional entrepreneurship often requires significant financial resources, which can be a deterrent for aspiring entrepreneurs. UBI eliminates the fear of financial instability, providing individuals with a reliable source of income regardless of their employment status. This stability allows entrepreneurs to allocate resources towards their ventures without the immediate pressure of generating income.
- **Encouraging Risk-Taking:** UBI offers a safety net that mitigates the risk associated with entrepreneurial ventures. With basic needs covered, individuals can take calculated risks without the fear of falling into financial hardship. This encourages experimentation and the pursuit of ambitious ideas that might otherwise seem too risky.
- **Fostering Creative Exploration:** The economic security provided by UBI enables individuals to explore unconventional and creative ideas that may not have immediate commercial viability. This fosters a culture of innovation, where individuals are free to engage in projects that push the boundaries of traditional

business models and contribute to the development of new industries.
- **Diversifying the Economy:** By nurturing a diverse range of entrepreneurial ventures, UBI contributes to a more resilient and dynamic economy. As individuals from various backgrounds and skill sets are empowered to start businesses, the economy becomes less reliant on a few sectors. This diversification helps buffer against economic downturns and promotes sustainable growth.
- **Nurturing Small and Medium Enterprises (SMEs):** UBI provides a fertile ground for the growth of small and medium-sized enterprises. These businesses often face challenges in accessing capital and resources. With a guaranteed income, entrepreneurs can focus on growing their businesses, hiring employees, and expanding their impact.
- **Stimulating Local Innovation Ecosystems:** UBI can lead to the development of thriving local innovation ecosystems. As more individuals engage in entrepreneurial activities, communities are likely to witness an increase in collaboration, knowledge sharing, and the establishment of support networks. These local ecosystems contribute to regional economic development and create a sense of community.

Universal Basic Income reimagines the landscape for innovation and entrepreneurship by offering individuals the economic security needed to pursue their ideas and ventures. By removing financial barriers, encouraging risk-taking, and fostering creative exploration, UBI transforms the entrepreneurial landscape, leading to a more diverse, innovative, and dynamic economy. As individuals are empowered to turn their visions into reality, UBI becomes a driving force behind economic growth and societal progress.

7.2.1.4. A Springboard for Reskilling and Lifelong Learning

Universal Basic Income (UBI) serves as a springboard for reskilling and lifelong learning, empowering individuals to embrace continuous education and adapt to the ever-changing demands of the job market. By providing a reliable source of income, UBI creates an environment conducive to personal and professional development.

- **Breathing Room for Learning:** One of the challenges individuals often face when considering reskilling or upskilling is the financial strain associated with taking time off work or investing in education. UBI alleviates this concern by offering a safety net that covers basic needs, allowing individuals to allocate time and resources toward acquiring new skills and knowledge.
- **Adaptability in an Evolving Economy:** In a rapidly evolving economy, the demand for new skills emerges quickly, and old skill sets can become obsolete. UBI ensures that individuals have the financial security to adapt to these changes without the fear of financial instability. This adaptability is vital for remaining relevant in industries that undergo continuous transformation.
- **Encouraging Exploration of New Fields:** UBI enables individuals to explore different fields and industries that align with their interests and aptitudes. This flexibility encourages individuals to venture into areas they might not have considered otherwise, fostering a diverse skill set that can be valuable in multiple contexts.
- **Promoting Lifelong Learning:** Lifelong learning is essential for personal growth and professional success in the modern economy. UBI creates an environment where individuals view education as a continuous journey, rather than a one-time event. The financial

security provided by UBI allows individuals to invest in courses, workshops, and training programs that enhance their skills over time.
- **Supporting Non-Traditional Learning Paths:** With UBI, individuals are more likely to pursue non-traditional forms of education, such as online courses, self-directed learning, and mentorship programs. These alternative learning paths provide flexibility and personalized learning experiences that cater to individual preferences and schedules.
- **Promoting Self-Driven Learning:** UBI empowers individuals to take ownership of their learning journey. With financial stability in place, individuals can proactively seek out opportunities for growth and skill development, enhancing their competitiveness in the job market.

Universal Basic Income serves as a catalyst for reskilling and lifelong learning by providing the financial stability needed to pursue educational opportunities. UBI's support enables individuals to adapt to changing job market demands, explore new fields, and embrace continuous learning. By promoting adaptability and self-driven learning, UBI contributes to the development of a workforce equipped with the skills needed to thrive in an ever-evolving economy.

7.2.1.5. Social Equity and Inclusion

Universal Basic Income (UBI) has emerged as a potential tool to bridge societal inequalities and create a more inclusive and just society. By providing a consistent income floor to all individuals, regardless of their background or employment status, UBI addresses financial disparities and fosters social cohesion.

- **Reducing Income Disparity:** One of the fundamental challenges in many societies is income inequality. UBI

directly addresses this issue by providing every citizen with a guaranteed income, thereby reducing the gap between the wealthy and the marginalized. This redistribution of resources promotes a more equitable distribution of wealth.
- **Equal Opportunities:** UBI ensures that everyone has access to a basic level of financial security. This financial cushion offers individuals the opportunity to make choices that align with their aspirations, such as pursuing education, starting a business, or engaging in meaningful community activities. Equal opportunities lead to greater social mobility and reduced barriers to success.
- **Mitigating Poverty:** UBI has the potential to lift people out of poverty and alleviate the challenges associated with financial hardship. This is particularly impactful for vulnerable populations, such as single parents, the elderly, and individuals with disabilities, who often face greater economic challenges. UBI provides them with a stable foundation upon which to build their lives.
- **Fostering Social Cohesion:** The economic divide in society can lead to feelings of exclusion and alienation. UBI creates a sense of unity by providing all citizens with a shared economic resource. This shared benefit fosters a sense of common purpose and solidarity among individuals from diverse backgrounds.
- **Empowering Marginalized Communities:** Marginalized communities often face systemic barriers that limit their opportunities. UBI empowers these communities by providing them with the financial means to overcome some of these barriers. It enables individuals to invest in education, healthcare, and skills development, breaking the cycle of disadvantage.

- **Enhancing Well-Being and Mental Health:** Financial stress is a significant contributor to mental health issues. UBI can alleviate this stress by ensuring that individuals have their basic needs met. This financial stability contributes to overall well-being and reduces anxiety related to economic insecurity.

Universal Basic Income (UBI) holds the potential to foster social equity and inclusion by addressing income disparity, providing equal opportunities, mitigating poverty, and empowering marginalized communities. By creating a more financially secure and inclusive society, UBI contributes to the well-being and prosperity of all citizens, regardless of their socioeconomic background.

7.2.1.6. Challenges and Considerations

The concept of Universal Basic Income (UBI) holds immense promise in addressing the challenges posed by technological disruption and job displacement in the AI era. However, its implementation is not without its share of challenges and considerations that demand careful thought and strategic policy design.

- **Funding Mechanisms:** One of the central challenges of UBI is identifying sustainable funding sources to support the regular cash payments to citizens. Financing UBI requires careful economic analysis to ensure that it does not lead to an unsustainable burden on government budgets or hinder other essential public services. Finding a balanced funding mechanism that aligns with economic realities is a critical consideration.
- **Disincentives to Work:** Critics argue that providing a guaranteed income through UBI could potentially create disincentives for individuals to engage in productive work. Concerns arise that people might opt

for a basic income rather than seeking employment, leading to a decline in overall workforce participation. Striking a balance between providing a safety net and maintaining incentives for productivity is a delicate challenge that policy-makers must address.
- **Economic Implications:** UBI's impact on the broader economy is a matter of debate. Some proponents believe that it could stimulate consumer spending and drive economic growth by providing individuals with greater purchasing power. However, critics argue that UBI might lead to inflation and disrupt market dynamics. Understanding the potential economic implications and analyzing how UBI interacts with existing social welfare programs is crucial.
- **Income Distribution and Social Equity:** While UBI aims to provide a basic income to all citizens, the question of whether it adequately addresses income inequality and social disparities remains. Without proper design, UBI might inadvertently benefit higher-income individuals more than those in greater need. Ensuring that UBI contributes to social equity and poverty reduction requires careful consideration.
- **Cultural and Behavioral Impact:** The introduction of UBI could have cultural and behavioral effects on society. It might influence how individuals perceive work, value, and personal responsibility. Analyzing these potential shifts in societal norms and values is essential to predict the long-term impact of UBI on workforce dynamics and individual behavior.
- **Implementing Pilot Programs:** Given the complexity of UBI, pilot programs and experiments can provide valuable insights into its potential benefits and challenges. These pilot initiatives allow governments and researchers to test UBI in controlled settings and

gather data on its effects on employment rates, poverty reduction, and overall well-being.

While Universal Basic Income offers a promising solution to the challenges of job displacement and economic instability in the AI era, its successful implementation requires a nuanced approach that addresses funding, incentives, economic implications, equity, and broader societal impact. Striking the right balance between providing financial security and maintaining incentives for productive engagement is essential to harness the full potential of UBI and ensure its positive impact on individuals, communities, and economies.

Conclusion: 7.2.1. Universal Basic Income (UBI)

Universal Basic Income transcends traditional welfare models, embodying a vision of a future where economic stability and individual empowerment go hand in hand. By providing a steady income floor, UBI redefines the relationship between work, income, and human potential. As societies grapple with the evolving nature of work, UBI stands as a testament to innovation in social policy, offering a path towards economic resilience and a more inclusive, adaptable, and equitable future.

7.2.2. Reskilling Initiatives: As jobs evolve and new roles emerge, reskilling becomes essential for individuals to remain competitive in the job market. Reskilling initiatives involve training programs and educational opportunities designed to equip workers with the skills needed for emerging industries. These programs help individuals transition into new roles by updating their skillsets and ensuring they can contribute effectively in AI-driven environments. Governments, educational institutions, and businesses can collaborate to offer reskilling programs that empower individuals to adapt to changing job requirements.

7.2.2.1. Adapting to Change: The rapid advancement of AI technology often renders certain skills obsolete while elevating the demand for new competencies. Reskilling initiatives recognize this dynamic and provide a pathway for individuals to transition from roles that are becoming redundant to ones that align with the demands of the future job market.

7.2.2.2. Key Features of Reskilling Initiatives:

- **Tailored Skill Development:** Reskilling initiatives are tailored to the needs of specific industries and job roles. These programs focus on providing individuals with the skills that are in demand, ensuring they remain relevant and competitive.
- **Lifelong Learning:** Reskilling initiatives foster a culture of lifelong learning, acknowledging that skill acquisition is an ongoing process. Workers are encouraged to continuously update their skills to adapt to changing technological landscapes.
- **Collaborative Efforts:** Governments, educational institutions, and businesses collaborate to offer comprehensive reskilling programs. Partnerships between these entities leverage their unique strengths to create holistic learning experiences.
- **Diverse Learning Formats:** Reskilling initiatives embrace various learning formats, including online courses, workshops, seminars, and practical training. This diverse approach accommodates different learning preferences and schedules.
- **Recognition of Prior Experience:** Many reskilling programs recognize and build upon individuals' existing

skills and experience, making the transition to new roles smoother and more efficient.

7.2.2.3. Empowering Individuals in AI-Driven Environments:

- **Transitioning to Emerging Roles:** Reskilling initiatives enable individuals to pivot into emerging roles within industries that are adopting AI technologies. These roles may require a combination of technical skills, soft skills, and domain-specific knowledge.
- **Adapting to Automation:** For workers whose current roles are becoming automated, reskilling provides an avenue to shift into roles that require human-centric skills, such as creativity, critical thinking, and emotional intelligence.
- **Filling Skill Gaps:** Reskilling initiatives address skill gaps that arise as industries adopt AI. For instance, industries like AI programming, data science, and cybersecurity require specialized skills that can be acquired through targeted reskilling programs.
- **Future-Proofing Careers:** By participating in reskilling initiatives, individuals are better equipped to future-proof their careers, staying ahead of technological disruptions and remaining competitive in the job market.

7.2.2.4. Challenges and Considerations

Reskilling initiatives are crucial for equipping individuals with the skills needed to thrive in the evolving job landscape shaped by AI and technological advancements. However, these initiatives come with a set of challenges and considerations that must be carefully addressed to ensure their effectiveness, accessibility, and long-term impact. Here are some key challenges and considerations that stakeholders involved in reskilling initiatives should take into account:

1. Access and Inclusivity:

- Ensuring that reskilling opportunities are accessible to individuals from diverse backgrounds, including marginalized communities and disadvantaged groups, is essential to promote equitable outcomes.
- Addressing barriers to access, such as geographic location, financial constraints, and digital literacy, is crucial for reaching a wide range of participants.

2. Funding and Resources:

- Developing and sustaining reskilling programs requires financial investments. Balancing the need for funding with the demand for accessible and affordable programs can be challenging.
- Collaborating with government agencies, private companies, and educational institutions to secure funding and resources is often necessary.

3. Scalability and Customization:

- Reskilling initiatives should be designed with scalability in mind to accommodate a large number of participants. However, scalability should not compromise the quality of education and training.
- Customizing programs to cater to different industries, job roles, and skill levels enhances their relevance and impact.

4. Curriculum Design and Relevance:

- Developing curricula that align with industry demands and emerging technologies is essential for ensuring that reskilled individuals have skills that are in demand.
- Regularly updating curricula to keep pace with technological advancements and industry shifts is crucial for maintaining the relevance of reskilling programs.

5. Training Delivery Methods:

- Choosing the appropriate delivery methods, such as online courses, in-person workshops, or a combination of both, requires consideration of participants' preferences and accessibility.
- Effective training methods that engage learners and promote active participation are key to successful reskilling outcomes.

6. Lifelong Learning Culture:

- Encouraging a culture of lifelong learning is important for individuals to remain adaptable in the face of evolving technologies. Promoting the value of continuous learning and upskilling is a challenge that requires awareness-building efforts.

7. Monitoring and Evaluation:

- Regularly assessing the effectiveness of reskilling programs, tracking participants' outcomes, and collecting feedback is necessary for continuous improvement.
- Monitoring the success of participants in securing new employment opportunities or advancing within their careers provides insights into the impact of reskilling efforts.

8. **Collaboration and Partnerships:**

   - Collaborating with industry partners, educational institutions, government agencies, and nonprofit organizations enhances the quality and reach of reskilling initiatives.
   - Partnerships can provide access to expertise, resources, and job placement opportunities for reskilled individuals.

9. **Support for Displaced Workers:**

   - Tailoring reskilling programs to support workers who have been displaced due to technological changes or economic shifts requires a sensitive and comprehensive approach.

Reskilling initiatives serve as a lifeline in the rapidly evolving landscape shaped by AI. They empower individuals to adapt to changing job requirements, transition into emerging roles, and future-proof their careers. As technology continues to reshape industries, reskilling initiatives stand as a testament to society's commitment to equipping its workforce with the tools needed to thrive in an AI-driven world.

7.2.3. Social Safety Nets: Robust social safety nets are essential to support individuals during periods of job transition or unemployment. These safety nets encompass unemployment benefits, healthcare coverage, and other forms of assistance that ensure individuals maintain a dignified standard of living. Social safety nets provide a buffer against economic shocks and uncertainties, enabling individuals to navigate career shifts or job losses without falling into financial hardship.

7.2.3.1. Ensuring Dignity in Times of Change:

- **Unemployment Benefits:** Social safety nets often include unemployment benefits, providing individuals who have lost their jobs with temporary financial assistance. These benefits offer a cushion to help individuals meet their basic needs and maintain a certain level of stability as they seek new opportunities.
- **Healthcare Coverage:** Access to healthcare is a fundamental aspect of maintaining well-being. Social safety nets may include healthcare coverage or subsidies, ensuring that individuals and their families can receive medical care and treatment even when they are in transition.
- **Assistance Programs:** Beyond monetary support, social safety nets may encompass various assistance programs that cater to specific needs. These could range from housing assistance and food support to childcare services, helping individuals sustain a reasonable quality of life during periods of uncertainty.

7.2.3.2. Key Features of Social Safety Nets:

- **Universal Accessibility:** Effective social safety nets are accessible to all individuals, regardless of their employment status, ensuring that everyone has a safety net to rely on in times of need.
- **Temporary Support:** Social safety nets provide temporary support, acknowledging that job transitions and economic fluctuations are often short-term challenges. This support helps individuals bridge the gap while they regain their footing.
- **Dignified Standard of Living:** The goal of social safety nets is to maintain a dignified standard of living for

individuals and their families, even during periods of job loss or change.

7.2.3.3. Empowering Individuals to Navigate Change:

- **Mitigating Financial Hardship:** Social safety nets offer a safety valve that prevents individuals from falling into severe financial hardship during times of job displacement or economic downturns.
- **Enabling Career Transitions:** With the assurance of financial support, individuals are more likely to pursue reskilling, upskilling, or transitioning into new roles without the fear of financial insecurity.
- **Economic Stability:** Robust social safety nets contribute to overall economic stability by reducing the negative impact of job losses on individuals and communities. This stability supports consumer spending and minimizes the ripple effects of economic downturns.

7.2.3.4. Challenges and Considerations:

The design and implementation of effective social safety nets are essential for maintaining social stability and providing a safety net for individuals facing economic uncertainties. However, creating these safety nets involves navigating a range of challenges and considerations to ensure that they are sustainable, equitable, and conducive to individual empowerment. Here are some key challenges and considerations that policymakers, governments, and organizations must address:

1. Funding and Resource Allocation:

- Adequate funding is crucial to sustain social safety nets. Balancing the need for financial support with other budgetary priorities requires careful allocation of resources.

- Identifying sustainable funding sources, such as taxation, government revenues, or contributions from employers and employees, is a challenge that policymakers must grapple with.

2. Coverage and Accessibility:

- Ensuring that social safety nets are accessible to all individuals, including marginalized and vulnerable populations, is essential. Coverage should extend to various sectors of society to prevent exclusion.
- Geographic coverage should also be considered, as safety nets should be accessible in both urban and rural areas.

3. Temporary vs. Long-Term Support:

- Striking a balance between providing temporary assistance and encouraging workforce participation is a delicate task. Social safety nets should offer support during periods of transition without inadvertently discouraging individuals from seeking employment or upskilling opportunities.

4. Targeting and Equity:

- Designing safety nets that target those most in need while avoiding dependency requires precise targeting mechanisms. Overly generous benefits can disincentivize work, while insufficient support can perpetuate inequality.

5. Incentivizing Upskilling and Reskilling:

- Social safety nets should be designed in a way that supports individuals' efforts to acquire new skills and transition into new roles. This involves creating programs that encourage and incentivize upskilling and reskilling.

6. Technological and Economic Changes:

- Rapid technological advancements can lead to shifts in industries and job markets. Safety nets should be flexible enough to adapt to these changes and support individuals in adjusting to new economic realities.

7. Avoiding Welfare Traps:

- The design of social safety nets should consider the potential for creating welfare traps—situations where individuals might choose to remain dependent on benefits rather than seeking employment.

8. Public Perception and Political Support:

- Garnering public support for social safety nets is essential. Educating the public about the benefits and necessity of safety nets can contribute to a favorable political environment for their implementation.

9. Continuous Monitoring and Evaluation:

- Safety nets should be subject to regular monitoring and evaluation to assess their effectiveness, identify areas for improvement, and ensure that they remain aligned with their intended goals.

10. International and Cultural Context:

- Different countries have varying cultural norms, economic structures, and social systems. Tailoring social safety nets to the unique needs and contexts of each country is essential.

The challenges and considerations in designing social safety nets highlight the complexity of creating systems that effectively support individuals in an era of economic and technological change. Thoughtful policy development, collaboration among stakeholders, and a commitment to equitable and sustainable solutions are key to navigating these challenges. By addressing these considerations, societies can build safety nets that not only provide financial stability but also foster economic resilience, individual empowerment, and social cohesion.

Conclusion: 7.2.3. Social Safety Nets

In an AI era characterized by technological disruptions and job transformations, social safety nets play a crucial role in safeguarding individuals and families from economic instability. By providing financial support, healthcare coverage, and assistance during transitions, these safety nets uphold human dignity and contribute to the resilience of societies. In embracing the future, social safety nets stand as a testament to society's commitment to ensuring that the benefits of technological progress are shared by all, fostering a more inclusive and compassionate world.

By combining strategies such as Universal Basic Income, reskilling initiatives, and social safety nets, societies can address the challenges posed by AI-driven job displacement. These approaches not only provide economic stability but also empower individuals to embrace new opportunities, acquire new skills, and contribute to the evolving job landscape. In a rapidly changing work environment, proactive measures are key to ensuring a resilient and adaptable workforce.

7.3 Cultural and Societal Transformations: Work, Leisure, and Human Identity

The advent of Artificial Intelligence (AI) has ignited profound shifts in cultural and societal norms, challenging traditional concepts of work, leisure, and even human identity. As AI technologies permeate various aspects of our lives, they bring about transformative changes that require us to reevaluate our perceptions and values.

7.3.1 Redefining Work

The integration of Artificial Intelligence (AI) into various industries has ushered in a redefinition of work, challenging traditional notions and transforming the way we approach employment and productivity. As AI technologies continue to advance, the landscape of work is evolving in profound ways.

7.3.1.1. Automation and Task Shifting

In the process of redefining work, one of the pivotal components is the automation of routine and repetitive tasks. The integration of AI-powered systems into various industries has led to the transformation of tasks that were once time-consuming and monotonous for human workers. This shift in task allocation not only enhances efficiency but also shapes the nature of human involvement in the workforce.

- **Liberating Human Potential:** Automation relieves human workers from the burden of performing tasks that can be efficiently executed by AI. Repetitive and rule-based tasks, which were once a significant part of many job roles, are now handled by technology. This liberation of human potential allows individuals to redirect their energies toward more strategic, creative, and complex aspects of their roles.

- **Fostering Higher-Order Thinking:** With routine tasks taken off their plate, human workers can engage in higher-order thinking and problem-solving. The cognitive capacity that was previously spent on mundane activities can now be directed towards analyzing complex data, making informed decisions, and devising innovative strategies. This shift elevates the value of human contributions within the workforce.
- **Enhancing Creativity and Innovation:** By automating routine tasks, AI-driven systems create space for human creativity and innovation to flourish. When individuals are not bogged down by repetitive activities, they can dedicate their cognitive resources to generating novel ideas, designing new solutions, and exploring uncharted territories. This synergy between human imagination and AI precision leads to groundbreaking advancements.
- **Adapting to Dynamic Roles:** As automation streamlines routine tasks, job roles evolve to encompass a more diverse and multidimensional set of responsibilities. Human workers find themselves in roles that require a combination of technical expertise, critical thinking, creativity, and emotional intelligence. These multifaceted roles are tailored to harness the unique strengths that humans bring to the table.

Automation and the subsequent shifting of tasks are redefining the work landscape in profound ways. As AI takes on routine tasks, human workers are liberated to engage in higher-order thinking, problem-solving, creativity, and innovation. This transformation not only enhances individual job satisfaction but also positions the workforce to adapt to the dynamic demands of an AI-augmented world. The collaboration between AI and human ingenuity paves the way for a more enriched and purposeful work experience.

7.3.1.2. The Evolving Workforce

The concept of the traditional 9-to-5 workday is undergoing a remarkable transformation in the era of AI. The integration of technological advancements and shifting cultural norms are reshaping how individuals engage with work, leading to the emergence of new work paradigms that prioritize flexibility, connectivity, and balance.

- **Seamless Connectivity and Remote Work:** AI-powered communication and collaboration tools have revolutionized the way work is conducted. Remote work, once considered an exception, has now become a viable and even preferred option for many professionals. With the ability to seamlessly connect with colleagues and stakeholders regardless of geographical boundaries, individuals can contribute to projects from the comfort of their own spaces.
- **Flexibility and Gig Economy Platforms:** The gig economy, characterized by short-term contracts and freelance work, is expanding rapidly with the aid of AI platforms. These platforms match individuals with tasks or projects that align with their skills and availability. As AI streamlines the process of finding gigs and managing contracts, workers have the flexibility to engage in diverse projects and tailor their work schedules to their preferences.
- **Breaking the Boundaries of Location:** AI has shattered the geographical limitations that once confined work to specific locations. Professionals can now collaborate

and contribute from anywhere in the world, transcending physical office spaces. This newfound flexibility not only allows organizations to tap into a global talent pool but also empowers individuals to work in environments that suit their lifestyles.

- **Work-Life Balance and Personalization:** The evolution of the workforce is leading to a redefinition of work-life balance. With the ability to choose flexible schedules and remote work options, individuals can design their work routines to accommodate personal commitments and priorities. This personalized approach to work enhances overall well-being and reduces the stress associated with traditional work structures.
- **Implications for Identity and Productivity:** As the boundaries between work and personal life blur, individuals are presented with opportunities to craft a holistic sense of identity that encompasses both professional and personal aspirations. This shift challenges the notion of a linear career trajectory and encourages a more dynamic and multidimensional approach to one's life path. Additionally, the newfound flexibility can boost productivity by allowing individuals to work during their most productive hours.

The evolving workforce is characterized by flexibility, connectivity, and a departure from the conventional 9-to-5 work model. AI-driven technologies enable remote work, gig economy participation, and the breaking of geographical barriers. This transformation not only redefines the relationship between work and personal life but also empowers individuals to design work routines that align with their unique preferences and aspirations. As the workforce becomes more diverse and dynamic, the synergy between AI and human autonomy drives a new era of work that is adaptable, personalized, and empowering.

7.3.1.3. Collaboration with AI

The evolution of work is closely intertwined with the collaboration between humans and AI systems. In contrast to the notion of AI replacing humans, the prevailing trend is one of augmentation—AI technologies enhancing human capabilities and expanding the horizons of what can be achieved.

- **Complementary Capabilities:** AI excels at processing and analyzing vast amounts of data, identifying patterns, and generating insights. Humans, on the other hand, possess intuitive reasoning, emotional intelligence, and creative thinking. The collaboration between humans and AI leverages these complementary strengths, creating a synergy that outperforms what either can achieve in isolation.
- **Data-Driven Decision-Making:** AI's ability to process and analyze data at unprecedented speeds empowers individuals to make more informed and accurate decisions. By providing data-driven insights, AI systems help humans navigate complex scenarios and assess potential outcomes with greater precision. This data-driven decision-making process enhances the efficacy of strategic choices.
- **Enhancing Creativity and Innovation:** While AI can automate routine and repetitive tasks, it can also contribute to the creative process. AI-generated suggestions, ideation, and even artistic creations complement human creativity. The fusion of AI's data-driven insights and human ingenuity yields innovative solutions that transcend what each can achieve independently.
- **Empowering Empathy and Human Judgment:** AI's analytical prowess is invaluable, but it lacks the nuanced

understanding of human emotions and context. In collaborative settings, humans bring empathy, intuition, and ethical judgment to the table. Whether in customer service interactions or ethical decision-making, the human touch remains indispensable.
- **Augmenting Problem-Solving:** Complex challenges often require a multifaceted approach. AI systems excel at breaking down intricate problems into manageable components and suggesting potential solutions. Humans contribute by evaluating these solutions, considering broader implications, and incorporating ethical considerations.

The collaboration between humans and AI is not about relinquishing human control, but about leveraging the strengths of both entities to achieve outcomes that transcend individual capabilities. The amalgamation of data-driven insights, human intuition, creativity, and empathy ushers in a new era of problem-solving and innovation. As AI continues to evolve, its role as a collaborator amplifying human potential emphasizes the importance of human judgment, values, and emotional intelligence in shaping the future of work.

7.3.1.4. Lifelong Learning and Adaptability

The ongoing transformation of work under the influence of AI underscores the significance of lifelong learning and adaptability. As AI takes on routine tasks, a fundamental shift occurs in the nature of work, necessitating a corresponding evolution in the skills and mindsets of individuals.

- **Dynamic Skill Landscape:** The rise of AI-driven automation creates a demand for specialized skills that complement the capabilities of AI systems. Proficiencies in AI programming, data analysis, machine learning, and other technical domains become increasingly valuable.

However, the dynamic nature of technology requires individuals to not only acquire these skills but also remain adaptable to rapid changes in the technological landscape.

- **Adapting to Change:** Adaptability is no longer a desirable trait; it's an essential survival skill in the modern workforce. As job roles evolve, individuals must be prepared to transition between industries, learn new technologies, and embrace emerging opportunities. The ability to pivot and acquire new skills becomes paramount to maintaining relevance in a competitive job market.
- **Continuous Learning as a Norm:** The traditional notion of education ending with a formal degree is being replaced by a culture of continuous learning. The pace of technological advancement demands ongoing skill development, which is no longer confined to specific stages of life. Whether through online courses, workshops, or self-directed learning, individuals are now expected to engage in continuous educational pursuits.
- **Education and Training Evolution:** Educational institutions and training programs play an integral role in equipping individuals for the AI-driven work environment. Curricula must evolve to incorporate technical competencies and foster critical thinking, problem-solving, and adaptability. Moreover, training initiatives need to be responsive to industry needs, ensuring that individuals are well-prepared for the demands of emerging job roles.

In an era characterized by AI-driven disruption, the journey of learning is unceasing. The ability to adapt, embrace change, and continually acquire new skills becomes the linchpin of professional success. Lifelong learning is not merely a choice;

it's a necessity. As AI transforms work, the individual's commitment to staying informed, acquiring new proficiencies, and remaining adaptable defines their capacity to thrive in the evolving landscape of opportunities and challenges.

Conclusion: 7.3.1 Redefining Work

The redefinition of work in the age of AI is a multifaceted transformation that presents both opportunities and challenges. Automation of routine tasks, flexible work arrangements, collaborative efforts with AI, and the emphasis on lifelong learning are reshaping the way we engage with employment. As AI continues to evolve, so too will our understanding of work and its role in our lives, underscoring the importance of adaptability, creativity, and continuous growth in the modern workforce.

7.3.2. Leisure in the Age of Automation

The era of automation and Artificial Intelligence (AI) brings forth a reimagining of leisure and how individuals engage with their free time. As AI technologies alleviate the burden of mundane tasks and reshape the workforce, leisure experiences are undergoing a transformation characterized by enrichment, creativity, and enhanced well-being.

7.3.2.1. Freedom from Mundane Tasks

The integration of AI into various aspects of life brings about a profound transformation in the way individuals experience leisure and free time. As AI systems adeptly manage routine tasks, individuals find themselves unburdened from the shackles of mundane activities, creating space for a renaissance in how leisure is embraced and cherished.

- **Reclaiming Precious Time:** The once-ubiquitous routine tasks that consumed a significant portion of daily life—sorting emails, managing schedules, organizing data—are now efficiently handled by AI. This liberation of time allows individuals to engage in activities that resonate with their true passions, aspirations, and creative inclinations.
- **Rediscovering Passions:** AI's ability to alleviate the tedium of repetitive chores paves the way for a revival of dormant interests and hobbies. Individuals can immerse themselves in artistic pursuits, delve into literature, explore culinary endeavors, or indulge in outdoor adventures that were previously sidelined by the demands of mundane tasks.
- **Cultivating Fulfillment:** The newfound freedom from mundane activities nurtures a sense of fulfillment. Engaging in activities driven by personal interest rather than necessity elevates one's sense of purpose and well-being. This enrichment of leisure time contributes to a more balanced and rewarding lifestyle, enhancing mental and emotional satisfaction.
- **Innovative Pursuits:** With AI taking on routine responsibilities, individuals are presented with the opportunity to channel their energy into innovative ventures. Entrepreneurial endeavors, creative projects, and community initiatives gain traction, fostering an environment of exploration and transformation.
- **Fostering Meaningful Connections:** AI's role in alleviating routine tasks allows individuals to allocate more time to meaningful interactions and relationships. The quality of relationships improves as individuals can invest their attention and energy in fostering deeper connections with loved ones.

AI's role in liberating individuals from the clutches of mundane tasks heralds a new era of leisure enriched by personal fulfillment and exploration. The evolution of leisure time from a mere respite to a canvas for creativity, innovation, and meaningful connections signifies the profound impact of AI on the human experience. As AI becomes an ally in managing the minutiae of daily life, it creates a space where passions flourish, purpose is cultivated, and leisure becomes a gateway to a life truly well-lived.

7.3.2.2. Exploration and Creativity

The integration of AI into the workforce has unveiled a transformative landscape, where the contours of creativity and exploration have been redefined. The impact of automation, relieving individuals from the drudgery of routine tasks, heralds an era where the pursuit of creative endeavors takes center stage, fostering a newfound sense of liberation and innovation.

- **Empowering Artistic Pursuits:** As AI takes over repetitive and time-consuming tasks, individuals are liberated to dedicate themselves to the pursuit of artistic passions. Hobbies such as painting, music composition, writing, and crafting are no longer constrained by the pressures of daily work. This unleashes a wave of creativity, allowing talents to flourish and artistic expressions to flourish.
- **Cultivating Entrepreneurial Dreams:** With the weight of administrative tasks lifted by automation, aspiring entrepreneurs find themselves in an environment conducive to realizing their business aspirations. The extra time and mental bandwidth can be channeled into devising innovative business strategies, refining product offerings, and forging meaningful customer relationships.

- **AI as the Muse of Creativity:** AI's role transcends mere task automation; it actively contributes to the creative process. By generating novel ideas, suggesting design concepts, and providing inspiration, AI serves as a muse to artists and creators. This collaborative synergy produces a dynamic fusion of human ingenuity and AI-generated insights.
- **Elevating Design and Inspiration:** AI's analytical prowess has far-reaching implications for design and innovation. By analyzing vast datasets and extracting insights, AI informs the design of products, services, and experiences that resonate with target audiences. This data-driven approach to design fuels innovation that caters to evolving consumer preferences.
- **Fostering Interdisciplinary Synergy:** AI's versatility extends across domains, fostering cross-disciplinary collaborations. Experts from various fields converge to solve complex challenges, leveraging AI's analytical capabilities to break new ground. This convergence of perspectives fuels innovation by weaving together insights from disparate fields.
- **Unveiling Unconventional Solutions:** AI's impartial approach to data analysis often yields unconventional solutions that elude traditional methodologies. By breaking free from preconceived notions, individuals are encouraged to explore uncharted territories of problem-solving, leading to innovative breakthroughs.
- **A Harmonious Future:** The synergy between AI and creative exploration is a symphony of innovation, pushing the boundaries of imagination and unleashing unprecedented levels of creativity. By shouldering the weight of repetitive tasks, AI offers a canvas of possibilities, inviting individuals to explore passions, embark on entrepreneurial journeys, and reshape

industries through imaginative collaborations. As AI elevates human creativity, the future emerges as a realm where innovation knows no bounds.

7.3.2.3. Personalized Leisure Experiences

In the age of AI, leisure and entertainment have undergone a remarkable transformation, inviting individuals into a realm of personalized experiences that cater to their unique preferences and desires. AI's proficiency in analyzing intricate patterns of behavior and preferences has woven a tapestry of leisure activities that resonate with each individual.

- **Customized Content Curation:** Entertainment platforms have become adept at unraveling the threads of individual tastes, leveraging AI algorithms to curate content recommendations that align with personal preferences. Whether in the form of movies, TV shows, music, or articles, these platforms create a mosaic of leisure options that resonate on a personal level.
- **The Immersive Realm of Virtual and Augmented Reality:** Virtual reality (VR) and augmented reality (AR) have emerged as the brushstrokes of AI-driven leisure experiences. VR engulfs individuals in fully immersive digital worlds, transporting them to realms where imagination knows no bounds. AR, on the other hand, overlays digital enhancements onto the physical world, infusing leisure activities with layers of interactivity and wonder.
- **Seamless Integration of AI-Powered Assistants:** AI-powered virtual assistants have become the concierges of leisure, enhancing the experience by anticipating and fulfilling individual needs. These digital companions recommend restaurants, suggest activities, and make reservations, ensuring that leisure time is spent

indulging in experiences that align with personal preferences.
- **Transforming Gaming and Play:** The gaming landscape has witnessed a profound transformation through AI, which tailors gameplay experiences to individual players. AI adapts game difficulty based on player skill, creates dynamic in-game narratives, and generates personalized challenges, ensuring that each gaming session is a unique adventure.
- **Augmenting Creativity and Expression:** AI extends its hand to the realm of creative leisure, inspiring and assisting individuals in their artistic endeavors. From generating music compositions to aiding in writing novels and designing artwork, AI infuses the creative process with novel perspectives and possibilities.
- **Enriching Travel and Exploration:** AI-driven travel platforms craft personalized itineraries that align with travelers' preferences, from sightseeing to culinary experiences. These platforms leverage data to create tailored journeys that resonate with individual desires, fostering meaningful connections with new destinations.
- **Harmonizing with Human Aspirations:** The symphony of AI-driven personalized leisure experiences is a testament to technology's capacity to harmonize with human aspirations. By refining leisure activities to align with personal tastes, AI redefines leisure, ensuring that every moment spent in leisure becomes a canvas of enjoyment, exploration, and self-expression. As AI and individual desires dance in harmony, the stage is set for a new era of leisure that celebrates the uniqueness of each individual.

7.3.2.4. Learning and Skill Development

As automation reshapes the landscape of work, leisure emerges not only as a realm of relaxation but also as a gateway to profound personal and professional growth. With the gift of time, individuals have the opportunity to engage in a journey of continuous learning and skill development that enriches their lives and empowers their futures.

- **Unleashing the Quest for Knowledge:** In the realm of leisure, the pursuit of knowledge takes on a vibrant new form. Online courses, workshops, and educational platforms extend a welcoming hand, inviting individuals to embark on learning journeys that align with their passions and aspirations. The boundaries of subject matter dissolve, allowing learners to delve into fields they may have only dreamed of exploring.
- **Skill Mastery: A Labor of Love:** Leisure becomes a canvas upon which individuals can meticulously paint their aspirations. Whether it's acquiring a new language, mastering a musical instrument, honing artistic techniques, or delving into the intricacies of coding, leisure transforms into a laboratory for skill mastery. The unhurried hours allow for deliberate practice, enabling individuals to elevate their abilities to new heights.
- **Bridging the Gap: Personal and Professional Growth:** In the age of automation, the demarcation between personal and professional growth becomes fluid. Leisure time becomes a bridge that connects the pursuit of passions with the acquisition of skills that hold relevance in various spheres of life. Whether it's for career advancement, entrepreneurial ventures, or purely personal enrichment, the skills cultivated during leisure create ripples of impact across all domains.

- **Empowerment Through Autonomy:** The beauty of leisure-driven learning lies in the autonomy it provides. Individuals have the freedom to chart their own courses, following their curiosity and passion wherever they lead. This autonomy breeds a sense of ownership over the learning process, fueling intrinsic motivation and propelling individuals toward mastery.
- **From Consumption to Creation:** Leisure, once associated with passive consumption, transforms into a space of active creation. As individuals acquire new knowledge and skills, they gain the ability to create and contribute to their communities and industries. This shift from consumer to creator encapsulates the essence of empowerment that lies at the heart of leisure-driven learning.
- **A Symphony of Balance: Leisure, Learning, and Fulfillment:** In the orchestra of leisure, learning emerges as a powerful instrument that adds depth and dimension to the melody of life. The harmonious interplay between leisure, learning, and skill development paints a portrait of fulfillment—a life rich with experiences, growth, and the boundless pursuit of excellence.
- **The Canvas of Lifelong Learning:** In a world where automation accelerates progress, leisure becomes an artist's canvas on which individuals paint strokes of curiosity, passion, and relentless pursuit of self-improvement. The palette of online resources, educational platforms, and workshops enriches this canvas, allowing each individual to craft a masterpiece of lifelong learning and skill mastery, a testament to the infinite possibilities that lie within the realm of leisure.

7.3.2.5. Community and Connection

As the boundaries between work and leisure evolve in the era of AI, a vibrant tapestry of community and connection emerges. AI's transformative influence extends beyond personal activities, shaping the way individuals connect, collaborate, and foster meaningful relationships, redefining the very essence of community in the digital age.

- **Digital Campfires: Fostering Virtual Communities:** AI-enabled platforms act as modern-day campfires, drawing together individuals who share common passions and interests. Social networks, online forums, and niche communities provide virtual spaces where individuals converge to exchange ideas, share experiences, and engage in conversations that transcend borders and time zones.
- **Shared Interests, Global Bonds:** The digital landscape erases geographic limitations, allowing individuals to connect with like-minded souls from around the world. Whether it's a shared love for a particular hobby, a niche interest, or a cause close to the heart, AI-powered algorithms facilitate the discovery of kindred spirits, nurturing connections that transcend the physical realm.
- **Empathy Through AI-Fueled Dialogue:** AI-driven communication tools introduce a new dimension of empathy and connection. Natural language processing enables more fluid and nuanced conversations, enabling individuals to forge deeper connections and communicate their thoughts and emotions effectively. Virtual interactions become bridges that traverse the gaps between cultures and backgrounds, fostering a sense of global camaraderie.

- **Collaboration Beyond Borders:** AI's role in leisure goes beyond individual pursuits—it amplifies collective endeavors. Collaborative projects, whether in the realm of creative expression, problem-solving, or activism, find their wings in the digital realm. The ability to connect with individuals who bring diverse skills and perspectives to the table fuels innovative collaborations that push boundaries.
- **AI as a Matchmaker of Minds:** AI's matchmaking capabilities extend beyond romantic relationships. Algorithms that suggest potential connections based on shared interests and objectives facilitate the formation of dynamic partnerships. Collaborators, mentors, and mentees are brought together, their union fortified by AI's ability to identify synergy.
- **Ethnicity, Culture, and Inclusivity:** AI's ability to connect individuals also brings to the fore questions of diversity and inclusivity. Communities can be woven together across ethnicities, cultures, and socioeconomic backgrounds. However, AI's role in nurturing inclusivity requires vigilant oversight to ensure that biases are not perpetuated and that the digital landscape becomes a haven for all voices.
- **From Solitude to Solidarity:** In the ever-expanding realm of leisure, AI transforms individual leisure activities into collective experiences. It bridges the gap between solitude and solidarity, nurturing a sense of belonging and shared purpose. As individuals gather around digital campfires, forging connections and collaborations that transcend time and space, AI becomes a conduit that enriches the human experience by weaving together the threads of community and connection.

Conclusion: 7.3.2. Leisure in the Age of Automation

As AI continues to shape the landscape of work and productivity, leisure experiences are liberated from the constraints of routine tasks. The age of automation heralds a new era of enriched leisure, characterized by creative exploration, personalized engagement, skill development, and meaningful connections. Embracing these possibilities, individuals have the opportunity to redefine how they spend their leisure time, fostering a sense of fulfillment, growth, and well-being in an AI-augmented world.

7.3.3. Rethinking Human Identity

The advent of Artificial Intelligence (AI) prompts a profound reevaluation of human identity—a narrative that transcends traditional boundaries and intertwines with technology. As AI systems demonstrate capabilities once attributed solely to humans, the essence of what it means to be human is reshaped, giving rise to complex questions and transformative perspectives.

7.3.3.1. Blurring the Boundaries

In the ever-evolving landscape of AI, the traditional demarcation between humans and machines undergoes a profound transformation. The symbiotic collaboration between human ingenuity and AI capabilities transcends conventional boundaries, giving rise to an intricate ecosystem where intelligence is intertwined, redefining what it means to be human and challenging the very essence of creativity and cognition.

- **Beyond Binary Roles:** The narrative of human versus machine is replaced by a narrative of coexistence and co-creation. AI's ability to perform complex tasks, analyze vast datasets, and generate creative content challenges the notion of binary roles. Humans are no longer merely creators while machines execute; the roles intertwine as humans harness AI to amplify their creative, analytical, and problem-solving abilities.

- **Augmented Creativity:** AI-generated art, music, and literature blur the lines between human creativity and algorithmic innovation. Humans provide the inspiration, and AI refines, evolves, and synthesizes ideas. The result is an augmented form of creativity that transcends individual capacities, offering a glimpse into the synergistic potential of human-machine collaboration.
- **Co-Created Insights:** In data analysis and decision-making, humans and AI collaborate to derive insights that neither could achieve alone. AI's capacity to process and identify patterns in massive datasets is complemented by human intuition, context, and ethical judgment. Together, they create a holistic understanding that spans the quantitative and qualitative realms.
- **The Fusion of Rationality and Intuition:** AI augments human decision-making by providing data-driven insights, while humans bring their unique emotional intelligence and ethical considerations to the table. The fusion of rationality and intuition, logic and empathy, leads to well-rounded choices that align with human values and aspirations.
- **Elevating Human Potential:** The interconnected ecosystem of human-AI intelligence becomes a vehicle for amplifying human potential. Mundane tasks are automated, liberating humans to focus on higher-order thinking, creative expression, and compassionate endeavors. The dynamic interplay between humans and AI becomes a conduit for unlocking latent talents and pushing the boundaries of achievement.

- **Navigating Ethical Waters:** The harmonious coexistence of humans and AI gives rise to ethical considerations. Transparency, accountability, and bias mitigation become imperative to ensure that the collaborative ecosystem upholds fairness, respects privacy, and aligns with societal values. Ethical oversight becomes a shared responsibility that guides the evolution of this intricate partnership.
- **From Coexistence to Coevolution:** As AI and humans collaborate, they not only coexist but also coevolve. The relationship is reciprocal, with each informing the growth and capabilities of the other. AI systems learn from human interactions, adapt to nuances, and refine their algorithms. Simultaneously, humans expand their horizons by integrating AI-augmented skills and knowledge.
- **A Nexus of Innovation:** The blurring of boundaries between humans and AI is a nexus of innovation, a confluence that propels civilization forward. The interconnected ecosystem of intelligence heralds an era where the potential for creativity, discovery, and progress is boundless. It's a journey where human curiosity and AI precision converge to redefine what's possible—a journey that mirrors the essence of human evolution itself.

7.3.3.2. Collaborative Partnerships

In the era defined by the ascent of AI, the paradigm of collaboration replaces the narrative of replacement. Rather than being pitted against each other, humans and AI forge collaborative partnerships that harness the unique strengths of both entities. This transformative relationship recognizes AI not as a usurper, but as an extension of human capabilities—an intelligent tool that augments and magnifies human ingenuity.

- **Beyond Substitution to Amplification:** The conventional apprehension of AI as a replacement for human labor gives way to a new perspective—an AI that complements, enhances, and extends human potential. The partnership between humans and technology is characterized by a shared goal: to leverage the synergies of cognitive capacities and technical precision, fostering an environment of innovation and creativity.
- **Amplifying Creative Expression:** In creative domains, this collaborative partnership unfolds as a symphony of human imagination and AI's algorithmic prowess. Artists, writers, and designers collaborate with AI to explore uncharted artistic territories. AI suggests novel concepts, generates variations, and offers fresh perspectives, enriching the creative process and elevating the outcomes to unforeseen heights.
- **AI as the Catalyst for Innovation:** The fusion of human intuition and AI's analytical might catalyzes innovation. AI's capacity to analyze complex datasets and detect patterns complements human intuition and lateral thinking. Together, they decode intricate challenges and unravel solutions that lie at the intersection of data-driven insights and human insights.
- **Amplifying Human Reasoning:** AI assists in decision-making by processing vast information and offering insights, allowing humans to make informed choices. This collaboration combines AI's quantitative precision with human judgment, ethics, and contextual understanding. The result is decision-making that transcends mere data analysis, incorporating nuances that align with human values.
- **Symbiotic Learning and Growth:** The partnership between humans and AI extends to mutual learning and growth. AI systems learn from human inputs, adapt to

nuances, and evolve algorithms accordingly. Simultaneously, humans acquire AI-augmented skills, enhancing their problem-solving capabilities and expanding their intellectual horizons.

- **Navigating Ethical Horizons:** As this collaborative relationship matures, ethical considerations come to the forefront. Ensuring transparency, fairness, and accountability in AI's role becomes a shared responsibility. Human oversight guides AI's operations, mitigating biases, and safeguarding ethical principles.
- **A Tapestry of Possibilities:** The narrative of collaboration between humans and AI weaves a tapestry of possibilities—where technological precision harmonizes with human creativity, and analytical prowess converges with human intuition. This collaboration redefines the boundaries of achievement, uncovering innovative solutions and amplifying human potential beyond what was previously conceivable.
- **An Era of Symbiotic Intelligence:** In the grand tapestry of progress, the era of collaborative partnerships between humans and AI stands as a testament to the power of symbiotic intelligence. As we navigate the uncharted territories of possibility, the harmonious interaction between human ingenuity and AI's capabilities reshapes industries, fuels discoveries, and ushers in a future where the symphony of collaboration leads to symphonies of innovation.

7.3.3.3. A New Dimension of Potential

The advent of AI introduces a transformative chapter in the story of human potential, one that extends the boundaries of achievement and redefines the essence of what it means to be human. As AI takes on the mantle of mundane tasks, individuals are unshackled from the chains of routine, opening a new dimension of possibilities that expand the horizon of human endeavor.

- **Liberating Minds from Mundane Tasks:** AI's prowess in handling routine and repetitive tasks liberates human minds to soar to unprecedented heights. Freed from the confines of monotonous labor, individuals are empowered to focus on endeavors that demand higher-order thinking, creativity, and emotional intelligence.
- **Exploring Higher-Order Thinking:** With mundane tasks relegated to AI's domain, individuals ascend to the realm of higher-order thinking. Complex problem-solving, critical analysis, and strategic decision-making become the domains where human intellect thrives. As AI shoulders the burden of routine, the human mind is unburdened, allowing for deep dives into intellectual challenges.
- **Unleashing Emotional Intelligence:** AI's contribution to mundane tasks creates space for the flourishing of emotional intelligence—a uniquely human trait that infuses empathy, understanding, and interpersonal skills into interactions. Freed from administrative burdens, individuals engage in meaningful connections, fostering empathy and deepening relationships.
- **Pioneering New Frontiers of Knowledge:** The landscape of knowledge becomes an uncharted territory awaiting exploration. With AI managing routine information retrieval, humans embark on journeys of discovery, delving into unexplored subjects, fueling curiosity, and pushing the boundaries of intellectual exploration.
- **The Evolution of Human Identity:** As AI and humans forge a symbiotic partnership, the narrative of human identity evolves. Adaptability takes center stage as individuals navigate a dynamic landscape where AI is an ally, not an adversary. Empathy, once overshadowed by

mechanization, becomes a cornerstone of human interaction, shaping connections and relationships.
- **AI as a Catalyst for Progress:** Rather than supplanting human potential, AI catalyzes it. The synergy of human ingenuity and AI's computational precision sparks innovations previously deemed unreachable. Humans become orchestrators of AI's capabilities, infusing technology with their unique insights and values.
- **A Tapestry of Progress:** In this new dimension of potential, humans and AI coalesce to weave a tapestry of progress. The canvas of achievement is painted with strokes of creativity, compassion, and collaboration, interwoven with the precision of AI's analytical prowess.
- **A Future of Unbounded Horizons:** As we navigate this uncharted territory, the fusion of human and AI capabilities beckons a future where the symphony of collaboration between technology and humanity reaches crescendos of innovation. This convergence charts a trajectory where AI is not an endpoint, but a stepping stone towards a future where the heights of human potential meet the limitless expanse of technological advancement.

7.3.3.4. Ethical Considerations and Values

In the unfolding landscape of AI advancement, ethical contemplations ascend as guiding beacons, illuminating the path that intertwines technology with the values that define human society. As AI's capabilities reach new frontiers, the discourse transcends algorithms and data to encompass the very essence of our collective identity.

- **The Moral Imperative of AI Deployment:** The deployment of AI technologies carries a moral imperative that resonates with the values upheld by society. Decisions about how AI is harnessed wield the power to uplift humanity or inadvertently perpetuate inequalities. Ethical considerations are the compass that steers AI towards contributing positively to the human experience.

- **Safeguarding Human Values:** In the quest to harness AI's potential, safeguarding human values emerges as a cornerstone. The technology should mirror the virtues that humanity cherishes—fairness, justice, inclusivity, and empathy. Ethical frameworks ensure that AI remains aligned with these values, amplifying them rather than eroding their significance.
- **Impact on Social Dynamics:** The integration of AI permeates social dynamics, shaping interactions and relationships. Ethical deliberations encompass the potential for AI to bridge divides, foster connections, and engender shared experiences. Careful considerations mitigate risks of inadvertently isolating individuals or undermining human connections.
- **Human Values as the North Star:** In the age of AI, human values serve as the North Star guiding the navigation of the uncharted territory. These values are not eclipsed by technology; rather, they are amplified as AI compels society to introspect on what it truly means to be human. The interplay between AI and values paints a portrait of human identity that radiates empathy, compassion, and collaboration.
- **The Canvas of Identity:** The narrative of human identity finds expression on the canvas where AI and ethics converge. The strokes of ethical considerations shape the contours of human dignity, respect for diversity, and the nurturing of a just and inclusive society. This canvas is not static; it evolves with each deliberation, decision, and action that intertwines AI with human values.

- **Human Identity Redefined:** In this juncture of AI and ethics, human identity is redefined not by technology's shadows, but by the values that AI amplifies. The moral reflections, the ethical compass, and the pursuit of shared well-being engrave the identity of a species that is more than its creations—a species that melds progress with conscience.
- **The Symphony of Progress and Ethics:** As AI continues its ascent, the symphony of progress finds its rhythm in the harmonious dance with ethics. The narrative of human identity evolves, blending technological prowess with moral compass. In this partnership, AI and human values join hands to shape a future where the tapestry of identity is woven with threads of integrity, purpose, and shared humanity.

7.3.3.5. Redefined Purpose

As the horizon of human identity broadens in the era of AI, the tapestry of purpose unfurls with new hues, inviting introspection into the essence of existence. With the delegation of mundane tasks to AI, the canvas of purpose transforms into a landscape that beckons individuals to venture beyond the confines of convention.

- **Transcending Mundane Obligations:** The liberation from routine tasks amplifies the pursuit of purpose beyond the realm of obligations. The shackles of repetition are loosened, allowing individuals to delve into pursuits that resonate deeply—ones that foster connection, creativity, and contribution.
- **Nurturing Relationships and Connection:** The redefined purpose finds its expression in the cultivation of relationships. With time freed from the grasp of monotonous tasks, individuals channel their energy into nurturing connections—deepening bonds with loved

ones, fostering collaborations, and fostering communities that flourish on shared values.
- **Contributing to Society's Tapestry:** The shift in identity mirrors a transformation in how individuals contribute to the fabric of society. The pursuit of purpose extends to weaving threads of positive impact—volunteering, mentoring, and addressing social challenges. The canvas of identity becomes adorned with strokes of collective betterment.
- **Unveiling Self-Discovery:** The redefinition of purpose also invites a journey of self-discovery. Freed from the obligations of routine, individuals embark on quests to uncover their passions, talents, and potentials. The pursuit of meaning intertwines with the quest to understand oneself on a deeper level.
- **Expanding Horizons of Contribution:** In the tapestry of redefined purpose, traditional roles no longer solely define one's contributions. The orchestra of humanity harmonizes diverse talents and perspectives—be they in arts, sciences, caregiving, or innovation. Purpose is no longer confined by roles but is an orchestra of myriad harmonies.
- **Harmony of Purpose and Identity:** In this symphony, purpose and identity harmonize in a dance of meaning and fulfillment. The canvas of redefined identity is splashed with colors of purpose that stretch across the spectrum of human endeavor. The narrative that unfolds is one where individuals find resonance in the pursuit of collective good, personal growth, and the enrichment of the human experience.
- **An Uncharted Journey of Purpose:** As AI redefines work and identity, the journey into purpose is a frontier of limitless exploration. It is an odyssey where individuals navigate uncharted waters to unearth the jewels of

personal fulfillment, human connection, and meaningful impact. The narrative of purpose is etched in the annals of human history as a testament to resilience, adaptability, and the evolving tapestry of identity.

Conclusion: 7.3.3. Rethinking Human Identity

The evolution of human identity in the era of AI is a narrative in flux—one that intertwines human qualities with technological prowess. The narrative goes beyond the dichotomy of human versus machine, embracing a collaborative and transformative partnership. As AI shapes the landscape of work, creativity, and interaction, humanity's essence remains rooted in its ability to adapt, collaborate, and define its role in a world where human and machine coexist in a harmonious symphony of progress.

The interplay between AI and culture underscores the need for thoughtful reflection and adaptation. As AI technologies continue to reshape work, leisure, and human identity, societies must grapple with questions of value, meaning, and ethics. Embracing these changes requires a balance between harnessing the benefits of AI and maintaining the core values that define us as individuals and communities. As we navigate this dynamic landscape, a nuanced understanding of cultural and societal transformations will guide us toward a harmonious coexistence with AI.

Conclusion: Chapter 7: Navigating Ethical and Societal Challenges

Embarking on the journey into the AI era, navigating the intricate nexus of ethical and societal challenges becomes an overarching narrative. While AI's potential is vast, its impact must be harnessed to resonate with core human values. Ethical considerations provide the compass, steering AI developments toward principles of fairness, transparency, and accountability. As the horizon of job displacement looms, innovative strategies including UBI and retraining initiatives offer compass points guiding societies towards resilient workforces. In the realm of cultural and societal implications, AI challenges us to redefine not only the tenets of work and leisure but also the essence of human identity itself. In traversing this uncharted terrain, a collective commitment to ethical AI implementation and a compassionate approach to societal metamorphosis will serve as beacons guiding the way toward an equitable, harmonious, and sustainable future.

Chapter 8: Preparing for the AI-Driven Future

As the dawn of the AI-driven future approaches, the path ahead beckons us to navigate uncharted waters with foresight and deliberate action. In this transformative era, our collective preparedness hinges upon strategic thinking, collaborative efforts, and an unwavering commitment to growth and adaptation.

8.1. Business Strategies: Catalyzing Innovation and Resilience

In the dynamic landscape of the AI-driven future, businesses stand at the forefront of transformation. They hold the key to harnessing the power of AI to drive innovation, enhance operations, and create lasting value. This chapter explores essential business strategies that enable organizations to not only adapt to change but also thrive in an era marked by technological disruption and unprecedented possibilities.

8.1.1. Embracing AI as an Innovation Catalyst

In the ever-evolving landscape of the AI-driven future, businesses find themselves at a pivotal juncture where innovation is not just a choice—it's a necessity. Embracing AI goes beyond implementing a new technology; it signifies a profound cultural shift that redefines the very essence of innovation. Rather than being viewed as a mere tool, AI becomes the catalyst that propels organizations toward creative problem-solving and novel opportunities.

- **AI-Powered Insights:** One of AI's remarkable contributions is its ability to unveil insights from vast troves of data that were once insurmountable for human analysis. Businesses that recognize this potential harness AI to discern market trends, customer preferences, and emerging patterns. These AI-powered insights serve as guiding stars for strategic decision-making, empowering organizations to make informed choices that resonate with their target audience.

- **Cultivating a Culture of Experimentation:** Embracing AI translates to more than just adopting a technology—it's about fostering a culture of experimentation. Successful businesses encourage their teams to explore AI's potential across various facets of their operations. This culture of experimentation encourages calculated risks, creative thinking, and a willingness to venture into uncharted territories. The result is an environment that thrives on curiosity, where failure is not a setback but a stepping stone toward innovation.
- **Continuous Improvement:** AI's integration heralds an era of continuous improvement. By analyzing real-time data and generating actionable insights, AI enables businesses to fine-tune their strategies swiftly. This iterative approach, fueled by AI's capabilities, transforms organizations into dynamic entities that adapt rapidly to changing market dynamics and consumer behavior.
- **Propelling Businesses to the Vanguard:** The convergence of AI and innovation propels businesses to the forefront of their industries. Those that embrace AI as an innovation catalyst stand out as pioneers, leading the charge toward new horizons. They reimagine traditional processes, harness the power of AI-driven insights, and make strategic leaps that were previously unimaginable.

Embracing AI as an innovation catalyst marks the beginning of a transformative journey. As businesses leverage AI-powered insights, foster cultures of experimentation, and champion continuous improvement, they propel themselves to the vanguard of their industries. In the uncharted landscape of the AI-driven future, organizations that view AI as a beacon of innovation are not just adapting to change—they are shaping it.

8.1.2. Reshaping Workforce Dynamics with AI

In the dynamic landscape of the AI-driven future, the impact on the workforce is not limited to automation—it's a profound redefinition of roles and responsibilities. Businesses at the forefront of this transformation recognize that AI is not just a tool; it's a catalyst for unleashing human potential and reshaping the nature of work itself.

- **Identifying Efficiency Gaps:** A strategic approach to AI implementation involves a meticulous analysis of business operations. It's about identifying areas where AI can seamlessly integrate to streamline processes, enhance productivity, and alleviate employees from mundane and repetitive tasks. AI-powered automation, when applied thoughtfully, liberates human workers from routine activities, enabling them to channel their efforts toward tasks that require critical thinking, creativity, and emotional intelligence.
- **Elevating Workforce Planning:** Workforce planning evolves into a strategic endeavor in the age of AI. It entails not just the identification of roles that can be automated, but a holistic assessment of the skills and competencies that will be most valuable in an AI-augmented environment. This proactive approach to workforce planning ensures that the organization remains adaptable, ready to seize emerging opportunities, and equipped with the human talent necessary to lead in an evolving landscape.
- **Reskilling Initiatives:** The integration of AI necessitates reskilling initiatives that empower employees to thrive in the changing work ecosystem. Businesses recognize that reskilling isn't just about preparing for the future;

it's about equipping employees with the skills needed to excel in the present. These initiatives foster a continuous learning culture, ensuring that employees are agile, versatile, and capable of seamlessly collaborating with AI technologies.

- **Adaptability:** As AI redefines workforce dynamics, adaptability becomes a cornerstone of success. The workforce of the AI-driven future isn't just skilled; it's agile, ready to pivot in response to shifting demands and seize new opportunities as they arise. This adaptability stems from the alignment of AI's capabilities with human ingenuity, creating a harmonious partnership that leverages the strengths of both.

- **Seizing the AI-Driven Opportunities:** In embracing AI to reshape workforce dynamics, businesses embark on a journey that goes beyond efficiency—it's about tapping into the full spectrum of human potential. By thoughtfully integrating AI, businesses create an environment where employees thrive, contribute, and lead with innovation. As the AI-augmented future unfolds, organizations that master this transformation are not just navigating change—they're shaping a new paradigm of work, collaboration, and success.

AI's role in reshaping workforce dynamics is transformative. By identifying efficiency gaps, elevating workforce planning, implementing reskilling initiatives, and embracing adaptability, businesses are poised to harness AI's potential to the fullest. The convergence of human capabilities and AI technologies paves the way for a future where the workforce is not merely adapting to change, but actively driving it toward unprecedented heights.

8.1.3. Fostering Innovation Ecosystems

In the rapidly evolving landscape of the AI-driven future, innovation isn't just a buzzword—it's the lifeblood of businesses that aspire to lead and create lasting impact. To foster innovation ecosystems is to create an environment that nurtures collaboration, sparks experimentation, and propels knowledge sharing.

- **Collaboration Beyond Boundaries:** Innovation rarely thrives in isolation. Businesses that seek to foster innovation ecosystems recognize the power of collaboration. This extends beyond internal teams to encompass partnerships with startups, academic institutions, and research centers. These collaborations serve as a conduit for the exchange of ideas, perspectives, and expertise. By bringing together diverse minds, businesses tap into a wellspring of creativity that accelerates problem-solving and fuels forward-looking initiatives.
- **Embracing Emerging Technologies:** Partnerships within innovation ecosystems offer more than just brainstorming sessions; they provide access to cutting-edge research and emerging technologies. Startups, often at the forefront of innovation, introduce businesses to novel solutions and disruptive ideas. Academic institutions contribute research insights that inform strategic decisions. Research centers offer deep dives into technological advancements that can reshape industries. By embracing these technologies, businesses stay on the cutting edge and remain primed to seize the opportunities of the AI-driven future.
- **Cultivating Curiosity and Experimentation:** Innovation ecosystems thrive on experimentation. They provide the space and support for businesses to test new

concepts, refine ideas, and iterate quickly. Failure, in this context, isn't a setback—it's a stepping stone toward refinement. By creating an environment that embraces calculated risk-taking, businesses unlock their potential for breakthrough innovations that have the power to reshape industries and pioneer new horizons.

- **Positioning for Future Leadership:** Fostering innovation ecosystems isn't just about staying ahead of the curve—it's about actively shaping the trajectory of industries. By cultivating a network of innovation, businesses position themselves as drivers of change rather than passive observers. They influence industry trends, challenge conventions, and lead with pioneering solutions. This proactive stance not only ensures relevance but also positions businesses as thought leaders that are shaping the very landscape they operate within.

In the era of AI-driven transformation, fostering innovation ecosystems is more than a strategy—it's a mindset that propels businesses toward growth and resilience. Collaboration, emerging technologies, experimentation, and the pursuit of industry leadership are the cornerstones of these ecosystems. Businesses that embrace this approach are not just navigating change—they're cultivating an environment where innovation flourishes, breakthroughs become the norm, and the future is one of boundless possibilities.

8.1.4. Balancing Automation with Human Touch

In the dynamic landscape of AI integration, businesses find themselves navigating a delicate equilibrium—leveraging automation for efficiency while safeguarding the irreplaceable human touch. This balance isn't just a strategy; it's a philosophy that defines how businesses engage with their customers and cultivate lasting relationships.

- **AI-Powered Personalization:** AI's ability to analyze vast amounts of data and predict customer preferences revolutionizes personalization. From tailored product recommendations to predictive insights, AI-enhanced interactions create seamless and tailored customer experiences. But amid these advances, a critical question emerges: how can businesses infuse the warmth and empathy that only human interactions can provide?

- **The Value of Human Empathy:** In the realm of customer interactions, empathy stands as an indispensable asset. The ability to understand emotions, empathize with concerns, and provide a human connection is a hallmark of exceptional service. While AI can analyze data, it lacks the ability to authentically understand and respond to human emotions. This is where the human touch becomes irreplaceable—a source of comfort, reassurance, and genuine connection.

- **Identifying Impactful Touchpoints:** The challenge lies in identifying the touchpoints where human interactions hold the greatest value. These are the moments when empathy, understanding, and nuanced communication make all the difference. Instead of replacing these touchpoints with AI, businesses should leverage automation to enhance them. This synergy allows businesses to provide efficient responses while ensuring that customers feel heard, valued, and understood.

- **Preserving Customer Satisfaction:** Efficiency gains from AI are undeniable, but they mustn't come at the cost of customer satisfaction. The key is to strike a balance that marries AI's analytical prowess with the emotional intelligence of human interactions. The result is a customer experience that combines the convenience of automation with the genuine connection that human engagement provides.

- **A Symphony of Efficiency and Empathy:** Balancing automation with the human touch isn't just a strategic imperative—it's a commitment to delivering exceptional customer experiences. It's an acknowledgment that while AI can predict preferences, analyze data, and provide insights, it's the human heart that truly understands, empathizes, and builds relationships. In this symphony of efficiency and empathy, businesses orchestrate an engagement model that resonates, creating connections that endure and loyalty that stands the test of time.

8.1.5. Investing in Ethical AI and Transparency

In the era of AI, businesses wield unprecedented power to transform industries, redefine customer experiences, and shape societal landscapes. Yet, this power comes with a profound responsibility—to ensure that AI technologies operate ethically, transparently, and without bias. This chapter delves into the critical role of ethical AI and transparency, exploring how businesses can cultivate trust while harnessing the potential of AI-driven innovation.

- **Transparency as a Foundation of Trust:** Transparency is the cornerstone upon which ethical AI is built. For AI systems to earn trust, their operations must be clear, comprehensible, and devoid of hidden agendas. Businesses must prioritize openness in disclosing how AI-driven decisions are made, the data they rely on, and the factors influencing outcomes. This transparency empowers users, customers, and stakeholders to understand the rationale behind AI's choices, fostering accountability and reinforcing trust.

- **Unmasking the Black Box:** While AI's algorithms can be highly complex, the lack of transparency in their functioning raises concerns. "Black box" AI, where decisions are made without clear explanations, is problematic. Businesses should invest in explainable AI—technologies that provide insights into how AI arrives at conclusions. This not only boosts transparency but also helps identify and rectify potential biases, ensuring that decisions are fair, just, and equitable.

- **Fighting Bias:** Bias, whether explicit or implicit, can perpetuate societal inequalities. Businesses must commit to eliminating bias in AI systems by carefully curating training data and implementing thorough testing. Regular audits of AI algorithms can identify and rectify discriminatory patterns, fostering a culture of fairness and equal opportunity. As AI technologies impact diverse communities, businesses' dedication to bias-free systems is a step toward creating a more inclusive society.

- **Responsible AI Development:** Investing in responsible AI development not only protects a business's reputation but also nurtures public confidence in technology. By adhering to ethical guidelines, businesses demonstrate a commitment to societal well-being. This, in turn, enhances brand loyalty and customer engagement. When businesses prioritize the welfare of individuals, the resulting trust becomes a bedrock of sustainable growth and innovation.

- **A Shared Responsibility:** Ethical AI is not solely the responsibility of businesses; it's a collective effort that involves governments, academia, and technology providers. Collaboration among stakeholders is vital in shaping AI regulations, standards, and best practices. By engaging in open dialogues and knowledge-sharing, businesses contribute to an ecosystem where ethical AI flourishes, benefitting society as a whole.

In the AI-driven landscape, businesses wield immense power to shape the future. However, this power must be wielded responsibly, guided by a moral compass that prioritizes fairness, transparency, and accountability. As businesses embrace ethical AI and transparency, they not only forge trust but also pave the way for a future where innovation uplifts humanity while preserving its core values.

Conclusion: 8.1. Business Strategies: Catalyzing Innovation and Resilience

The future is an uncharted landscape shaped by AI's transformative potential. For businesses, this era presents a canvas of innovation, where strategic thinking, adaptability, and ethical responsibility converge. By embracing AI as an innovation catalyst, reshaping workforce dynamics, fostering innovation ecosystems, balancing automation with human interactions, and investing in ethical AI, businesses forge a path towards resilience and growth. In the symphony of change, businesses lead the chorus of progress, crafting a harmonious future where the fusion of human ingenuity and technological advancement propels us towards uncharted horizons.

8.2. Government Policies: Balancing Innovation, Regulation, and Collaboration

In the ever-evolving landscape of AI, governments play a pivotal role in shaping the trajectory of innovation, ensuring ethical boundaries, and safeguarding societal interests. This chapter delves into the intricate dance between government policies, technological advancement, and ethical considerations—a dance that defines the AI landscape of the future.

8.2.1. The Regulatory Tightrope: Fostering Innovation While Ensuring Accountability

In the intricate dance between technological innovation and ethical accountability, government policies serve as a guiding light. This chapter unravels the challenges and opportunities of navigating the regulatory landscape in the AI era, illuminating the path towards fostering innovation while ensuring ethical standards are upheld.

8.2.1.1. Striking the Delicate Balance: Encouraging Innovation Without Compromising Ethics

In the ever-evolving landscape of AI, governments find themselves in a precarious balancing act—fostering innovation while safeguarding ethical considerations. This chapter delves into the intricate challenge of striking this balance, exploring the strategies governments employ to encourage AI innovation while upholding ethical standards.

8.2.1.1.1. The Innovation Imperative: Nurturing Technological Advancement

Innovation, often fueled by emerging technologies like AI, has the power to drive societies toward progress and prosperity. Governments worldwide acknowledge the potential of AI to reshape industries, enhance efficiency, and revolutionize human experiences. However, this enthusiasm for innovation must be tempered by a cautious and ethical approach that prioritizes integrity, fairness, and accountability.

- **The Promise of AI Innovation:** The promise of AI innovation is vast. It encompasses groundbreaking advances in healthcare, with AI-driven diagnostic tools and personalized treatments. It extends to the realm of autonomous vehicles, promising safer and more efficient transportation systems. In finance, AI models enable more accurate risk assessment and investment strategies. The applications are limitless, and governments rightly see AI as a powerful tool for societal betterment.

- **The Imperative of Ethical Considerations:** Amid the enthusiasm for innovation, it is imperative to weave ethical considerations into the fabric of AI development and deployment. These considerations revolve around fairness, transparency, accountability, and safeguarding individual rights. Governments play a pivotal role in setting the tone for ethical AI practices.
- **Ensuring Fairness and Mitigating Bias:** AI algorithms are only as fair as the data they are trained on. Governments must work alongside businesses to ensure that datasets used for AI training are diverse, representative, and free from bias. Regulatory frameworks can mandate audits of AI systems to identify and rectify biases, ensuring that AI-driven decisions do not perpetuate discrimination or inequalities.
- **Transparency and Accountability:** Transparency is central to earning public trust in AI systems. Governments can require that businesses provide clear explanations of how AI systems make decisions. This includes disclosing the sources of data, the algorithms used, and the criteria guiding AI-driven choices. Accountability mechanisms should be in place to hold individuals and organizations responsible for the actions of AI systems.
- **Data Privacy and Security:** AI relies on vast amounts of data, much of it personal and sensitive. Governments

must enact robust data protection laws that safeguard individuals' privacy and ensure that AI systems handle data responsibly. Adequate cybersecurity measures are essential to protect against data breaches and misuse.

- **Empowering Citizens Through Education:** Governments can empower citizens by promoting AI literacy and awareness. This involves educational initiatives that help individuals understand AI technologies, their implications, and their rights in an AI-driven society. Informed citizens are better equipped to engage in discussions about AI ethics and hold both governments and businesses accountable.
- **Collaborative Regulation:** Regulation should not stifle innovation but should act as a guide for responsible AI development. Governments can collaborate with industry experts, researchers, and ethicists to create adaptive and forward-looking regulatory frameworks. These frameworks should evolve with the rapid pace of AI advancement, ensuring that ethical considerations remain at the forefront.

The path forward in the age of AI is one where innovation and ethical integrity go hand in hand. Governments, as stewards of the public interest, have a crucial role in shaping this path. By fostering innovation within ethical boundaries, they can harness the full potential of AI to uplift societies while safeguarding the values that define them. In this way, innovation becomes a force for positive transformation, driving progress that is not only groundbreaking but also just, equitable, and sustainable.

8.2.1.1.2. Ethics as the Cornerstone: Mitigating Unintended Consequences

In the era of rapid AI advancement, innovation is celebrated as a driving force of progress. However, this exponential growth also raises a host of ethical dilemmas and potential risks. At the core of these concerns lies the recognition that ethical considerations are the cornerstone of responsible AI development. Governments, along with businesses and researchers, are tasked with navigating these challenges and mitigating unintended consequences.

- **Addressing Bias and Discrimination:** One of the primary ethical concerns in AI is the potential for bias and discrimination. AI systems, when trained on biased data or designed without adequate safeguards, can perpetuate and even amplify existing societal biases. Governments have a responsibility to enact regulations that ensure AI systems are trained on diverse, representative datasets and are regularly audited for bias. These regulations aim to create AI technologies that treat all individuals fairly, regardless of their background.
- **Mitigating Socioeconomic Inequalities:** AI's transformative potential can lead to socioeconomic inequalities if not managed carefully. Governments recognize that access to AI technologies and the benefits they offer should be equitable. To achieve this, they can implement policies that encourage the responsible deployment of AI in underserved communities and create pathways for marginalized groups to participate in AI development and decision-making.
- **Transparency and Accountability:** Transparency is a critical component of ethical AI. Governments can mandate that organizations using AI technologies disclose how AI systems make decisions and what data they use. This transparency not only builds public trust but also holds organizations accountable for their AI systems' actions. It ensures that individuals affected by

AI-driven decisions have insight into the decision-making process and recourse in case of errors or biases.
- **Data Privacy and Security:** AI's reliance on vast amounts of data raises significant concerns about data privacy and security. Governments play a vital role in enacting stringent data protection laws and cybersecurity measures to safeguard individuals' personal information. These laws ensure that data used in AI applications is handled responsibly and securely, mitigating the risks of data breaches or misuse.
- **Educating and Empowering Citizens:** Ethical AI development is a collective endeavor that involves individuals as informed stakeholders. Governments can invest in educational initiatives that promote AI literacy among citizens. When people understand AI technologies, their implications, and their rights, they become active participants in discussions about AI ethics. This education empowers individuals to advocate for ethical AI practices and hold both governments and businesses accountable.
- **Collaborative Regulation:** Regulating AI is a complex task that requires collaboration between governments, industry experts, researchers, and ethicists. Governments can create flexible regulatory frameworks that evolve with AI's rapid advancement. These frameworks should strike a balance between encouraging innovation and ensuring ethical accountability. Collaboration fosters an environment where AI ethics are continually refined and upheld.

Ethics is not an afterthought but the foundation upon which responsible AI innovation rests. Governments play a pivotal role in ensuring that AI technologies adhere to ethical principles that prioritize fairness, transparency, and accountability. In doing so, they help navigate the complexities of AI advancement and mitigate unintended consequences. Ethical AI becomes the North Star guiding society toward a future where innovation and responsibility are in harmonious balance.

8.2.1.1.3. Overregulation: Stifling the Flame of Innovation

In the realm of AI governance, the specter of overregulation looms as a potential obstacle to the flourishing of innovation. This section delves into the complexities of overregulation, its potential consequences, and the delicate balance governments must strike to ensure that regulation fosters rather than hampers technological progress.

- **The Risk of Stifling Creativity:** Overregulation carries the inherent risk of impeding creativity and invention. A flood of stringent regulations can create an environment where businesses are hesitant to explore uncharted territories and experiment with novel ideas. The fear of inadvertently violating complex regulations can discourage entrepreneurs from pursuing innovative AI solutions, thus stifling the dynamism that drives technological breakthroughs.
- **Sluggish Adaptation to Technological Evolution:** One of the foremost challenges of overregulation is its tendency to age poorly in the face of rapidly evolving technology. The speed at which AI is advancing surpasses the rate at which regulations can be enacted and revised. As a result, regulations designed to address today's challenges may quickly become outdated, hindering the adaptation of AI to emerging contexts and applications.
- **Barriers to Entry and Competition:** Excessive regulatory burdens can act as barriers to entry, particularly for startups and smaller businesses. Compliance with intricate regulations often requires substantial resources, which may not be feasible for new players in

the AI landscape. This can stifle competition and innovation by favoring established entities that can navigate the regulatory maze, thereby creating an environment that is less conducive to disruption.
- **Dampening Experimentation and Risk-Taking:** Innovation often thrives in environments that encourage experimentation and calculated risk-taking. Overregulation can result in a risk-averse culture, where businesses prioritize compliance over experimentation. The unwillingness to venture into unexplored territories limits the potential for groundbreaking advancements and hampers the development of AI technologies that could reshape industries.
- **Balancing Caution and Progress:** Governments recognize the delicate balancing act required to avoid overregulation. While the need for ethical and responsible AI deployment is critical, they also understand that fostering innovation demands a certain degree of freedom and flexibility. Striking the right balance involves crafting regulations that ensure public safety, ethical considerations, and fairness, while also leaving room for agile adaptation and experimentation.

The potential pitfalls of overregulation underscore the importance of finding a middle ground that supports innovation without compromising ethical and societal values. Governments must craft regulations that strike this equilibrium—providing guidance and safeguards while allowing AI technologies to evolve and flourish. By adopting a dynamic and adaptive approach, governments can help shape an AI landscape that nurtures innovation, embraces change, and contributes positively to society's progress.

8.2.1.1.4. Underregulation: Navigating the Uncharted Waters

While overregulation poses challenges to AI innovation, underregulation also raises significant concerns. This section explores the complexities of underregulation, its potential consequences, and the imperative for governments to find the right balance between fostering innovation and ensuring accountability.

- **The Risk of Unchecked AI Development:** Underregulation exposes the AI landscape to the risk of unchecked development. In the absence of clear guidelines and ethical boundaries, businesses may prioritize rapid deployment and profit over societal well-being. This can lead to AI systems that lack transparency, fairness, and accountability, potentially resulting in harmful consequences.
- **Ethical and Social Conundrums:** Unchecked AI development can give rise to a host of ethical and social conundrums. Biased algorithms, discriminatory decision-making, and violations of privacy can become prevalent without adequate oversight. This not only erodes public trust but also perpetuates inequalities and injustices, ultimately hindering the responsible and equitable growth of AI.
- **Safety and Security Concerns:** Underregulation can leave AI systems vulnerable to security breaches and misuse. Without robust security standards and accountability measures, AI technologies may be exploited for malicious purposes. This includes the potential for cyberattacks on critical infrastructure, dissemination of false information, and the proliferation of deepfakes.
- **Consumer Protection and Fair Competition:** Consumers and businesses alike rely on regulatory frameworks to ensure their rights and interests are protected. Underregulation can create an environment where

consumers are left without adequate safeguards, while businesses may engage in unfair or anticompetitive practices. This jeopardizes the principles of fair competition and consumer protection.

- **Balancing Innovation with Responsibility:** Governments face the challenge of finding a balance between nurturing innovation and ensuring that AI development aligns with ethical and societal values. While underregulation can foster rapid innovation, it must be tempered with a sense of responsibility. Regulatory frameworks should promote transparency, fairness, and accountability in AI deployment.

The potential perils of underregulation underscore the need for governments to navigate the middle path—one that encourages innovation while safeguarding the interests of society. Striking this balance involves crafting regulations that set clear ethical standards, promote transparency, and establish mechanisms for accountability. By doing so, governments can foster an AI landscape that thrives on innovation while upholding ethical principles and the well-being of all stakeholders.

8.2.1.1.5. Dynamic Regulatory Evolution: Adapting to Technological Progress

Governments acknowledge that AI's growth is characterized by rapid technological evolution and unforeseen challenges. To effectively navigate this dynamic landscape, they are adopting regulatory frameworks that evolve in tandem with technological progress. These dynamic regulatory approaches provide businesses with adaptable guidelines that respond to AI's maturation and emerging ethical concerns. Such an approach allows governments to balance fostering innovation with safeguarding ethical principles.

- **Guidelines for Ethical Innovation:** Dynamic regulatory frameworks offer guidelines that emphasize ethical innovation. They encourage businesses to embrace technological advancements while ensuring that the development and deployment of AI technologies adhere to ethical principles. This means that as AI continues to evolve, businesses must prioritize transparency, fairness, and accountability in their AI systems.
- **Adaptability in the Face of Emerging Ethical Concerns:** One of the key advantages of dynamic regulatory frameworks is their adaptability. Governments can swiftly respond to emerging ethical concerns or issues related to AI by updating regulations as needed. This adaptability ensures that AI technologies are continually held to high ethical standards, even as they advance.
- **Fostering Responsible AI Development:** Dynamic regulatory frameworks promote responsible AI development. They encourage businesses to remain vigilant about potential ethical pitfalls and provide mechanisms for addressing them. This fosters a culture of responsibility in the AI industry, where businesses are proactive in identifying and mitigating ethical risks.
- **Balancing Innovation with Ethical Considerations:** Balancing innovation with ethical considerations is a central tenet of dynamic regulatory frameworks. While they encourage technological progress, they also ensure that businesses remain accountable for the ethical implications of their AI technologies. This balance helps prevent AI from advancing at the expense of ethical integrity.
- **Encouraging Public Trust:** Dynamic regulatory frameworks contribute to building and maintaining public trust in AI technologies. By demonstrating a

commitment to ethical guidelines that evolve with technological progress, governments and businesses alike show that they prioritize the well-being and rights of individuals affected by AI systems.

The dynamic regulatory evolution is a strategic response to the ever-changing landscape of AI. It enables governments to strike a balance between fostering innovation and upholding ethical principles. As AI continues to advance, these regulatory frameworks will play a crucial role in ensuring that technology serves humanity's best interests, guided by ethical considerations that evolve in lockstep with technological progress.

8.2.1.1.6. Incentivizing Ethical Practices: Aligning Ethics and Innovation

In the era of AI, governments recognize the paramount importance of ethical AI development. To incentivize businesses to prioritize responsible practices, they are implementing strategies that align ethics and innovation. These strategies encompass various incentives designed to reward companies that integrate transparency, fairness, and accountability into their AI projects.

- **Financial Incentives: Grants and Subsidies:** One approach governments are taking is to offer financial incentives in the form of grants and subsidies. These funds are directed towards companies that demonstrate a commitment to ethical AI development. Businesses that prioritize transparency in AI decision-making processes, strive for fairness in AI algorithms, and implement robust accountability mechanisms can access these incentives. This financial support not only helps companies invest in ethical practices but also fosters an environment where responsible AI is actively encouraged.

- **Tax Incentives for Ethical AI Practices:** Tax incentives are another powerful tool governments use to promote ethical AI. By providing tax breaks or credits to companies that adhere to ethical AI guidelines, governments incentivize businesses to integrate responsible practices into their operations. These incentives reduce the financial burden on companies striving for ethical excellence in their AI projects.
- **Promoting a Culture of Ethical Innovation:** These incentives collectively promote a culture of ethical innovation. Businesses are encouraged to align their goals with societal well-being, placing ethics at the core of their AI endeavors. This cultural shift towards ethical AI is vital for ensuring that technological advancements are guided by principles that prioritize transparency, fairness, and accountability.
- **Long-Term Benefits of Incentivizing Ethical AI:** Incentivizing ethical practices in AI development has long-term benefits. It helps build public trust in AI technologies, fosters responsible innovation, and mitigates the risks associated with biased or discriminatory AI systems. Ultimately, these incentives contribute to the creation of AI technologies that not only advance industries but also benefit individuals and society as a whole.

The incentivization of ethical AI practices provides a robust framework for ethical innovation. Governments, by rewarding businesses that prioritize responsible AI development, play a pivotal role in shaping an AI landscape where ethics and innovation go hand in hand. This approach ensures that AI technologies are developed and deployed with a strong ethical foundation, promoting a future where technology serves the greater good.

Conclusion: 8.2.1.1. Striking the Delicate Balance: Encouraging Innovation Without Compromising Ethics

The path forward requires governments to tread carefully, nurturing a landscape where innovation flourishes hand in hand with ethical considerations. Striking the delicate balance between innovation and ethics involves a multifaceted approach, where regulatory frameworks adapt, incentives are aligned, and ethical integrity is at the forefront. As governments traverse this tightrope, they pave the way for a future where AI-driven innovation enriches lives while maintaining the highest ethical standards.

8.2.1.2. Flexible Frameworks for an Evolving AI Landscape

Flexible frameworks for AI regulation and governance are becoming imperative as the AI landscape evolves at an unprecedented pace. These frameworks are designed to accommodate the rapid advancements in AI technology while ensuring that ethical, legal, and societal considerations are not left behind. Here's an exploration of why flexible frameworks are crucial and how they can adapt to the ever-changing AI environment.

8.2.1.2.1. The Need for Flexibility

The need for flexibility in AI regulation and governance arises from the dynamic and rapidly evolving nature of artificial intelligence technologies. Here, we delve into the reasons why flexibility is crucial in adapting to the AI landscape's ever-changing challenges and opportunities.

- **1. Rapid Technological Advancements:** AI technologies are advancing at an unprecedented rate. What was considered state-of-the-art just a few years ago is now commonplace, and new breakthroughs are continually emerging. Fixed regulations can quickly become outdated, hindering innovation and growth.

- **2. Diverse AI Applications:** AI is applied across a wide range of industries and sectors, from healthcare to finance to transportation. Each application comes with its unique challenges and considerations. Fixed regulations may not adequately address the nuances and complexities of these diverse applications.
- **3. Evolving Ethical Concerns:** As AI systems become more sophisticated and integrated into daily life, they can give rise to unforeseen ethical dilemmas and risks. Flexibility is necessary to respond to emerging ethical concerns and adapt regulations accordingly.
- **4. Balancing Innovation and Accountability:** Striking the right balance between fostering innovation and ensuring accountability is a complex challenge. Flexible frameworks allow regulators to adjust regulations as needed, fostering innovation while maintaining ethical and legal standards.
- **5. Global Variability:** AI is a global phenomenon, and regulatory approaches vary from one country to another. Flexible frameworks can adapt to international standards and accommodate variations in regulatory approaches, facilitating international cooperation and trade.
- **6. User Feedback and Experience:** Users' experiences and feedback can provide valuable insights into AI system behavior and potential risks. Flexible regulations can incorporate user feedback to improve AI system safety and performance continually.
- **7. AI's Unpredictable Trajectory:** The future trajectory of AI is unpredictable. New breakthroughs and

applications may reshape the AI landscape in unforeseen ways. Flexible frameworks allow policymakers to respond to these changes agilely.
- **8. Encouraging Responsible Innovation:** By offering flexibility, regulations can encourage responsible innovation. Startups and smaller companies may find it easier to comply with adaptable rules, promoting a vibrant and competitive AI ecosystem.
- **9. Continuous Learning and Improvement:** The field of AI is marked by ongoing learning and improvement. Regulators must be open to updating their understanding of AI technologies and their implications continually.
- **10. Ethical and Societal Implications:** AI's impact extends beyond technology and into ethical and societal realms. Regulations must adapt to address not only technical issues but also broader societal implications, such as the impact on employment, privacy, and safety.

In conclusion, flexibility in AI regulation and governance is essential to keep pace with the ever-evolving landscape of artificial intelligence. These flexible frameworks enable regulators to strike the right balance between fostering innovation and ensuring accountability while addressing the unique challenges posed by AI technologies.

8.2.1.2.2. Components of Flexible Frameworks

Flexible frameworks in AI regulation and governance consist of various components and strategies aimed at adapting to the dynamic and evolving nature of artificial intelligence. These components are designed to ensure that regulations remain effective, relevant, and responsive to emerging challenges and opportunities. Here are key components of flexible frameworks:

- **1. Risk-Based Approach:** Flexible frameworks prioritize a risk-based approach to regulation. They focus resources and attention on high-risk AI applications and systems while allowing more leeway for lower-risk applications. This approach ensures that regulatory efforts are proportional to potential harms.
- **2. Adaptive Standards:** Regulations should incorporate adaptive standards that can be updated as AI technologies evolve. These standards provide guidelines for developers and operators, with built-in mechanisms for adjustments as needed.
- **3. Continuous Monitoring and Assessment:** Flexible frameworks include mechanisms for continuous monitoring and assessment of AI systems' performance, safety, and ethical considerations. This involves collecting data on AI deployments and evaluating their impact on various stakeholders.
- **4. Stakeholder Engagement:** Regulators actively engage with a diverse set of stakeholders, including industry experts, researchers, policymakers, and the public. This engagement helps in gathering insights, identifying risks, and refining regulations collaboratively.
- **5. Ethical Guidelines:** Ethical principles and guidelines are integral to flexible frameworks. They provide a foundation for addressing ethical concerns related to AI, such as bias, transparency, fairness, and accountability.
- **6. Regulatory Sandboxes:** Regulatory sandboxes are controlled environments where AI developers can test innovative solutions with relaxed regulatory requirements. They encourage experimentation while ensuring safeguards are in place.
- **7. Agility in Rulemaking:** Flexible frameworks enable regulatory bodies to adapt and revise rules in response to technological advancements and emerging

challenges swiftly. This agility ensures that regulations remain effective and up-to-date.
- **8. Transparency and Explainability:** Regulations promote transparency and explainability in AI systems. This includes requirements for developers to document their AI models and algorithms comprehensively.
- **9. Public Reporting:** Developers and operators of AI systems may be required to provide public reports detailing their AI systems' performance, safety, and impact on society. This transparency enhances accountability.
- **10. Enforcement Mechanisms:** Flexible frameworks include enforcement mechanisms that can be adjusted to the severity of non-compliance. These mechanisms may range from warnings and fines to more stringent actions like suspensions or shutdowns.
- **11. Data Governance:** Regulations address data governance issues, including data privacy, security, and ownership. They ensure that AI systems handle data responsibly and ethically.
- **12. International Collaboration:** Given the global nature of AI, flexible frameworks promote international collaboration and harmonization of standards. This ensures consistency and interoperability across borders.
- **13. Feedback Loops:** There are built-in feedback loops that allow stakeholders to provide input on the effectiveness and fairness of AI regulations. Feedback from real-world AI deployments informs regulatory adjustments.
- **14. Accountability and Liability:** Regulations define accountability and liability frameworks for AI systems. This includes specifying who is responsible for AI decisions and actions, especially in cases of harm or discrimination.

- **15. Public Awareness and Education:** Flexible frameworks support public awareness and education initiatives to inform citizens about AI, its benefits, and potential risks. Informed citizens can better engage in discussions about AI regulation and ethics.

These components collectively create a regulatory environment that adapts to the ever-changing AI landscape while ensuring that AI technologies are developed and deployed responsibly, ethically, and with a focus on minimizing risks to society.

8.2.1.2.3. Case-by-Case Assessment

A case-by-case assessment is a fundamental aspect of flexible regulatory frameworks for artificial intelligence (AI). It involves evaluating and regulating AI applications, systems, or deployments individually based on their unique characteristics, risks, and potential societal impacts. This approach acknowledges that not all AI technologies are the same and that a one-size-fits-all regulatory approach may not be appropriate.

Here are key aspects of a case-by-case assessment within flexible AI regulation:

- **1. Risk Analysis:** Each AI application undergoes a risk analysis to determine its potential for harm or negative societal impact. This analysis considers factors such as the AI's purpose, capabilities, data inputs, and deployment context.
- **2. Ethical Considerations:** Ethical principles and guidelines are applied to assess the ethical implications of the AI application. This includes evaluating issues

related to bias, fairness, transparency, accountability, and the protection of human rights.
- **3. Public Input:** Stakeholder engagement is essential in the case-by-case assessment. Regulators actively seek input from industry experts, researchers, affected communities, and the public to gather diverse perspectives and insights.
- **4. Transparency:** Developers and operators of AI systems are required to provide comprehensive information about the AI's design, data sources, algorithms, and intended use. Transparency is a key element in assessing the AI's fairness and accountability.
- **5. Real-World Impact:** The assessment includes an evaluation of the AI's real-world impact on individuals, organizations, and society as a whole. This involves monitoring and data collection during the AI's deployment.
- **6. Flexibility in Rules:** Regulatory rules and requirements can be adjusted based on the findings of the case-by-case assessment. This flexibility allows regulators to tailor regulations to specific AI applications and adapt them as needed.
- **7. Enforcement Mechanisms:** Enforcement mechanisms are designed to align with the assessed risk level. Higher-risk AI applications may face stricter enforcement, while lower-risk ones have more lenient requirements.
- **8. Continual Monitoring:** After an AI application is deployed, continual monitoring and assessment take place to ensure ongoing compliance with regulations and to address any emerging issues or risks.
- **9. Feedback Loops:** Regulators establish feedback loops with stakeholders to gather information about the AI's

performance and impact. Feedback from real-world use informs regulatory adjustments.

- **10. Adaptive Regulations:** Regulatory frameworks are adaptive and responsive to the outcomes of case-by-case assessments. If an AI application poses unforeseen risks or ethical concerns, regulations can be updated accordingly.
- **11. Comprehensive Documentation:** Developers are required to maintain comprehensive documentation of their AI systems, including data, algorithms, and model updates. This documentation aids in transparency and accountability.
- **12. International Collaboration:** When necessary, international collaboration is pursued to ensure consistency in the case-by-case assessment and regulatory approaches, particularly for AI applications with global implications.

A case-by-case assessment approach ensures that AI regulation is context-aware and responsive to the evolving AI landscape. It allows regulators to strike a balance between promoting innovation and safeguarding ethical and societal considerations. This flexibility is essential for addressing the diverse range of AI applications and their potential impacts on society.

8.2.1.2.4. Ethical Considerations

Ethical considerations are a crucial aspect of the case-by-case assessment within flexible regulatory frameworks for artificial intelligence (AI). These considerations ensure that AI technologies are developed, deployed, and used in ways that align with ethical principles, respect human values, and mitigate potential harm. Here are key ethical considerations in the context of AI regulation:

- **1. Bias and Fairness:** Regulators assess whether AI systems exhibit bias, particularly in terms of race, gender, age, or other protected characteristics. Ensuring fairness in AI decision-making is essential to prevent discrimination and promote equity.
- **2. Transparency:** Ethical AI should be transparent, meaning that its operations and decision-making processes are explainable and understandable to stakeholders. Transparency fosters accountability and trust.
- **3. Accountability:** Developers and operators of AI systems must be accountable for the actions and decisions made by their systems. Clear lines of responsibility ensure that those who deploy AI are held responsible for its consequences.
- **4. Privacy:** The protection of individuals' privacy is a paramount ethical concern. Regulators examine how AI systems handle personal data and ensure compliance with privacy regulations and norms.
- **5. Human Rights:** AI applications should respect fundamental human rights, including the right to life, liberty, and security. Assessments consider whether AI could infringe upon these rights, especially in sensitive areas like surveillance.
- **6. Explainability:** Regulators assess whether AI systems are capable of providing explanations for their decisions. This is particularly important in contexts such as healthcare and finance, where decisions have significant consequences.
- **7. Safety:** Ensuring the safety of AI systems, especially in applications like autonomous vehicles and healthcare, is an ethical imperative. Regulators consider whether adequate safety measures are in place.

- **8. Accessibility:** Ethical AI should be accessible to all individuals, including those with disabilities. Regulators evaluate whether AI applications are designed with inclusivity in mind.
- **9. Informed Consent:** In cases where AI systems interact with individuals, obtaining informed consent is essential. Regulators assess whether users are adequately informed about how AI systems operate and their potential impact.
- **10. Social Impact:** The broader societal impact of AI is scrutinized. Regulators consider how AI might affect employment, income distribution, and social dynamics, with an emphasis on mitigating negative consequences.
- **11. Dual Use:** AI systems with potential dual-use, meaning they can be used for both beneficial and harmful purposes, undergo careful scrutiny to prevent misuse.
- **12. Stakeholder Engagement:** Public and stakeholder input is sought to gather diverse perspectives on the ethical implications of AI applications. This engagement ensures that regulatory decisions are informed by a broad range of voices.
- **13. International Standards:** Regulators may reference international ethical standards and guidelines, such as those put forth by organizations like the OECD or the United Nations, to inform their assessments.
- **14. Adaptability:** Regulatory frameworks must be adaptable to evolving ethical considerations and emerging AI technologies. Flexibility allows regulations to respond to new challenges and ethical dilemmas.

Ethical considerations are at the core of responsible AI development and regulation. By addressing these considerations within flexible regulatory frameworks, regulators aim to strike a balance between promoting innovation and ensuring that AI technologies benefit society while minimizing potential harms.

8.2.1.2.5. Balancing Innovation and Accountability

Balancing innovation and accountability is a central challenge in the regulation of artificial intelligence (AI). While fostering innovation is crucial for technological advancement and economic growth, accountability is essential to prevent potential risks and ensure ethical AI development. Here's how regulators can strike a balance:

- **1. Clear Ethical Guidelines:** Regulators can establish clear ethical guidelines that outline the expected standards for AI development and usage. These guidelines should emphasize fairness, transparency, accountability, and safety. Businesses and developers can then innovate within these boundaries.
- **2. Ethical Impact Assessments:** Before deploying AI systems, businesses can be required to conduct ethical impact assessments. These assessments evaluate the potential ethical implications and consequences of AI applications, helping to identify and mitigate risks.
- **3. Sector-Specific Regulations:** Regulators can adopt a sector-specific approach to AI regulation. For instance, industries with a higher risk of AI-related harm, such as healthcare and finance, might have more stringent accountability requirements.
- **4. Regulatory Sandboxes:** Regulatory sandboxes provide a controlled environment where businesses can test innovative AI applications under regulatory supervision. This allows for experimentation while ensuring that ethical and safety standards are met.
- **5. Independent Audits:** Independent audits by third-party organizations or regulatory bodies can verify that

AI systems comply with ethical and safety standards. These audits enhance accountability by providing objective assessments.

- **6. Transparency and Reporting:** Regulators can mandate that businesses report on the development, deployment, and performance of AI systems. Transparency requirements ensure that accountability can be enforced.
- **7. Liability Frameworks:** Establishing liability frameworks clarifies who is responsible in case of AI-related harm. It encourages businesses to take responsibility for their AI systems and fosters a culture of accountability.
- **8. Public Input:** Inviting public input and consultation in the regulatory process ensures that a broad range of perspectives is considered. This inclusivity can lead to regulations that balance innovation and accountability effectively.
- **9. International Collaboration:** Given the global nature of AI, international collaboration on regulatory standards is essential. Aligning regulations across borders can create a more consistent framework for innovation and accountability.
- **10. Flexibility and Adaptation:** Regulatory frameworks should be designed to adapt to evolving AI technologies and ethical considerations. Flexibility allows regulations to keep pace with innovation while remaining accountable.
- **11. Education and Awareness:** Regulators can play a role in educating businesses and the public about AI ethics and accountability. This awareness can lead to more responsible AI development and usage.
- **12. Incentives for Ethical AI:** Governments can provide incentives, such as tax benefits or grants, to businesses

that prioritize ethical AI development. These incentives encourage innovation that aligns with accountability.

Balancing innovation and accountability in AI regulation is an ongoing process that requires collaboration between regulators, businesses, researchers, and the public. The goal is to foster innovation while ensuring that AI technologies are developed and used in ways that benefit society and minimize potential harm.

Conclusion: 8.2.1.2. Flexible Frameworks for an Evolving AI Landscape

In an era of rapid AI advancement, flexible frameworks for regulation and governance are essential. They provide a way to adapt to evolving technology, address ethical dilemmas, and balance innovation with accountability. By prioritizing principles and risk-based approaches, these frameworks offer a path forward in harnessing the potential of AI for the benefit of society.

8.2.1.3. Guiding Businesses on the Ethical Journey

Government policies can play a pivotal role in guiding businesses on their ethical journey in AI development and deployment. Here are some key ways in which governments can provide guidance to businesses:

- **1. Clear Ethical Frameworks:** Governments can establish clear ethical frameworks and principles that businesses should follow when developing and deploying AI technologies. These frameworks can include guidelines on fairness, transparency, accountability, privacy, and bias mitigation.

- **2. Transparency Requirements:** Regulators can mandate that businesses be transparent about the use of AI in their products and services. This includes providing clear explanations of how AI systems make decisions and disclosing the data sources used.
- **3. Data Usage Guidelines:** Governments can set guidelines for the collection, storage, and usage of data in AI systems. This includes ensuring that data used for training AI models is obtained ethically and respects individuals' privacy rights.
- **4. Algorithmic Accountability:** Regulators can require businesses to implement measures for algorithmic accountability. This involves regular audits and assessments of AI systems to identify and mitigate biases and discriminatory outcomes.
- **5. Public Impact Assessments:** Before deploying AI systems with significant public impact, businesses can be required to conduct impact assessments. These assessments evaluate the potential social, ethical, and legal consequences of AI applications.
- **6. Ethical Review Boards:** Governments can establish independent ethical review boards or committees to assess the ethical implications of AI projects, especially those with high stakes, such as healthcare or criminal justice applications.
- **7. Liability and Responsibility:** Regulators can define liability frameworks that specify who is responsible for AI-related harm. This clarity encourages businesses to take responsibility for the ethical use of their AI technologies.
- **8. International Alignment:** To ensure consistency and facilitate global business operations, governments can work towards aligning their AI ethics and regulations with international standards.

- **9. Incentives for Ethical AI:** Governments can provide incentives, such as tax benefits or grants, to businesses that prioritize ethical AI development. This encourages businesses to invest in ethical practices.
- **10. Education and Training:** Governments can support educational initiatives that promote AI ethics and responsible AI development within businesses. This includes training programs and resources on ethical AI.
- **11. Stakeholder Engagement:** Governments can facilitate dialogues and engagements between businesses, civil society, academia, and the public to gather diverse perspectives and input on AI ethics.
- **12. Periodic Audits and Compliance Checks:** Regulatory bodies can conduct periodic audits and compliance checks to ensure that businesses are adhering to ethical guidelines and policies.

By providing a regulatory framework that promotes ethical AI, governments can help businesses navigate the complex landscape of AI ethics and ensure that AI technologies are developed and used in ways that benefit society while maintaining public trust. This partnership between governments and businesses is essential for responsible AI innovation.

8.2.1.4. Ethics by Design: Nurturing Ethical AI Culture

Government policies can incentivize the integration of ethics into AI development processes. Encouraging the adoption of ethical AI principles from the inception of projects promotes responsible innovation. By requiring regular ethical assessments and audits of AI systems, governments ensure that potential biases, discriminatory patterns, and privacy concerns are addressed proactively.

Here's how government policies can support and promote an "Ethics by Design" approach:

- **1. Mandatory Ethical Impact Assessments:** Governments can require organizations to conduct Ethical Impact Assessments (EIAs) at the outset of AI projects. These assessments would evaluate the potential ethical implications of the AI system, including fairness, bias, privacy, and societal impact. Organizations would need to address these concerns before proceeding.
- **2. Ethics Training and Certification:** Governments can mandate that individuals involved in AI development, including data scientists and engineers, undergo ethics training and certification. This ensures that AI professionals are equipped with the knowledge and tools to consider ethical implications in their work.
- **3. Ethical AI Guidelines:** Regulatory bodies can establish clear guidelines for ethical AI development. These guidelines can cover aspects such as transparency, fairness, accountability, and the handling of sensitive data. They can serve as a reference for organizations to follow throughout the development lifecycle.
- **4. Regular Ethical Audits:** Governments can require organizations to conduct regular ethical audits of their AI systems. These audits would assess whether the AI system aligns with ethical guidelines and identify any emerging ethical issues that need attention.
- **5. Transparency Requirements:** Regulations can mandate that organizations be transparent about their AI systems' ethical considerations. This includes disclosing how data is used, how decisions are made, and how biases are addressed.
- **6. Ethics Review Boards:** Governments can establish independent ethics review boards that evaluate AI projects for ethical compliance. These boards can

consist of experts in ethics, AI, and related fields to provide objective assessments.
- **7. Whistleblower Protections:** To encourage ethical reporting, governments can enact whistleblower protections specific to AI ethics. This ensures that individuals who identify ethical concerns within their organizations can report them without fear of retaliation.
- **8. Ethical Certification Labels:** Governments can introduce certification programs that label AI systems as "ethically certified" when they meet specific ethical standards. This can help consumers and businesses make informed choices about which AI systems to use.
- **9. Public Accountability Reports:** Organizations could be required to publish annual reports on the ethical aspects of their AI systems. These reports would detail steps taken to address ethical concerns and provide transparency to the public.
- **10. Penalties for Ethical Violations:** Regulatory bodies can impose penalties for organizations found in violation of ethical AI guidelines. Penalties serve as a deterrent and ensure accountability.

By incorporating these measures into government policies, organizations are encouraged to consider ethics at every stage of AI development. This not only helps prevent ethical issues but also promotes a culture of responsible AI innovation.

8.2.1.5. Building Public Trust Through Accountability

Transparent accountability mechanisms reinforce the public's trust in AI technologies. Governments can mandate that businesses provide explanations for AI-driven decisions, enhancing transparency and reducing the "black box" nature of AI systems. This accountability fosters a culture of responsible

AI development and aligns technological progress with societal values.

Building and maintaining public trust in AI is crucial for its widespread acceptance and responsible use. Here are some ways governments can help reinforce public trust through accountability mechanisms:

- **1. Explainable AI (XAI) Requirements:** Governments can require that AI systems provide explanations for their decisions. This is especially important in critical domains like healthcare, finance, and criminal justice. XAI techniques make AI systems more transparent and understandable, helping users and stakeholders trust the technology.
- **2. Transparency Reporting:** Regulatory bodies can mandate that organizations using AI regularly publish transparency reports. These reports would detail how AI systems are trained, the data sources used, and the steps taken to address bias and fairness. Transparency reporting holds organizations accountable for their AI practices.
- **3. Algorithm Audits:** Independent audits of AI algorithms can be required to assess their fairness, bias, and ethical considerations. These audits ensure that AI systems meet predefined ethical standards and aren't inadvertently discriminating against specific groups.
- **4. Data Governance:** Governments can establish data governance frameworks that outline the responsible collection, use, and sharing of data. Clear rules for data handling contribute to the ethical use of AI.
- **5. Whistleblower Protections:** To encourage the reporting of ethical violations, governments can enact strong whistleblower protection laws specific to AI. This

gives individuals within organizations the confidence to report unethical practices without fear of retaliation.
- **6. Ethics Review Boards:** Independent ethics review boards can evaluate AI systems for compliance with ethical guidelines. These boards may include experts in ethics, AI, and other relevant fields.
- **7. Consumer-Facing Information:** For AI systems used by consumers, governments can require that plain-language explanations of how AI systems work, what data is used, and how decisions are made are provided. This empowers users to make informed choices.
- **8. Privacy Regulations:** Strong data privacy regulations can ensure that personal data used by AI is handled responsibly and that individuals have control over their data.
- **9. Penalties for Violations:** Regulatory bodies should have the authority to impose fines and penalties on organizations found to be in violation of ethical and transparency standards. Penalties serve as a deterrent and ensure accountability.
- **10. Public Awareness Campaigns:** Governments can run public awareness campaigns to educate citizens about AI, its benefits, and potential risks. An informed public is better equipped to hold organizations and governments accountable for ethical AI use.

These accountability mechanisms not only foster trust but also promote responsible AI development and usage, ensuring that AI technologies align with societal values and ethical standards.

Conclusion: 8.2.1. The Regulatory Tightrope: Fostering Innovation While Ensuring Accountability

As the AI landscape continues to evolve, governments stand as guardians of ethical innovation. By establishing balanced regulatory frameworks, they create an environment where innovation thrives without compromising ethical considerations. In this intricate dance, governments inspire businesses to navigate the complex terrain of AI deployment while fostering a culture that upholds transparency, fairness, and accountability. As we journey into the AI-driven future, it is the harmonious balance between innovation and ethics that paves the way for a transformative and responsible technological era.

8.2.2. Ethical AI at the Core: Ensuring Fairness and Bias Mitigation

The proliferation of AI technologies across various sectors underscores the importance of ethical AI development. Governments play a crucial role in establishing policies that prioritize fairness, transparency, and bias mitigation in AI systems. Here's a deeper dive into how these principles can be integrated into regulatory frameworks:

8.2.2.1. Transparency and Explainability Requirements: Fostering Ethical AI

Government regulations play a pivotal role in ensuring the ethical development and deployment of AI systems, particularly in sensitive domains like finance, healthcare, and criminal justice. The mandate for transparency and explainability is a foundational element of these regulations:

- **1. Clear Decision-Making Processes:** Regulations can stipulate that AI systems used in critical applications must have clearly defined decision-making processes. This means that organizations and developers must provide a detailed account of how the AI arrives at

specific conclusions or recommendations. Transparent processes enable users, regulators, and affected individuals to gain insights into AI reasoning.
- **2. Understandable Explanations:** AI algorithms should be required to provide explanations that are understandable by non-experts. This ensures that individuals affected by AI decisions can comprehend why a particular choice was made. For example, in healthcare, an AI system diagnosing a medical condition should be able to explain the reasoning behind its diagnosis in a way that both patients and healthcare providers can grasp.
- **3. Algorithmic Accountability:** Regulations can introduce the concept of algorithmic accountability, where organizations using AI systems are held responsible for the decisions those systems make. If an AI system denies a loan application, for instance, the organization must be able to explain the factors and criteria that led to that decision. This enhances accountability and ensures that AI is not used as a "black box."
- **4. Mitigating Unintended Consequences:** To prevent unintended consequences, organizations should be required to conduct impact assessments that evaluate how AI systems might affect different groups or communities. If potential biases or unfair outcomes are identified, corrective actions must be taken.
- **5. Human Oversight:** Regulations should also emphasize the importance of human oversight in AI decision-making. While AI can provide recommendations and insights, ultimate decisions in critical domains should remain under human control. This ensures that ethical considerations, empathy, and context are not overlooked.

- **6. Accessibility of Explanations:** Explanations generated by AI should be accessible to all, including individuals with disabilities. Ensuring that explanations are available in multiple formats, such as text, audio, or visual aids, enhances inclusivity and makes AI systems more widely usable.
- **7. Periodic Audits:** To ensure ongoing compliance, regulations can require organizations to conduct regular audits of their AI systems. These audits should assess the transparency and explainability of AI processes and identify areas for improvement.
- **8. Continuous Improvement:** Ethical AI development should be a dynamic process. Regulations can encourage organizations to continuously enhance the transparency and explainability of their AI systems as technology evolves and best practices emerge.

By incorporating these transparency and explainability requirements into regulations, governments can promote ethical AI practices, enhance trust in AI systems, and ensure that AI is used to benefit society responsibly and fairly.

8.2.2.2. Bias Identification and Rectification: Enforcing Fairness in AI

To uphold fairness and equity in AI systems, government regulations can play a pivotal role by instituting comprehensive bias identification and rectification measures:

- **1. Regular Audits and Assessments:** Regulations should mandate that organizations conducting AI operations regularly audit and assess their algorithms for bias. These assessments should encompass both data and decision-making processes to detect any discriminatory patterns or disparities.

- **2. Bias Detection Algorithms:** Organizations should be required to implement bias detection algorithms that scan AI systems for potential biases. These algorithms can flag instances where AI decisions disproportionately impact certain groups or exhibit discriminatory behavior.
- **3. Bias Reporting Mechanisms:** Regulations can stipulate the establishment of mechanisms for reporting and addressing bias concerns. Individuals or groups who suspect bias in AI systems should have accessible channels to voice their concerns.
- **4. Corrective Actions:** When biases are identified, organizations must take prompt corrective actions. These actions may include retraining AI models on more diverse and representative datasets, adjusting decision-making criteria, or fine-tuning algorithms to reduce bias.
- **5. Transparency in Bias Mitigation:** Organizations should transparently communicate their efforts to mitigate bias and the results of those efforts. This transparency builds trust and allows for external evaluation of their fairness measures.
- **6. Impact Assessments:** Regulations should encourage organizations to conduct impact assessments to understand how AI decisions affect different groups. If disparities are identified, organizations must address them and ensure that AI systems do not perpetuate discrimination.
- **7. Fairness Testing:** Fairness should be a core component of testing AI systems. Regulations can require organizations to demonstrate that their AI algorithms perform consistently across various demographic groups and do not discriminate.

- **8. Ongoing Monitoring:** Bias identification and rectification should not be viewed as a one-time task but as an ongoing commitment. Regulations can mandate continuous monitoring and improvement to ensure that AI systems remain fair and equitable.
- **9. Independent Audits:** To enhance accountability, regulations can also allow for independent audits of AI systems. Independent third parties can assess an organization's efforts to detect and rectify bias, providing an additional layer of oversight.
- **10. Ethical AI Officers:** Organizations may be required to designate individuals or teams responsible for ethical AI oversight. These officers can ensure that bias identification and rectification efforts are integrated into AI development and deployment processes.

By enforcing these bias identification and rectification regulations, governments can help mitigate the risk of AI perpetuating discrimination and bias, thereby promoting fairness and equity in AI systems.

8.2.2.3. Audits for Algorithmic Fairness: Ensuring Fair AI Outputs

To safeguard fairness in AI systems, government regulations can mandate the regular auditing of algorithms to assess and rectify bias or discrimination. Here's how such audits can be implemented:

- **1. Independent Auditing Bodies:** Regulations should require organizations to engage independent auditing bodies or experts with expertise in algorithmic fairness. These auditors can impartially assess AI systems for bias and discrimination.
- **2. Regular Auditing Schedule:** Organizations must conduct audits on a predetermined schedule, ensuring

that AI systems are consistently evaluated for fairness. The frequency of audits should align with the criticality and impact of the AI application.
- **3. Comprehensive Data Review:** Audits should encompass a comprehensive review of the data used to train and test AI models. This includes assessing the representativeness and diversity of training data to identify potential biases.
- **4. Bias Detection Algorithms:** Auditors can employ specialized bias detection algorithms to scan AI systems for any disparities in their outputs. These algorithms can help pinpoint instances where bias or discrimination may exist.
- **5. Explainability Assessment:** Auditors should evaluate the explainability of AI decisions, ensuring that the rationale behind AI outputs can be understood and justified.
- **6. Impact Assessment:** Audits should include an impact assessment to determine whether AI systems disproportionately affect specific demographic groups or communities. If disparities are detected, corrective actions must be taken.
- **7. Corrective Measures:** When bias or discrimination is identified, organizations should be required to take corrective measures. This may involve retraining AI models on more diverse datasets, modifying decision criteria, or fine-tuning algorithms to reduce bias.
- **8. Transparency and Reporting:** Auditing results, along with any corrective actions taken, should be transparently reported to relevant stakeholders, regulatory bodies, and the public.
- **9. Continuous Improvement:** Organizations should demonstrate a commitment to continuous improvement by addressing any issues identified in

audits and actively working to enhance algorithmic fairness.

- **10. Remediation Plans:** In cases where significant bias or discrimination is found, regulations can require organizations to develop and implement remediation plans. These plans should outline steps to rectify the issues and prevent their recurrence.
- **11. Accountability Measures:** Regulations should establish accountability measures for organizations that fail to address bias or discrimination adequately. Penalties, fines, or other consequences can incentivize compliance with auditing requirements.

By enforcing audits for algorithmic fairness, governments can promote transparency, accountability, and ethical AI practices, ultimately ensuring that AI systems produce fair and unbiased outcomes. These audits serve as a critical safeguard against discriminatory AI behavior.

8.2.2.4. Inclusive Training Data: Ensuring Fair and Representative AI Learning

To prevent bias in AI systems, government regulations can stipulate the use of inclusive and representative training data. Here's how such regulations can be implemented:

- **1. Data Sourcing Guidelines:** Regulations should provide guidelines for sourcing training data that is diverse and representative of the population or domain the AI system will operate in.
- **2. Data Auditing:** Organizations should conduct audits of their training data to identify potential biases or underrepresentation of specific groups or characteristics.
- **3. Demographic and Contextual Diversity:** Regulations can require organizations to ensure that training data

includes demographic diversity (e.g., age, gender, race) and contextual diversity (e.g., geographic locations, cultural factors).
- **4. Bias Mitigation Strategies:** Organizations must implement strategies to mitigate bias in training data, such as data preprocessing techniques or the use of debiasing algorithms.
- **5. Data Documentation:** Organizations should maintain detailed documentation of their training data sources, preprocessing steps, and any bias mitigation measures applied. This documentation should be available for review by auditing bodies.
- **6. Third-Party Verification:** To ensure compliance, regulations can allow for third-party verification or auditing of training data practices.
- **7. Periodic Data Review:** Organizations should conduct periodic reviews of their training data to account for evolving demographics and contexts, updating the data as needed.
- **8. Diverse Data Experts:** Regulations can encourage organizations to seek input from diverse teams of data experts who can provide insights into potential biases or gaps in training data.
- **9. Accountability Measures:** Establishing consequences for organizations that fail to adhere to inclusive training data requirements can incentivize compliance.
- **10. Transparency:** Regulations should mandate transparency in the use of training data, ensuring that stakeholders and the public have insight into the data sources and processing methods.

By enforcing the use of inclusive and representative training data, government regulations can significantly reduce the risk of bias in AI systems. This approach fosters fairness, accuracy, and equitable outcomes in AI decision-making processes.

8.2.2.5. Reporting, Accountability, and Bias Mitigation in AI: Building Trust Through Transparency

To ensure fairness and bias mitigation in AI systems, government regulations can mandate reporting and accountability measures. Here's how such regulations can be structured:

- **1. Reporting Requirements:** Organizations that deploy AI systems in critical applications must be required to submit regular reports on their efforts to ensure fairness and bias mitigation. These reports should include:
    - Details of the steps taken to identify and rectify biases in AI algorithms.
    - Outcomes of audits and assessments related to bias detection.
    - Actions taken to address identified bias issues.
    - Updates on the organization's ongoing efforts to prevent and mitigate bias.
- **2. Frequency of Reporting:** Regulations should specify the frequency of reporting, such as quarterly or annually, to ensure that organizations provide consistent updates on their bias mitigation measures.
- **3. Independent Audits:** To maintain transparency and accountability, organizations may be required to undergo independent audits of their AI systems and bias mitigation practices. These audits can be conducted by third-party organizations with expertise in AI ethics.
- **4. Penalties for Non-Compliance:** Regulations should establish penalties for organizations that fail to address biases adequately or provide inaccurate or incomplete reports. Penalties can include fines, restrictions on AI system usage, or legal consequences.

- **5. Public Accessibility:** Reports on bias mitigation efforts should be made publicly accessible, allowing stakeholders, researchers, and the general public to scrutinize organizations' actions and progress.
- **6. Whistleblower Protection:** Regulations can include provisions to protect whistleblowers who report bias or unethical practices within organizations. This protection encourages individuals to come forward with concerns.
- **7. Review and Accountability Boards:** Establishing review boards or committees responsible for overseeing organizations' compliance with bias mitigation regulations can ensure impartial assessment and enforcement.
- **8. Remediation Plans:** Organizations found in violation of bias mitigation regulations should be required to develop and implement remediation plans to rectify identified issues.
- **9. Continuous Improvement:** Regulations should encourage organizations to continuously improve their bias mitigation efforts by incorporating lessons learned from audits and assessments.
- **10. Public Awareness Campaigns:** Governments can run public awareness campaigns to inform citizens about AI bias, their rights in AI interactions, and how to report instances of bias.

By enforcing reporting and accountability measures, government regulations can promote transparency and trust in AI systems, reducing the risk of bias and discrimination in critical applications. These measures also provide a means for organizations to demonstrate their commitment to ethical AI development.

8.2.2.6. Promoting Ethical AI through Ongoing Education and Training: A Regulatory Framework

To uphold ethical AI practices, regulations can emphasize the importance of ongoing education and training for AI professionals. Here's how such regulations can be structured:

- **1. Mandatory Training Programs:** Regulations should require organizations developing or deploying AI systems to establish mandatory training programs for AI developers, data scientists, and operators. These programs should cover topics such as AI ethics, bias mitigation techniques, and responsible AI development.
- **2. Curriculum Requirements:** Regulations can specify the curriculum content for AI ethics and bias mitigation training programs. This content should be comprehensive and regularly updated to align with evolving ethical considerations and best practices.
- **3. Continuing Education:** Organizations should be mandated to provide opportunities for AI professionals to engage in continuing education. This ensures that individuals stay current with the latest developments in AI ethics and responsible AI practices.
- **4. Certification Standards:** Regulations can establish certification standards for AI professionals, indicating their proficiency in ethical AI development and bias mitigation. Certification can serve as a benchmark for ethical expertise within the industry.
- **5. Reporting and Compliance:** Organizations should be required to report on the number of professionals who have undergone training and provide evidence of compliance with mandatory education and certification standards.
- **6. Third-Party Audits:** Independent third-party organizations or regulatory bodies can conduct audits to assess organizations' compliance with education and training requirements. These audits ensure that

organizations are not only offering training but also effectively implementing it.
- **7. Whistleblower Protection:** Regulations should include provisions to protect whistleblowers who report instances of inadequate training or ethical violations within organizations. This protection encourages transparency and accountability.
- **8. Penalties for Non-Compliance:** Regulations can establish penalties for organizations that fail to provide adequate training or comply with certification standards. Penalties may include fines, suspension of AI system usage, or legal consequences.
- **9. Public Awareness Initiatives:** Governments can run public awareness campaigns to inform citizens about the importance of AI ethics and the role of education and training in ensuring responsible AI development.
- **10. Research and Development:** Regulations can encourage organizations to allocate resources for research and development in AI ethics, promoting innovation in ethical AI practices.

By implementing these regulatory measures, governments can promote a culture of ethical AI development and ensure that AI professionals are well-equipped to address bias and ethical considerations throughout the AI development lifecycle.

8.2.2.7. Public Oversight and Input in AI Ethics: A Regulatory Framework

To ensure that AI ethics policies are aligned with public values and concerns, regulations can establish mechanisms for public oversight and input. Here's how such regulations can be structured:

- **1. Advisory Boards:** Governments can mandate the creation of AI ethics advisory boards comprising

experts, stakeholders, and members of the public. These boards can provide guidance and recommendations on AI ethics policies, ensuring a diverse range of perspectives.
- **2. Public Consultations:** Regulations can require government agencies and organizations developing or deploying AI systems to conduct public consultations on AI ethics issues. These consultations can solicit input on topics such as bias mitigation, data privacy, and AI transparency.
- **3. Transparency Requirements:** Regulations should stipulate transparency requirements for AI developers and operators. This includes disclosing information about AI system functionality, data usage, and decision-making processes to the public.
- **4. Accessibility:** Public consultations and advisory board meetings should be accessible to a wide range of participants, including those with disabilities or language barriers. Accommodations should be made to facilitate inclusive participation.
- **5. Reporting Mechanisms:** Organizations deploying AI systems should establish mechanisms for the public to report concerns related to AI ethics. These mechanisms should be easily accessible and provide assurance that reported issues will be addressed.
- **6. Periodic Reviews:** Regulations can mandate periodic reviews of AI ethics policies with a focus on public input. These reviews ensure that policies remain relevant and responsive to evolving societal values and technological advancements.
- **7. Whistleblower Protection:** Regulations should include provisions to protect whistleblowers who report ethical violations or concerns related to AI systems.

Protection encourages individuals to come forward with information.
- **8. Public Awareness Initiatives:** Governments can run public awareness campaigns to educate citizens about the importance of AI ethics and their role in providing input and oversight. These campaigns promote informed participation.
- **9. Impact Assessments:** Regulations can require organizations to conduct AI ethics impact assessments, including the potential societal, ethical, and legal implications of AI systems. The results of these assessments should be made public.
- **10. Enforcement:** Regulations should outline the consequences for organizations that do not comply with public oversight and input requirements. Penalties may include fines, suspension of AI system usage, or legal action.

By implementing these regulatory measures, governments ensure that AI ethics policies are not developed in isolation but in collaboration with the public, fostering trust and accountability in AI technologies.

By embedding ethics, fairness, and bias mitigation into regulatory frameworks, governments not only provide clear guidelines for responsible AI development but also foster a culture of inclusivity and fairness. These policies help ensure that AI technologies benefit all members of society and do not perpetuate or exacerbate existing inequalities or biases.

8.2.3. Incentivizing Technological Advancement: AI Research and Implementation Incentives

To incentivize AI research and implementation, governments can employ a multifaceted approach that encourages a broad spectrum of stakeholders to engage in AI-driven growth. Here's a strategic framework for these incentives:

1. Research Grants and Funding:

- **Competitive Research Grants:** Government agencies can offer competitive grants to research institutions, universities, and AI-focused startups. These grants can fund AI research projects with the potential for significant societal impact.

- **Collaborative Research Initiatives:** Encourage collaboration between public and private sectors by providing matching funds for joint AI research ventures.

2. Tax Benefits and Credits:

- **R&D Tax Credits:** Establish tax credits for businesses engaged in AI research and development activities. These credits can offset a portion of R&D expenses, reducing the financial burden on companies.

- **Investment Tax Incentives:** Offer tax incentives for investments in AI technologies, including hardware, software, and infrastructure. These incentives stimulate private-sector investment in AI.

3. Innovation Hubs and Clusters:

- **AI Innovation Hubs:** Create physical or virtual AI innovation hubs where startups, researchers, and businesses can collaborate and access resources. These hubs facilitate knowledge exchange and innovation.

- **Cluster Development:** Support the formation of AI clusters or ecosystems in specific regions, encouraging knowledge sharing and talent retention.

4. Education and Talent Development:

- **Scholarships and Grants:** Offer scholarships and grants to students pursuing AI-related fields to foster a pipeline of skilled AI professionals.

- **Training and Skill Development:** Fund training programs and initiatives that upskill the existing workforce in AI-related competencies.

5. Intellectual Property Support:

- **Patent Acceleration:** Implement expedited patent examination processes for AI-related inventions, reducing the time-to-market for innovative AI technologies.

- **IP Protection:** Enhance IP protection for AI innovations, reassuring businesses that their investments in AI will be safeguarded.

6. Public-Private Partnerships:

- **Joint Initiatives:** Establish collaborative projects between government agencies and private companies to address societal challenges using AI solutions.

- **Innovation Challenges:** Organize innovation challenges and competitions that encourage AI startups and researchers to develop solutions for pressing issues.

7. Access to Data and Resources:

- **Data Sharing Initiatives:** Create platforms for sharing anonymized datasets for AI research, promoting data-driven innovation.

- **AI Infrastructure:** Provide access to high-performance computing resources and AI-specific infrastructure for research and development.

8. Export and Trade Support:

- **Export Promotion:** Assist AI companies in reaching global markets by offering export support programs and market entry facilitation.

- **Trade Agreements:** Negotiate international agreements that facilitate the cross-border exchange of AI-related technologies and services.

9. Regulatory Sandboxes:

- **AI Regulatory Sandboxes:** Establish regulatory sandboxes where AI startups and innovators can test their solutions in a controlled environment with reduced regulatory barriers.

10. Impact Assessment Funds:

- **Societal Impact Assessment:** Allocate funds for research that evaluates the societal impact of AI technologies, ensuring responsible deployment.

By strategically implementing these incentives, governments can create an environment where AI research and implementation thrive, contributing to economic growth, technological advancement, and societal well-being.

8.2.4. Collaboration for a Flourishing Ecosystem: Government-Industry-Academia Synergy

Effective collaboration among government, industry, and academia is instrumental in fostering a thriving AI ecosystem. Here's a framework outlining key areas of synergy:

1. Research and Development Collaborations:

- **Joint Research Projects:** Facilitate partnerships between academia and industry for collaborative research endeavors. Government funding can support these projects, addressing real-world challenges with AI solutions.

- **Technology Transfer:** Create mechanisms for the seamless transfer of AI technologies developed in academic institutions to the private sector, promoting innovation and commercialization.

2. Talent Development and Education:

- **Curriculum Alignment:** Collaborate with universities and industry to align educational curricula with the skills required for the AI job market. Ensure that academic programs reflect industry needs.

- **Internship Programs:** Promote internship and apprenticeship programs that connect students with industry professionals, offering real-world experience in AI-related roles.

3. Innovation Hubs and Incubators:

- **Establishment of Innovation Centers:** Create innovation hubs or centers where startups, researchers, and industry experts can collaborate. These hubs offer shared resources and facilitate knowledge exchange.

- **Incubation Support:** Provide funding and resources to AI-focused incubators and accelerators, nurturing the growth of startups in the AI sector.

4. Data Sharing and Access:

- **Secure Data Sharing Platforms:** Develop secure and standardized platforms for sharing anonymized data between government agencies, industry, and researchers. These platforms facilitate data-driven AI research.

- **Data Access Policies:** Implement policies that enable AI researchers, while respecting privacy and security, to access government-held data for research purposes.

5. Regulatory Frameworks and Standards:

- **Collaborative Regulation:** Engage industry and academia in the development of AI regulatory frameworks. Leverage their expertise to create balanced regulations that foster innovation while ensuring ethical AI deployment.

- **Standardization Committees:** Establish committees that bring together stakeholders to define AI standards, ensuring interoperability and safety in AI technologies.

6. Public-Private Funding Initiatives:

- **Joint Funding Programs:** Collaborate with industry partners to co-fund AI research and development projects. These programs can focus on addressing specific societal challenges or advancing cutting-edge technologies.

- **Venture Funds:** Establish venture funds that combine public and private capital to invest in AI startups and innovative AI projects.

7. Policy Feedback Mechanisms:

- **Industry and Academic Input:** Create channels for industry and academia to provide input and feedback on AI-related policies and regulations. This ensures that policies align with practical needs and emerging trends.

8. Ethical AI Initiatives:

- **Ethics Committees:** Form multidisciplinary ethics committees that include representatives from academia, industry, and government to address ethical considerations in AI development.

- **Ethical Guidelines:** Collaboratively develop ethical guidelines for AI development and deployment, emphasizing transparency, fairness, and accountability.

9. Knowledge Dissemination:

- **Conferences and Seminars:** Support AI-related conferences, seminars, and knowledge-sharing events that bring together stakeholders from government, industry, and academia to exchange insights and best practices.

10. Public Awareness and Education:

- **Collaborative Awareness Campaigns:** Collaborate on public awareness campaigns to educate citizens about AI's potential and its ethical implications. This ensures informed public discourse.

By fostering synergy among government, industry, and academia, governments can create a dynamic AI ecosystem that encourages innovation, responsible AI development, and knowledge dissemination. This collaborative approach accelerates AI adoption, drives economic growth, and addresses societal challenges in a coordinated manner.

8.2.5. Data Privacy and Security: Safeguarding Digital Sovereignty

Governments play a pivotal role in ensuring data privacy and security in the AI-driven era. Here's a framework for enacting robust regulations to safeguard digital sovereignty:

1. Comprehensive Data Privacy Laws:

- **Legislation Development:** Create and regularly update comprehensive data privacy laws that establish clear guidelines for the collection, processing, and storage of personal data.

- **Data Ownership:** Clarify data ownership rights, emphasizing that individuals have control over their personal data, including the right to access, modify, and delete it.

2. Consent and Transparency:

- **Informed Consent:** Enforce strict requirements for obtaining informed consent from individuals before collecting and processing their data. Make it mandatory for organizations to clearly explain the purposes of data collection.

- **Transparency Obligations:** Mandate transparency in data processing, ensuring that individuals can easily access information about what data is collected and how it is used.

3. Data Minimization and Purpose Limitation:

- **Data Minimization Principle:** Promote the principle of data minimization, where organizations only collect and retain data that is necessary for the stated purpose.

- **Purpose Limitation:** Specify that data can only be used for the purpose for which it was collected, preventing unauthorized or secondary uses.

4. Strong Security Measures:

- **Data Encryption:** Encourage the use of encryption technologies to protect data during storage and transmission.

- **Incident Reporting:** Require organizations to promptly report data breaches and security incidents to both affected individuals and regulatory authorities.

5. Cross-Border Data Transfers:

- **International Data Transfer Agreements:** Establish agreements and standards for cross-border data transfers to ensure that data remains protected when it crosses jurisdictional boundaries.

- **Data Localization:** Consider policies that require certain sensitive data to be stored within national borders.

6. Data Protection Officers (DPOs):

- **Appointment of DPOs:** Require organizations handling large volumes of personal data to appoint Data Protection Officers responsible for ensuring compliance with data privacy laws.

7. Penalties and Enforcement:

- **Fines and Penalties:** Institute significant fines for organizations found in violation of data privacy regulations, with penalties escalating for repeat offenses.

- **Independent Regulators:** Establish independent data protection authorities responsible for enforcing data privacy laws.

8. Ethical AI Impact Assessments:

- **Ethical Review Boards:** Encourage organizations, especially those developing AI systems, to establish ethical review boards that assess the potential ethical implications of data usage and AI deployment.

9. Public Awareness and Education:

- **Data Literacy Programs:** Invest in public awareness campaigns and educational programs that enhance citizens' understanding of data privacy and security, empowering them to protect their digital sovereignty.

10. International Collaboration:

- **Harmonization Efforts:** Collaborate with international counterparts to align data privacy standards, fostering consistency and coherence in global data protection.

These comprehensive regulations ensure that individuals' digital sovereignty is upheld, personal data is handled responsibly, and trust in the AI ecosystem is maintained. Balancing data utilization with privacy rights is critical for a sustainable and ethical AI-driven future.

Conclusion: 8.2. Government Policies: Balancing Innovation, Regulation, and Collaboration

In the intricate tapestry of the AI landscape, governments wield the brush that paints the canvas of the future. By crafting policies that prioritize ethical AI, foster innovation, and encourage collaboration, governments lay the foundation for a future where technology and humanity coexist harmoniously. As governments navigate this uncharted territory, their policies become the blueprint that guides innovation, preserves societal values, and shapes a world where AI serves as a force for progress and human betterment.

8.3. Individual Actions: The Transformative Role of Lifelong Learning and Adaptability

In the AI-driven future, individual actions are transformative, shaping personal and professional success. Here's a closer look at how lifelong learning and adaptability play a pivotal role:

1. Lifelong Learning

Lifelong learning is the cornerstone of personal and professional growth in the age of AI. Here's an expanded view of how individuals can embrace this concept:

- **Continuous Skill Acquisition:** Lifelong learning begins with the recognition that acquiring new skills and knowledge should be an ongoing journey, not limited to formal education. Individuals should cultivate a mindset that values learning throughout their lives, regardless of age or career stage.
- **Diverse Learning Channels:** To support lifelong learning, individuals should leverage a wide range of learning channels and resources. This includes traditional education, online courses, workshops, seminars, webinars, books, podcasts, and mentorship programs.

The diversity of these channels allows individuals to tailor their learning experiences to their specific needs and interests.

- **Self-Directed Learning:** Lifelong learners take ownership of their education. They set personal learning goals, identify areas they want to explore, and create structured plans to achieve those goals. Self-directed learning empowers individuals to pursue knowledge and skills that are meaningful to them.
- **Adaptive Learning:** With technology playing a significant role in education, individuals can benefit from adaptive learning platforms. These systems use AI algorithms to personalize learning experiences, adapting content and pacing to the individual's abilities and needs.
- **Interdisciplinary Learning:** The AI-driven future is interdisciplinary, and individuals can thrive by gaining expertise in multiple domains. Lifelong learners should be open to exploring subjects beyond their immediate fields, fostering creativity and the ability to connect ideas from various disciplines.
- **Credentialing and Certification**: Many online courses and programs offer certifications and credentials. These can be valuable for career advancement and demonstrate expertise in specific areas. Lifelong learners should consider earning certifications that align with their goals.
- **Professional Networks:** Participation in professional organizations, industry conferences, and networking events can provide valuable learning opportunities. Engaging with peers and experts in one's field fosters knowledge exchange and keeps individuals informed about industry trends.

- **Learning from Failure:** Lifelong learning also involves embracing failure as a learning opportunity. When individuals encounter setbacks or challenges, they should reflect on these experiences, identify lessons learned, and apply that knowledge to future endeavors.
- **Mentorship and Coaching:** Seeking guidance from mentors and coaches can accelerate the learning process. Experienced mentors can offer insights, share their experiences, and provide valuable feedback to help individuals on their learning journeys.
- **Balancing Formal and Informal Learning:** Lifelong learners should strike a balance between formal and informal learning. While formal education and structured courses are important, informal learning through reading, exploring hobbies, or engaging in discussions with peers can also expand one's horizons.
- **Digital Literacy:** In an increasingly digital world, individuals should develop digital literacy skills. This includes the ability to navigate online resources, critically evaluate information, and use digital tools for learning effectively.

By embracing lifelong learning through these strategies, individuals can adapt to the evolving demands of the AI-driven future, remain competitive in the job market, and find fulfillment in their personal growth journeys.

2. Adaptability

Adaptability is a crucial trait for individuals in the AI-driven future. Here's an extended perspective on how adaptability can empower individuals:

- **Embracing Change:** Adaptability begins with a willingness to embrace change rather than resist it. Individuals should recognize that change is inevitable in a world driven by AI and technology. Instead of fearing change, they should view it as an opportunity for growth and innovation.
- **Flexibility in Career Paths:** The careers of the future may not follow linear paths. Adaptability involves being open to exploring diverse career trajectories. Individuals should be willing to pivot, switch industries, and take on new roles as technology reshapes job markets. This flexibility can lead to exciting opportunities and personal reinvention.
- **Resilience in the Face of Challenges:** Challenges and setbacks are part of any journey. Adaptability equips individuals with the resilience to bounce back from failures and setbacks. It involves maintaining a positive outlook, learning from experiences, and using adversity as a stepping stone to future success.
- **Continuous Self-Assessment:** Self-assessment is a critical component of adaptability. Individuals should regularly evaluate their skills, strengths, and areas for improvement. This self-awareness enables them to proactively identify areas where they need to adapt and grow.
- **Agility in Learning:** Adaptability and lifelong learning go hand in hand. An agile learner quickly acquires new skills and knowledge as circumstances evolve. This agility enables individuals to stay relevant in dynamic industries and take advantage of emerging opportunities.
- **Openness to Feedback:** Adaptability requires an openness to feedback. Constructive criticism from mentors, peers, or supervisors can provide valuable

insights for improvement. Individuals should actively seek feedback and use it to refine their skills and approaches.

- **Cultivating a Growth Mindset:** A growth mindset is the belief that abilities and intelligence can be developed with effort and learning. Cultivating a growth mindset encourages individuals to see challenges as opportunities to learn and improve. It fosters resilience and a willingness to adapt.
- **Networking and Collaboration:** Adaptability often involves collaboration and networking. Building a diverse professional network can expose individuals to different perspectives and ideas. Collaborating with others can lead to innovative solutions and adaptability through collective knowledge.
- **Staying Informed:** Remaining informed about industry trends, technological advancements, and global developments is crucial for adaptability. Individuals should proactively seek information through various sources, including news, research, and professional networks.
- **Seeking New Experiences:** Adaptability can be enhanced by seeking new experiences outside one's comfort zone. This might involve taking on challenging projects, volunteering for leadership roles, or pursuing opportunities in different locations or cultures.
- **Balancing Tradition and Innovation:** In an AI-driven future, individuals can balance tradition and innovation. While embracing new technologies and approaches, they can also draw on timeless principles, ethics, and values that remain relevant in a changing world.
- **Mental and Emotional Resilience:** Adaptability involves mental and emotional resilience. Individuals should develop coping strategies to manage stress,

uncertainty, and ambiguity effectively. Practices such as mindfulness, meditation, and emotional intelligence can enhance adaptability.

By cultivating adaptability, individuals can navigate the ever-changing landscape of the AI-driven future with confidence, creativity, and a sense of purpose. Adaptability is not just a skill; it's a mindset that empowers individuals to thrive in the face of complexity and transformation.

3. Overcoming the Fear of Change

Overcoming the fear of change is a critical aspect of adaptability, especially in the context of an AI-driven future. Here's a more in-depth exploration of this important point:

- **Understanding the Fear of Change:** The fear of change is a natural human response to uncertainty. It often stems from the unknown and the perceived risks associated with departing from the familiar. In an AI-driven world, where technological advancements are rapid, change is constant. Acknowledging this fear is the first step in addressing it.
- **Cultivating a Growth Mindset:** A growth mindset, as coined by psychologist Carol Dweck, involves believing that abilities and intelligence can be developed through dedication and hard work. Embracing a growth mindset can help individuals see change as an opportunity for learning and improvement rather than a threat. This mindset shift can make change more approachable and less intimidating.

- **Setting Realistic Expectations:** Change often involves challenges and setbacks. It's important to set realistic expectations and recognize that not every change will lead to immediate success. Understanding that there might be obstacles along the way allows individuals to persevere through difficulties.
- **Breaking Change into Manageable Steps:** Change can be overwhelming when viewed as a massive, all-encompassing transformation. To overcome this fear, individuals can break change into smaller, manageable steps or milestones. This incremental approach makes progress tangible and less intimidating.
- **Seeking Support and Guidance:** Individuals should not hesitate to seek support and guidance when facing change. This support can come from mentors, coaches, colleagues, or friends who have experience navigating similar transitions. Their insights and encouragement can be invaluable.
- **Visualizing Success:** Visualization techniques involve mentally picturing a successful outcome. Visualizing a positive result of the change can reduce anxiety and build confidence. This practice can be especially helpful in overcoming the fear of change.
- **Developing Resilience:** Resilience is the ability to bounce back from adversity. Building resilience involves developing coping strategies to manage stress and setbacks effectively. Techniques such as mindfulness, meditation, and exercise can enhance emotional resilience and help individuals face change with greater equanimity.
- **Staying Informed:** Knowledge is a powerful antidote to fear. Staying informed about the changes, their reasons, and their potential benefits can demystify the process.

Understanding the context and purpose behind the change can make it more palatable.

- **Recognizing Past Successes:** Reflecting on past experiences of successfully navigating change can boost confidence. Individuals should remind themselves of their past accomplishments and how they overcame challenges. This reminder reinforces the belief in their ability to adapt.
- **Embracing a Supportive Environment:** Creating or seeking out a supportive environment can ease the fear of change. This includes having open and transparent communication within organizations or communities undergoing change. When individuals feel that their concerns are heard and addressed, they are more likely to embrace change positively.
- **Continuous Learning:** As mentioned earlier, lifelong learning is an essential aspect of adaptability. When individuals continuously acquire new skills and knowledge, they become better equipped to face change confidently. Learning can demystify the unknown and empower individuals to navigate new terrain.

Overcoming the fear of change is not a one-time effort but an ongoing journey. It requires self-awareness, patience, and a willingness to step out of one's comfort zone. In an AI-driven future, where change is the norm, individuals who can conquer this fear are better positioned to thrive and contribute meaningfully to their personal and professional lives.

4. Adapting to Technological Progress

Adapting to technological progress is essential in an era where AI is rapidly reshaping industries and societies. Here's an expanded discussion on this topic:

- **Understanding the Pace of Technological Progress:** The speed at which technology, including AI, is advancing is unprecedented. Innovations that used to take decades are now occurring within years, if not months. This pace of progress can be both exciting and intimidating. Understanding this pace is crucial for individuals to adapt effectively.
- **Continuous Learning and Upskilling:** One of the most practical ways to adapt to technological progress is through continuous learning and upskilling. This involves regularly updating one's knowledge and skills to stay relevant in a changing job market. It's not limited to formal education; it can also include online courses, workshops, and self-directed learning.
- **Tech Literacy:** In a tech-driven world, being tech literate is increasingly important. This doesn't mean becoming a computer programmer, but rather understanding the basics of how technology works, including AI. Tech literacy empowers individuals to make informed decisions about the technology they use and to communicate effectively in a tech-savvy environment.
- **Embracing Change as an Opportunity:** Adapting to technological progress requires a mindset shift. Instead of viewing change as a threat, individuals can embrace it as an opportunity for growth and innovation. This mindset encourages curiosity, exploration, and a willingness to experiment with new technologies.
- **Networking and Collaboration:** Adapting to technological progress is not a solitary endeavor. Networking and collaboration are vital. Engaging with peers, industry groups, and professional networks can

provide insights, support, and opportunities for collaboration on projects that leverage new technologies.
- **Cross-Disciplinary Skills:** Many of the most transformative innovations happen at the intersections of different fields. Individuals who can apply their expertise across multiple disciplines are often better equipped to harness the potential of new technologies. For example, combining knowledge of AI with healthcare or environmental science can lead to groundbreaking solutions.
- **Anticipating Trends:** Keeping an eye on technological trends is essential for proactive adaptation. Individuals can anticipate how emerging technologies might impact their field or industry and prepare accordingly. For example, understanding the potential applications of AI in healthcare can help medical professionals adapt to AI-assisted diagnostics and treatments.
- **Ethical Considerations:** As technology advances, ethical considerations become increasingly important. Adapting to technological progress should involve a deep understanding of the ethical implications of new technologies. Individuals who can navigate these ethical challenges are in high demand.
- **Entrepreneurship and Innovation:** For some, adapting to technological progress may involve entrepreneurship and innovation. Identifying unmet needs and creating solutions, often tech-driven ones, can be a way to thrive in a changing landscape.
- **Resilience:** Adaptation also requires resilience. It's important to recognize that not every attempt to adapt will be immediately successful. There will be setbacks and failures along the way. Resilience involves bouncing

back from these challenges and using them as opportunities for learning and growth.
- **Embracing Lifelong Learning:** Lifelong learning, which was mentioned earlier, is a fundamental part of adapting to technological progress. It's not a one-time effort but a lifelong commitment to staying informed and relevant in an ever-changing world.

In conclusion, adapting to technological progress is not just about acquiring new technical skills; it's about adopting a mindset of curiosity, learning, and adaptability. It's a commitment to embracing change as an opportunity rather than a threat and a recognition that in an AI-driven future, the ability to adapt will be one of the most valuable skills an individual can possess

5. Personal Growth and Fulfillment

Personal growth and fulfillment are at the heart of adapting to technological progress in an AI-driven world. Here's an expanded discussion on this topic:

- **Self-Discovery:** Adapting to technological progress often involves a journey of self-discovery. As individuals explore new skills, technologies, and opportunities, they may uncover hidden passions and talents. This process of self-discovery can be deeply fulfilling and lead to more purposeful career choices.
- **Exploring Interests:** AI and automation can alleviate the burden of routine tasks, freeing up time for individuals to explore their interests. Whether it's pursuing a hobby, starting a side business, or engaging in creative endeavors, technology can be an enabler of personal passions.

- **Flexibility in Work-Life Integration:** The traditional boundaries between work and personal life are evolving, thanks to AI and remote work. Individuals can adapt by finding a work-life balance that suits their needs and allows for personal growth. This might involve flexible work hours or remote work arrangements.
- **Lifelong Learning as a Source of Fulfillment:** Lifelong learning, as discussed earlier, is not just about career advancement. It can also be a source of personal fulfillment. Learning new languages, exploring the arts, or delving into history can enrich one's life and provide a sense of accomplishment.
- **Meaningful Contributions:** Adapting to technological progress can also mean seeking more meaningful and purposeful work. AI can handle many routine tasks, but it often falls short in areas that require empathy, creativity, and complex problem-solving. Individuals can find fulfillment in roles that leverage these uniquely human qualities.
- **Building Resilience:** Personal growth involves building resilience to navigate the challenges that come with technological change. Resilience enables individuals to bounce back from setbacks and view failures as opportunities for learning and growth.
- **Mental and Emotional Well-Being:** Adapting to technological progress includes taking care of mental and emotional well-being. The fast-paced nature of change can be stressful, and mindfulness practices, meditation, and seeking support from mental health professionals can contribute to overall fulfillment.
- **Community and Connection:** Technology can facilitate connections with like-minded individuals and communities. Engaging with communities that share

common interests or goals can enhance personal growth and provide a sense of belonging.
- **Contribution to Society:** Many find fulfillment in contributing to the betterment of society. Adapting to technological progress may involve using one's skills and resources to address pressing societal challenges, such as climate change, healthcare disparities, or education access.
- **Balancing Technology Use:** While adapting to technology, it's essential to strike a balance. Overuse of technology, such as excessive screen time or social media consumption, can hinder personal growth and fulfillment. Being mindful of technology use is part of the adaptation process.

In conclusion, adapting to technological progress is not solely about career advancement or technical skills. It's a holistic journey that encompasses self-discovery, personal growth, and fulfillment. Embracing the opportunities that technology offers while maintaining a focus on well-being and meaningful contributions can lead to a rich and satisfying life in an AI-driven future.

6. Amplifying Contributions

Amplifying contributions in an AI-driven world involves leveraging technology to make a more significant impact in various areas of life. Here's an expanded discussion:

- **Leveraging Technology for Impact:** Technology, including AI, provides tools and platforms that can amplify an individual's contributions. For example, AI-driven data analysis can help nonprofit organizations make more informed decisions and allocate resources

more efficiently, ultimately increasing their impact on pressing social issues.
- **Scaling Efforts:** Technology enables individuals to scale their efforts beyond what would be possible manually. Entrepreneurs can use e-commerce platforms and digital marketing to reach a global audience, while educators can deliver online courses to students worldwide. AI can automate repetitive tasks, allowing professionals to focus on strategic and creative aspects of their work.
- **Collaboration with AI:** Collaboration with AI systems can lead to amplified contributions. AI can assist professionals in various fields, from healthcare to research, by providing insights and recommendations based on vast datasets. This collaboration between human expertise and AI capabilities can result in breakthroughs and innovations that might not be achievable by humans alone.
- **Entrepreneurship and Innovation:** AI can empower entrepreneurs to develop innovative solutions to societal challenges. Startups and innovators can leverage AI to create products and services that address unmet needs, from healthcare diagnostics to sustainability solutions. These innovations have the potential to disrupt industries and drive positive change.
- **Social Impact Initiatives:** Many individuals are drawn to social impact initiatives, such as addressing environmental issues, poverty, or access to education. AI can be a powerful tool in advancing these causes. For instance, AI-powered sensors can monitor environmental conditions, while machine learning algorithms can analyze data to identify patterns and potential solutions.

- **Education and Awareness:** Technology, including social media and online platforms, provides a means to raise awareness about important issues. Advocates and activists can use digital channels to reach a broad audience and mobilize support for various causes, amplifying their voices and impact.
- **Philanthropy and Giving:** Technology has transformed philanthropy, making it easier for individuals to contribute to charitable causes. Online fundraising platforms, crowdfunding, and digital wallets enable people to donate to organizations and initiatives they care about, amplifying the resources available for charitable work.
- **Supporting Grassroots Movements:** Grassroots movements often rely on technology for organization, communication, and advocacy. Social media platforms can help grassroots activists connect with supporters, coordinate events, and amplify their messages, leading to more significant social and political impact.
- **Research and Innovation:** In fields like science and healthcare, AI accelerates research and innovation. Scientists and researchers can use AI algorithms to process and analyze vast datasets, leading to discoveries and advancements that have far-reaching implications.
- **Global Connectivity:** The interconnectedness of the world through technology means that individuals can have an impact on a global scale. Collaboration with people from diverse backgrounds and regions can lead to innovative solutions and a broader perspective on pressing global challenges.

In summary, amplifying contributions in an AI-driven world involves harnessing technology and AI capabilities to extend one's reach, scale efforts, and drive positive change in various domains, from entrepreneurship and innovation to social impact and philanthropy. It's about using technology as a force multiplier for meaningful and impactful endeavors.

7. Community and Support

Community and support are essential elements for individuals looking to thrive in an AI-driven world. Here's a more detailed exploration:

- **Building Support Networks:** In an era of rapid technological change, individuals benefit from building support networks. These networks can consist of mentors, colleagues, friends, and fellow learners who provide guidance, encouragement, and a sense of belonging. Support networks are particularly crucial for those engaged in lifelong learning and adaptation.
- **Peer Learning and Collaboration:** Collaborative learning and peer support are powerful tools for personal growth and adaptation. Online communities, forums, and social platforms facilitate connections with like-minded individuals. These digital spaces enable knowledge sharing, collaboration on projects, and the exchange of experiences, contributing to collective learning and resilience.
- **Mentorship and Guidance:** Mentorship from experienced professionals can significantly accelerate an individual's learning and adaptation journey. Mentors offer valuable insights, share their expertise, and provide guidance on navigating the evolving landscape. Mentorship programs, both formal and informal, connect learners with mentors who can offer valuable perspectives.

- **Continuous Education and Training:** As technology evolves, continuous education and training are critical. Individuals should seek out educational opportunities, whether through formal courses, online platforms, workshops, or self-study. Lifelong learners stay ahead of the curve, acquire new skills, and adapt to changing job requirements.
- **Embracing Diversity and Inclusion:** Inclusive communities and support networks recognize the value of diversity. Embracing individuals from various backgrounds, perspectives, and skillsets fosters creativity and innovation. It also promotes a sense of belonging and ensures that a wide range of voices is heard in discussions about AI's impact.
- **Emotional and Psychological Support:** The pace of technological change can sometimes be overwhelming. Emotional and psychological support, including stress management and resilience-building, is essential. Strategies like mindfulness, self-care, and seeking professional help when needed contribute to mental well-being.
- **Support for Transition and Career Changes:** AI-driven changes in the job market may necessitate career transitions. Support for career changes, such as career counseling, skills assessment, and job placement services, can ease the process and provide a safety net during transitions.
- **Advocacy for Ethical AI:** Engaging in advocacy for ethical AI practices and policies can be a form of community involvement. Individuals can join or support organizations that advocate for fairness, transparency, and accountability in AI development. This advocacy extends the individual's impact to a broader societal level.

- **Giving Back to the Community:** As individuals grow and adapt, they can contribute to their communities and support others in their journeys. Whether through mentorship, volunteering, or sharing knowledge, giving back is a way to strengthen the support ecosystem.
- **Balancing Digital and In-Person Interactions:** While digital communities offer valuable support, balancing digital interactions with in-person connections is essential for well-rounded support networks. Face-to-face interactions provide unique opportunities for deeper relationships and collaboration.

In conclusion, community and support are vital components of an individual's ability to thrive in an AI-driven world. These networks and resources provide guidance, emotional well-being, learning opportunities, and a sense of belonging, enabling individuals to adapt, grow, and contribute meaningfully to society.

By embracing lifelong learning and adaptability, individuals can not only thrive in the AI era but also contribute to a society marked by innovation, resilience, and personal growth. These actions empower individuals to shape their destinies, maximize their potential, and actively participate in the ever-evolving world.

8.4. A Tapestry of Preparedness: Weaving Together Businesses, Government, and Individuals

The tapestry of preparedness is woven through the harmonious collaboration of businesses, government bodies, and individuals. Each thread, when thoughtfully interlaced, forms a fabric that is not only strong but also incredibly flexible and resilient—a fabric that can effectively weather the winds of change and, in doing so, seize the boundless opportunities that the AI-driven future presents.

8.4.1. Businesses as Catalysts of Innovation and Resilience

At the heart of this tapestry stand businesses, the engines of innovation. They are the driving force behind AI's transformative potential. When businesses wholeheartedly embrace AI, they not only adopt a new technology but embark on a cultural shift towards innovation. They realize that AI is not merely a tool; it's a catalyst for creative problem-solving, a wellspring of new opportunities, and a beacon guiding strategic decision-making. Through AI-powered insights, organizations can discern market trends, decode customer preferences, and spot emerging patterns that provide the foundation for sound strategic choices.

But innovation is not solely about technology; it's also about workforce dynamics. Businesses must understand that AI's impact on the workforce transcends automation; it necessitates a holistic reshaping of roles. To navigate these uncharted waters successfully, organizations need to scrutinize their operations, pinpoint areas where AI can streamline processes and enhance productivity, and reduce the burden of routine tasks. Simultaneously, they must engage in strategic workforce planning, including reskilling initiatives aimed at equipping employees with the skills demanded in an AI-augmented environment. This proactive approach ensures that the workforce remains adaptable and ready to embrace emerging opportunities, making businesses not just adopters of AI but champions of innovation and resilience.

8.4.2. Government Policies: Balancing Innovation, Regulation, and Collaboration

As vital as businesses are, the tapestry of preparedness extends to government policies that serve as the very loom upon which the fabric of AI's future is woven. Government policies are tasked with the delicate balancing act of fostering innovation while ensuring ethical AI development and safeguarding public interests. Regulatory frameworks must be designed to accommodate the boundless potential of AI while simultaneously shielding society from potential risks, biases, and discriminatory outcomes. It's a high-wire act where overregulation can stifle progress and underregulation can lead to unintended consequences. To walk this tightrope successfully, governments can establish flexible frameworks that evolve in lockstep with AI's growth, thereby enabling nimble responses to emerging ethical concerns and remaining open to technological advancements.

Collaboration is key to creating a thriving AI ecosystem. Government-industry-academia synergy is the linchpin that propels innovation forward. By fostering partnerships and collaborations among these stakeholders, governments create an environment where best practices are shared, cutting-edge research flourishes, and AI adoption is facilitated. This results in an ecosystem that not only nurtures responsible AI development but also champions innovation and sustainable progress.

8.4.3. Individual Actions: The Transformative Role of Lifelong Learning and Adaptability

Yet, the most intricate threads in the tapestry of preparedness are the individual actions of citizens. In this paradigm shift ushered in by AI, individuals play pivotal roles. Lifelong learning becomes their guiding star, leading them to continuously acquire new skills and knowledge. This commitment to personal growth and adaptation ensures that individuals remain relevant and agile in a swiftly evolving landscape. Cultivating adaptability equips them to navigate uncertainties, embrace change, and thrive in a world marked by constant transformation. By relinquishing the fear of change and embracing AI as an enabler, individuals can harness its potential to enrich their lives and amplify their contributions.

In conclusion, the tapestry of preparedness is not merely a metaphor; it's a living reality. Businesses, government bodies, and individuals are the master weavers, each contributing their unique threads to create a fabric that is not just strong but adaptable, not just resilient but visionary. As businesses innovate and adapt, as governments craft policies that guide responsible AI development, and as individuals commit to lifelong learning and adaptability, a symphony of transformation emerges. In this symphony, AI is not the conductor but a harmonious note, and together, we weave a future where humans and AI coexist, innovate, collaborate, and shape a world that is ever-evolving and filled with boundless possibilities.

8.5. A Dynamic Future Unveiled: Navigating the Uncharted with Unity

The AI-driven future is not some distant, nebulous horizon that lies beyond our reach; it is the realm we are stepping into today. This isn't a mere prediction; it's a present reality. It's a future that we, as a collective, have the power to shape through our actions, decisions, and collaboration—a future where AI and humans converge, not as competitors, but as partners in crafting a world that is dynamic, innovative, and infinitely adaptable.

This future, brimming with boundless possibilities, is not handed to us on a silver platter; we must actively participate in its creation. It's a future where businesses play a pivotal role by leveraging AI as a tool for innovation and transformation. In this narrative, AI isn't a replacement for human ingenuity but a complementary force that amplifies our creative potential. Through strategic business endeavors, organizations harness the capabilities of AI to optimize processes, enhance customer experiences, and unearth new vistas of opportunity. They recognize that AI isn't merely a technology but a profound cultural shift that beckons them towards innovation, experimentation, and growth.

Government policies are the guiding stars in this journey towards an AI-infused future. These policies, if thoughtfully crafted, serve as the rudders that steer our course. They must strike a delicate balance, encouraging innovation while ensuring ethical AI development and safeguarding the interests of society. Regulatory frameworks, akin to a sturdy vessel navigating turbulent waters, must be flexible enough to adapt to the ever-evolving landscape of AI, accommodating its limitless potential while guarding against potential pitfalls, biases, and discriminatory outcomes. Governments play a crucial role in fostering collaboration among stakeholders—industry, academia, and their own institutions—creating an ecosystem where best practices are shared, knowledge flows freely, and AI adoption is nurtured. This synergy amplifies innovation, fuels sustainable progress, and ensures responsible AI development.

But the most intricate and potent thread in this tapestry of transformation is the individual. Each person's actions, commitments, and choices collectively shape the future. Lifelong learning becomes the compass guiding individuals through uncharted territories, instilling the habit of continuously acquiring new skills and knowledge. This commitment to personal growth and adaptability ensures that individuals remain agile and relevant in a rapidly evolving world. By embracing change instead of fearing it, individuals can fully harness AI's potential as an enabler, not a threat. This personal commitment to growth aligns with the broader vision of a dynamic, innovative future.

Moreover, individuals play a vital role in the ethical development of AI. By advocating for fairness, transparency, and accountability in AI systems, they contribute to the creation of technologies that align with human values and societal well-being. Grassroots movements, informed discussions, and public engagement are integral components of this ethical journey, ensuring that AI-driven progress is just, inclusive, and considerate of diverse perspectives.

In unity, through these strategic business endeavors, well-crafted government policies, and the personal commitment of individuals to growth and ethics, we navigate the uncharted waters of the AI-driven future. Together, we craft a future that is more than a destination; it's a journey. It's a journey where humans and AI collaborate not only to redefine progress and innovation but to reshape the very essence of what it means to thrive. In this future, AI is not a distant force to be feared but a partner to be embraced—a future where the possibilities are as limitless as our collective imagination, where progress knows no bounds, and where unity propels us into a dynamic and inspiring era of human-AI partnership.

Conclusion: Chapter 8: Preparing for the AI-Driven Future

Preparing for the AI-driven future is not a passive endeavor; it's an active pursuit of growth and readiness. Businesses must not only integrate AI but also strategize to harness its transformative power. Government policies should nurture innovation while safeguarding ethical considerations. On the individual front, a commitment to lifelong learning, adaptability, and a willingness to embrace change shapes personal preparedness. In unity, these strategies guide us towards a future where humans and AI thrive together, innovating, collaborating, and shaping a world that is ever-evolving and filled with boundless possibilities.

Chapter 9: Case Studies of AI Implementation

In this enlightening chapter, we delve into real-world examples of how companies have successfully integrated Artificial Intelligence (AI) into their operations. These case studies provide a profound understanding of the challenges, benefits, and unexpected outcomes of AI implementation, offering invaluable insights for those embarking on their AI journey.

Case Study 1: Amazon's AI-Powered Supply Chain Optimization

Amazon's AI transformation stands as a testament to the e-commerce giant's unwavering commitment to innovation and operational excellence. By embracing a potent mix of machine learning algorithms, predictive analytics, and robotics, Amazon has orchestrated a profound supply chain revolution that has reverberated across the global retail landscape.

The AI-Powered Revolution: Amazon's journey into the realm of AI-driven supply chain optimization commenced with the recognition that in a world where customer expectations for fast deliveries and product availability are ever-increasing, traditional supply chain models could no longer suffice. To address this, Amazon turned to AI as a strategic enabler.

Forecasting Demand Patterns: One of the crown jewels in Amazon's AI arsenal is its ability to predict consumer demand with remarkable precision. Through sophisticated machine learning algorithms, Amazon analyzes historical data, market trends, and even external factors like weather patterns to forecast demand patterns. This foresight empowers the company to position products strategically, ensuring that popular items are readily available, thus minimizing stockouts and maximizing sales.

Inventory Optimization: AI has transformed how Amazon manages its inventory. Traditionally, managing an inventory as vast and diverse as Amazon's would be a logistical nightmare. However, AI algorithms now handle this intricate task, determining the optimal quantity and location of products within the supply chain. This optimization has streamlined operations, leading to substantial cost reductions.

Proactive Maintenance: In Amazon's bustling warehouses, efficiency is paramount. Here, AI-driven predictive analytics shine. Amazon's robots, used extensively in its fulfillment centers, are equipped with sensors that collect data on their performance. AI algorithms then analyze this data in real-time, predicting when maintenance is required. This proactive approach minimizes downtime, ensuring that Amazon's fulfillment centers operate at peak efficiency.

Remarkable Results: The impact of Amazon's AI-powered supply chain optimization has been nothing short of astounding.

Faster deliveries have become the norm, delighting customers and bolstering loyalty. Concurrently, the cost savings achieved through inventory optimization and proactive maintenance have contributed to Amazon's ability to remain competitive while investing in further innovations. This virtuous cycle has significantly elevated customer satisfaction and propelled Amazon's position as a retail juggernaut.

Lessons Learned:

- **AI as a Transformative Force:** Amazon's case demonstrates that AI isn't just a tool but a transformative force that can overhaul even the most complex operational landscapes.

- **Continuous Innovation:** Maintaining a competitive edge in the AI-driven era requires sustained investment in AI technology and talent.

- **Ethical Considerations:** Amazon's case underscores the importance of ethical considerations, particularly concerning labor practices and the implications of AI for workers.

Amazon's journey into AI-driven supply chain optimization serves as a resounding example of how a visionary approach to technology adoption can yield remarkable results, transforming not just a company's operations but entire industries.

Case Study 2: Netflix's Personalized Content Recommendations

Netflix, the global streaming giant, has harnessed the power of Artificial Intelligence to redefine the viewer experience. Its recommendation system, underpinned by sophisticated machine learning algorithms, stands as a testament to how AI can profoundly impact user engagement and content consumption.

The Power of Personalization: Netflix understands that in today's digital age, viewers demand personalized experiences. The vast library of content available can be overwhelming, and this is where AI steps in. Netflix's recommendation system is designed to cut through the noise, helping viewers discover content that aligns with their unique tastes.

Understanding User Behavior: At the heart of Netflix's recommendation system lies an intricate understanding of user behavior. Every click, pause, rewind, or fast-forward is meticulously tracked and analyzed. Machine learning algorithms process this data to discern patterns, preferences, and even the most subtle cues about a viewer's viewing habits.

Creating Viewer Profiles: Netflix leverages this wealth of data to create detailed viewer profiles. These profiles are enriched with information about preferred genres, actors, directors, and viewing history. The more a user watches, the more accurate the profile becomes.

Recommendation Algorithms in Action: Netflix's recommendation algorithms work tirelessly behind the scenes. When a viewer logs in, the system instantly compares their profile to a vast database of content. It identifies shows, movies, or documentaries that align with the viewer's preferences. The recommendations are presented in a personalized feed, making it easier for viewers to find content that resonates.

Driving User Engagement and Retention: The impact of this AI-driven personalization is striking. Viewers are not only more likely to discover content they enjoy but also spend more time engaged with the platform. This increased user engagement translates directly into higher customer retention rates, a critical metric in the fiercely competitive streaming industry.

Balancing Personalization and Privacy: While personalization is a powerful tool, Netflix is acutely aware of the importance of user privacy. The company has established robust privacy controls, allowing users to adjust their viewing profiles and control data sharing. This balance between personalization and privacy is pivotal to maintaining user trust.

Lessons Learned:

- **Enhancing User Experience:** Netflix's case underscores how AI can be leveraged to enhance user experiences dramatically.

- **Privacy Considerations:** Maintaining user trust necessitates a commitment to data privacy and transparency.

- **Continuous Refinement:** Ongoing data collection and analysis are essential for refining AI algorithms and recommendations.

Netflix's personalized content recommendation system is a testament to the transformative power of AI in the entertainment industry. It has not only elevated user engagement and retention but has also set a benchmark for how viewers expect content to be delivered in the digital age—tailored to their unique tastes and preferences.

Case Study 3: Tesla's Autonomous Driving Technology

Tesla, the trailblazing electric car manufacturer, has embarked on a remarkable journey toward redefining the future of transportation with the integration of autonomous driving technology. This case study illuminates Tesla's pioneering approach, the intricacies of its AI-driven systems, and the lessons it imparts to the automotive industry.

The Promise of Autonomous Driving: Tesla envisions a future where vehicles are not merely means of transportation but intelligent companions that enhance safety, convenience, and overall driving experience. The foundation of this vision lies in autonomous driving technology powered by Artificial Intelligence.

AI-Infused Vehicle Sensors: Tesla's vehicles are equipped with an array of sensors, cameras, and radar systems. These sensors act as the eyes and ears of the vehicle, continuously scanning the surrounding environment. This wealth of data is fed into powerful AI algorithms, which analyze and interpret the information in real-time.

Autopilot and Full Self-Driving (FSD): Tesla's AI-driven systems are phased into two primary modes—Autopilot and Full Self-Driving (FSD). Autopilot provides advanced driver-assistance features, such as adaptive cruise control and lane-keeping assistance. FSD, on the other hand, is a more ambitious suite of capabilities designed to enable full autonomy, allowing the vehicle to handle complex driving tasks without human intervention.

Iterative Development Process: Tesla's journey to autonomous driving is characterized by its iterative approach. The AI systems continuously learn from billions of miles of real-world driving data. This process involves refining algorithms, enhancing sensor technology, and addressing edge cases to improve the system's safety and reliability.

Regulatory and Safety Challenges: The pursuit of autonomous driving is not without its challenges. Regulatory hurdles and safety concerns require careful navigation. Tesla collaborates with regulatory authorities and conducts rigorous safety assessments to ensure its autonomous technology complies with the highest safety standards.

Continuous Updates and Improvements: Tesla's approach emphasizes continuous improvement through over-the-air software updates. These updates not only introduce new features but also enhance the safety and functionality of existing ones. This agile development model enables the company to adapt to evolving challenges and opportunities.

Lessons Learned:

- **Complexity of Autonomous Systems:** Building AI-driven autonomous systems is a complex and iterative process that demands long-term commitment and expertise.

- **Regulatory Considerations:** Navigating regulatory landscapes and ensuring compliance is paramount in the development of self-driving technology.

- **Ongoing Development:** Continuous updates and improvements are essential to enhance safety and functionality.

Tesla's foray into autonomous driving technology showcases the transformative potential of AI in the automotive sector. While the road to full autonomy remains ongoing, Tesla's iterative and data-driven approach positions it at the forefront of the autonomous vehicle revolution. It also underscores the importance of safety, regulatory compliance, and constant innovation in realizing the promise of self-driving cars.

Case Study 4: IBM Watson's Healthcare Applications

IBM Watson, a prominent AI system, has made significant inroads into the healthcare sector, where its natural language processing capabilities have proven instrumental in supporting medical professionals and advancing the field of medicine. This case study explores how IBM Watson has transformed healthcare practices, emphasizing its applications, challenges, and the lessons it offers.

The Power of AI in Healthcare: Healthcare is a domain where timely, accurate decision-making can be a matter of life and death. IBM Watson steps into this critical arena as a sophisticated AI tool with the potential to augment human expertise.

Data Analysis at Unprecedented Speed: IBM Watson's remarkable capability lies in its ability to process and understand vast amounts of medical data, including academic journals, clinical studies, patient records, and medical literature. Traditional methods of manual data analysis pale in comparison to Watson's speed and precision.

Assisting in Diagnosis and Treatment: One of Watson's primary roles in healthcare is to assist doctors in diagnosing diseases and suggesting treatment options. It does this by swiftly scanning and interpreting patient records, symptoms, and test results, cross-referencing them with a wealth of medical knowledge. This process not only expedites diagnosis but also reduces the chances of errors.

Efficient Drug Discovery: Beyond diagnosis and treatment recommendations, IBM Watson plays a pivotal role in drug discovery and development. It can analyze extensive datasets to identify potential drug candidates and assess their efficacy, significantly expediting the research and development process.

Challenges and Considerations: Despite its transformative potential, the integration of AI like IBM Watson in healthcare comes with challenges. Ensuring the accuracy and reliability of AI-driven medical recommendations is paramount. The need for ethical data handling, patient privacy, and regulatory compliance adds layers of complexity. Additionally, there's a learning curve for healthcare professionals in effectively utilizing AI tools like Watson.

Collaboration Between AI and Human Expertise: IBM Watson's success in healthcare highlights the potential of AI-human collaboration. Rather than replacing doctors, it serves as a tool that complements their expertise. The synergy between AI and healthcare professionals enables more informed decisions and improved patient outcomes.

Lessons Learned:

- **Augmenting Human Expertise:** AI can serve as a valuable tool in augmenting human expertise, particularly in complex fields like medicine.

- **Ethical and Regulatory Considerations:** Ensuring the ethical handling of patient data, privacy, and regulatory compliance is crucial.

- **Collaboration is Key:** Effective integration of AI in healthcare relies on collaboration between AI developers and healthcare domain experts.

IBM Watson's foray into healthcare showcases the potential of AI to enhance decision-making, accelerate research, and improve patient care. While challenges exist, including ethical and regulatory considerations, it underscores the transformative power of AI-human collaboration in the pursuit of better healthcare outcomes.

Conclusion: Chapter 9: Case Studies of AI Implementation

These illuminating case studies unveil the diverse ways AI is catalyzing transformation across industries. They underscore the potential benefits of AI, from revolutionizing supply chains and elevating user experiences to advancing autonomous technologies and enhancing healthcare. However, they also spotlight the imperative of addressing multifaceted challenges related to data privacy, ethics, regulation, and sustaining investments in AI development. The invaluable lessons drawn from these case studies provide an invaluable compass for businesses and organizations embarking on their own AI implementation journeys, guiding them toward a future enriched by the transformative power of artificial intelligence.

Chapter 10: Envisioning Tomorrow's Workforce

As we peer into the horizon of the future, the contours of work and the workforce are poised to undergo profound transformations. In this chapter, we embark on a speculative journey into the realms of tomorrow's workforce, exploring the potential landscapes of remote work, augmented reality (AR) offices, the evolving facets of leadership, the dynamics of collaboration and teamwork, and the intricate interplay between AI, human creativity, and innovation.

10.1. Remote Work and Augmented Reality Offices: Bridging Distances

The concept of the workplace is in the midst of a radical transformation. Remote work, which has been accelerated by technological advancements and the lessons learned from the COVID-19 pandemic, is steadily becoming the new norm. However, the future of work may not be solely confined to remote or physical locations; instead, it might offer a harmonious blend of both, facilitated by groundbreaking technologies such as augmented reality (AR).

10.1.1. Remote Work: A Paradigm Shift

Remote work has rapidly evolved from being an occasional perk to a mainstream mode of employment. The widespread adoption of video conferencing, cloud computing, and collaboration tools has enabled organizations to seamlessly extend their operations beyond the confines of traditional offices. Employees have experienced the benefits of greater flexibility, reduced commuting, and improved work-life balance.

As remote work continues to mature, it's poised to encompass a wider range of industries and roles. Jobs that were once considered inseparable from physical presence are being reimagined. The traditional 9-to-5 workday is giving way to a more flexible approach, where productivity is measured by output rather than hours logged.

10.1.2. Augmented Reality Offices: A Vision of the Future

While remote work provides flexibility, it can also introduce challenges related to isolation, disconnection from colleagues, and difficulties in replicating the collaborative atmosphere of a physical office. This is where augmented reality (AR) steps in to potentially revolutionize the concept of the workplace.

AR offices, powered by technologies like mixed reality headsets, are virtual workspaces that have the potential to merge the best aspects of remote and in-person work. In these immersive digital environments, employees can interact with each other and their work in ways that go far beyond what traditional video conferencing and collaboration tools can offer.

Imagine attending a virtual meeting where your colleagues' avatars are seated around a conference table, and you can engage in natural conversations as if you were in the same room. Or envision working together on a project where digital 3D models and data visualizations are overlaid onto your physical surroundings, allowing for real-time collaboration and brainstorming.

10.1.3. Redefining the Boundaries of the Traditional Office

AR offices have the potential to redefine the very essence of the traditional office. They can provide a sense of presence and connection that bridges the geographical distances between team members. With AR, the boundaries between physical and virtual spaces blur, creating opportunities for more dynamic and interactive collaboration.

Moreover, these AR environments could accommodate flexible work arrangements. Employees might choose to work from the comfort of their homes, a co-working space, or even a beachside cafe, all while being seamlessly connected to their colleagues in the AR office. This flexibility could open doors to a more diverse and inclusive workforce, with talent sourced from a global pool.

10.1.4. Fostering Collaboration and Innovation

The potential benefits of AR offices extend beyond convenience. They hold the promise of fostering collaboration and innovation. The ability to interact with digital content and data in a spatial context can enhance problem-solving, design thinking, and creative brainstorming.

Imagine architects collaborating on the design of a new building, with holographic blueprints floating in their AR workspace. Or scientists exploring complex datasets by physically manipulating virtual representations. These are just glimpses of the transformative power of AR in redefining how work is done.

10.1.5. Challenges and Considerations

While the vision of AR offices is compelling, several challenges and considerations must be addressed. These include:

1. Technology Accessibility: Not all employees may have access to the necessary AR hardware or a suitable environment for immersive work.

2. Data Security and Privacy: Storing and transmitting sensitive business data in virtual environments must be done securely to protect against cyber threats.

3. Training and Adaptation: Employees will need training to navigate and make the most of AR office environments effectively.

4. Balancing Flexibility and Structure: Striking the right balance between flexibility and structure in remote work arrangements is crucial to ensure productivity and work-life balance.

In conclusion, the future of work is on the cusp of a paradigm shift, with remote work and AR offices at the forefront. These innovations promise to redefine how we collaborate, where we work, and how we access and interact with information. While challenges exist, the potential for more flexible, inclusive, and innovative work environments is both exciting and transformative. As technology continues to advance, the boundary between physical and digital workspaces may become increasingly indistinguishable, ushering in a new era of work that is as dynamic and adaptable as the workforce itself.

10.2. The Evolving Nature of Leadership: Adaptive and Empathetic

The landscape of leadership is undergoing a profound transformation in response to the integration of AI into the workforce. As AI takes on routine and data-driven tasks, leaders are poised to play a pivotal role in shaping the future of work. The emerging paradigm of leadership encompasses a dynamic equilibrium between adaptability and empathy.

1. Adaptability in Leadership

Leaders of the future must exhibit a high degree of adaptability. AI-driven technologies are evolving at an unprecedented pace, and leaders need to stay ahead of the curve to effectively harness these tools. This adaptability includes:

- **Tech-Savviness:** Leaders must be well-versed in AI and emerging technologies. They should understand the capabilities and limitations of AI to make informed

decisions about its implementation within their organizations.
- **Agility:** The ability to pivot and adapt to changing circumstances is essential. Leaders should be comfortable with uncertainty and open to adjusting strategies in response to evolving business landscapes.
- **Continuous Learning:** An ongoing commitment to learning is paramount. Leaders should model a culture of lifelong learning within their organizations, embracing new skills and knowledge to remain relevant in a rapidly changing world.
- **Innovation:** Leaders should encourage and empower their teams to innovate. AI can be a catalyst for creativity and problem-solving, and leaders should foster an environment where employees feel comfortable experimenting and proposing novel solutions.

2. Empathy as a Leadership Cornerstone

Empathy is another crucial component of future leadership. While AI can perform tasks efficiently, it lacks the emotional intelligence and human touch that are essential in many aspects of business and leadership. Empathy includes:

- **Understanding Employee Needs:** Empathetic leaders are attuned to the needs and concerns of their employees. They recognize the unique challenges individuals face and work to provide support and solutions.
- **Inclusive Leadership:** Leaders should embrace diversity and inclusion as core values. Empathy enables leaders to create inclusive environments where every voice is

heard and valued, regardless of background or perspective.
- **Supporting Well-Being:** The well-being of employees is a top priority for empathetic leaders. They understand the importance of work-life balance, mental health, and a supportive workplace culture.
- **Effective Communication:** Empathy enhances communication skills. Leaders who can connect on a human level with their teams build trust and rapport, leading to stronger collaborations and more engaged employees.

3. Cultivating a Culture of Learning and Inclusion

Future leaders play a critical role in cultivating workplace cultures that prioritize continuous learning, diversity, and inclusion:

- **Continuous Learning:** Leaders should model a commitment to ongoing learning and encourage their teams to do the same. This can involve supporting training and development programs and creating space for skill-building.
- **Diversity and Inclusion:** Empathetic leaders actively seek diverse perspectives and ensure that all voices are heard. They work to remove barriers to entry and advancement for underrepresented groups.
- **Resilience:** In times of change and uncertainty, leaders should exemplify resilience. This sets a positive example for their teams and helps organizations adapt to challenges effectively.

In conclusion, the evolving nature of leadership in the AI-driven future is characterized by a delicate balance between adaptability and empathy. Leaders must adapt to the changing technological landscape while retaining a deep understanding of human needs and emotions. By embodying these qualities and fostering cultures of continuous learning and inclusion, future leaders can guide their organizations towards success in an era where humans and AI collaborate harmoniously to achieve their fullest potential.

10.3. Collaboration and Team Dynamics: Beyond Boundaries

The future of work is marked by a fundamental shift in how teams collaborate and interact, transcending geographical boundaries and embracing the potential of technology-enabled collaboration. Here, we delve into the dynamics of this transformative landscape:

1. Borderless Collaboration

The traditional notion of teams confined to a physical office space is giving way to a borderless world of collaboration. Future teams are not defined by the constraints of location; instead, they are formed based on expertise and skills, regardless of where team members are situated. This borderless approach offers several advantages:

- **Access to Global Talent:** Organizations can tap into a global talent pool, bringing together experts from diverse backgrounds and cultures. This diversity of perspectives enriches problem-solving and innovation.

- **Around-the-Clock Productivity:** Teams distributed across time zones can work continuously, resulting in enhanced productivity and faster project turnaround times. Tasks can be handed off seamlessly from one team to another as the sun sets in one part of the world and rises in another.
- **Reduced Overhead Costs:** With fewer employees tied to a physical office, organizations can reduce office space and related expenses. This can lead to significant cost savings.

2. Evolution of Collaboration Tools

The tools and platforms that facilitate collaboration are evolving to meet the demands of remote and distributed teams. These developments include:

- **Immersive Virtual Environments:** Virtual reality (VR) and augmented reality (AR) are enabling teams to meet in immersive digital spaces that mimic physical meeting rooms. This technology provides a sense of presence and fosters more engaging interactions.
- **Integrated Communication Platforms:** Collaboration tools are becoming more integrated, offering features such as video conferencing, document sharing, project management, and chat within a single platform. This streamlines communication and improves efficiency.
- **AI-Powered Insights:** AI algorithms are being used to analyze collaboration data, providing insights into team dynamics and suggesting ways to improve productivity and collaboration.

3. The Power of Diverse Perspectives

Global teams, with members from different cultures, backgrounds, and experiences, are fertile grounds for innovation. The interplay of diverse perspectives can lead to:

- **Creative Solutions:** Diverse teams are more likely to generate innovative and creative solutions to complex problems. Varied viewpoints challenge conventional thinking and lead to breakthroughs.
- **Enhanced Decision-Making:** Diverse teams tend to make better decisions. They consider a wider range of factors and are less susceptible to groupthink.
- **Improved Problem-Solving:** Different cultural and professional backgrounds bring unique problem-solving approaches to the table. This can lead to more comprehensive and effective solutions.

Challenges and Considerations

While the future of collaboration is promising, it comes with its share of challenges:

- **Communication Barriers:** Managing communication in global teams can be complex, with language barriers, time zone differences, and cultural nuances to navigate.
- **Building Trust:** Trust is crucial in virtual teams. Building and maintaining trust among team members who may never meet in person requires deliberate effort.
- **Cybersecurity:** With remote work and digital collaboration comes the need for robust cybersecurity measures to protect sensitive information.

In conclusion, the future of collaboration and team dynamics is characterized by the breaking down of geographical boundaries and the embrace of technology-driven, borderless teamwork. This evolution promises enhanced productivity, innovation, and problem-solving capabilities. However, it also requires organizations to address communication challenges, build trust in virtual teams, and prioritize cybersecurity to ensure the success of this new era of collaboration.

10.4. The Interplay of AI, Creativity, and Human Ingenuity

The interplay between AI, creativity, and human ingenuity is poised to define the future of work and innovation. Here, we explore the dynamics of this transformative relationship:

1. Augmenting Human Creativity

AI is set to revolutionize creativity by serving as a powerful tool for idea generation, inspiration, and problem-solving. Key aspects of AI-driven augmentation include:

- **Idea Generation:** AI algorithms can analyze vast datasets and generate creative ideas or concepts based on patterns and trends. This capability can be harnessed in various creative fields, from art and design to content creation.
- **Predictive Creativity:** AI systems can predict emerging trends and consumer preferences, allowing creative professionals to stay ahead of the curve and tailor their work to evolving demands.
- **Enhanced Productivity:** AI tools can automate repetitive tasks, freeing up creative professionals to

focus on more innovative and high-value aspects of their work.

2. AI as a Creative Collaborator

The future of creativity may see AI as an active collaborator rather than a passive tool. AI can:

- **Generate Inspiration:** AI algorithms can curate content, images, or ideas that align with a creator's style or project requirements, acting as a source of inspiration.
- **Offer Creative Suggestions:** AI-driven systems can provide real-time feedback and suggestions to artists, writers, and designers, facilitating an iterative creative process.
- **Foster Cross-Disciplinary Collaboration:** AI can bridge gaps between different creative disciplines, facilitating collaboration between artists, scientists, engineers, and other professionals.

3. The Human Element in Creativity

While AI can excel in data-driven creativity and optimization, the essence of human creativity remains irreplaceable. Human creativity encompasses:

- **Emotional Depth:** Human creators infuse their work with emotional depth, drawing from personal experiences, values, and cultural contexts that AI cannot replicate.
- **Ethical and Moral Considerations:** Human creators bring ethical and moral considerations to the forefront of their work, ensuring responsible and socially conscious creativity.

- **Innovation Through Serendipity:** Human creativity often thrives on serendipitous discoveries and unexpected connections, which can be challenging for AI to replicate.

4. Catalyzing Breakthroughs Across Domains

The synergy between AI and human ingenuity has the potential to catalyze breakthroughs across diverse domains:

- **Art and Culture:** AI-driven art, music, and literature are pushing the boundaries of what is possible, challenging traditional definitions of creativity.
- **Science and Research:** AI accelerates scientific discoveries by analyzing vast datasets, simulating experiments, and identifying patterns that human scientists might overlook.
- **Business and Innovation:** AI-powered insights and predictive analytics enable businesses to innovate in product development, marketing, and customer engagement.

Challenges and Considerations

While the collaboration between AI and human creativity offers immense potential, it also raises challenges:

- **Ethical Boundaries:** Ensuring that AI-generated content respects copyright, cultural sensitivities, and ethical standards is a growing concern.
- **Human-AI Interaction:** Effective collaboration between humans and AI requires intuitive interfaces and tools that facilitate seamless interaction.

- **Education and Skill Development:** As AI takes on more creative tasks, there is a growing need to prepare individuals with the skills required to collaborate effectively with AI.

In conclusion, the future of work and innovation is marked by a harmonious interplay between AI, creativity, and human ingenuity. AI augments human creativity, offers inspiration, and streamlines processes, while humans contribute emotional depth, ethical considerations, and serendipitous discoveries. This synergy promises to drive breakthroughs across various domains, redefining how we approach art, science, business, and beyond. However, addressing ethical concerns, improving human-AI interaction, and investing in education are essential for realizing the full potential of this creative partnership.

Conclusion

In the kaleidoscope of tomorrow's workforce, we catch a glimpse of a future where the boundaries between physical and virtual workspaces blur into insignificance. Leadership evolves to embrace adaptability and empathy as its guiding tenets, forging a pathway for enlightened management. Collaboration, unshackled by geographical constraints, ushers in an era of globalized teamwork and the cross-pollination of diverse ideas. Meanwhile, AI stands as a stalwart creative partner, propelling human ingenuity to unprecedented heights.

While this future remains speculative, it is firmly anchored in the swift progression of technological innovation and the indomitable resilience of human adaptability. As we navigate this uncharted terrain, the vision of a harmonious fusion of AI and human potential beckons. It promises a workforce that is more interconnected, creative, and capable than ever before—a workforce that not only confronts the future but actively shapes it with unwavering ingenuity.

Conclusion: Embracing the AI-Enhanced Future

In this book, we embarked on a journey through the transformative landscape of Artificial Intelligence (AI) and its profound impact on industries, jobs, skills, ethics, and the very essence of work itself. As we conclude our exploration, let's recap some of the key findings and insights from our journey and encourage you, the reader, to view AI as a catalyst for positive change.

Recap of Key Findings and Insights

1. AI's Transformative Power: AI is not just a tool; it's a transformative force reshaping industries, jobs, and skills. It augments human capabilities and opens new frontiers of innovation.

2. AI Ethics: Ensuring AI operates ethically is paramount. Fairness, transparency, and accountability are essential principles to guide AI's development and deployment.

3. The Evolving Workforce: The workforce of tomorrow will require a blend of technical skills and soft skills like creativity, critical thinking, and adaptability.

4. Collaboration, Not Replacement: AI is not here to replace humans but to collaborate with us, freeing us from mundane tasks and amplifying our abilities.

5. Reskilling and Lifelong Learning: In the face of technological disruption, reskilling and lifelong learning are vital for staying relevant and thriving in the AI era.

6. Leadership and Cultural Transformation: Leadership in the AI-driven future will require adaptability and empathy, fostering a culture of continuous learning and innovation.

7. Collaboration Across Boundaries: Collaboration will transcend geographical boundaries as remote work and augmented reality offices become the norm, leading to diverse and innovative teams.

8. The Creative Partnership: AI will be a creative partner, enhancing human creativity and innovation across various fields.

Embracing AI as a Catalyst for Positive Change

As we conclude our journey, it's crucial to emphasize that AI is not a threat but an opportunity—a catalyst for positive change. It empowers us to tackle complex problems, enhance our lives, and push the boundaries of human knowledge. By embracing AI, we open the door to a future where technology and humanity collaborate to build a more prosperous, innovative, and equitable world.

The Importance of Adaptability and Continuous Learning

In this fast-evolving AI-enhanced future, adaptability and continuous learning are our greatest assets. They enable us to navigate uncertainty, seize opportunities, and shape our destinies. As we move forward, remember that the journey is ongoing, and the possibilities are limitless. Embrace change, cultivate resilience, and embark on a lifelong quest for knowledge.

Thank you for joining us on this journey through the AI-enhanced future. As we stand on the precipice of new horizons, let us harness the power of AI to build a future that is not just technologically advanced but also compassionate, inclusive, and filled with boundless opportunities for all.

The future is yours to shape, and with AI as your ally, the possibilities are boundless. Embrace this AI-enhanced world, and together, let's create a future that is brighter and more promising than we can imagine.